MENTORING MUSIC TEACHERS IN THE SECONDARY SCHOOL

Mentoring Music Teachers in the Secondary School helps mentors of trainee and newly qualified music teachers in both developing their own mentoring skills and providing the essential guidance their beginning teachers need as they navigate the roller-coaster of the first years of teaching. Offering tried and tested strategies based on research and evidence, this book covers the knowledge, skills, understanding, and practical tools every mentor needs.

This book is a vital source of support and inspiration for mentors involved in developing the next generation of outstanding music education teachers. Key topics explained include:

- What is meant by mentoring
- What a mentor does
- Supporting specific aspects of beginning music teachers' knowledge, skills, and understanding
- Moving beginning music teachers on in their professional practice

Filled with key tools for the mentor's individual development, this essential text offers an accessible guide to mentoring early career music education teachers with ready-to-use strategies that support and inspire both mentors and beginning teachers alike.

Motje Wolf is a Senior Lecturer in Education at De Montfort University Leicester where she teaches and researches music education.

Nikki Booth is currently a part-time Research Assistant for the Birmingham Music Education Research Group (BMERG) at Birmingham City University.

Sarah Younie is a Professor in Education Innovation at De Montfort University Leicester and Visiting Professor at Chichester University.

MENTORING TRAINEE AND EARLY CAREER TEACHERS

Series edited by: Susan Capel, Julia Lawrence and Sarah Younie

The **Mentoring Trainee and Early Career Teachers** Series are subject (or age)-specific, practical books designed to reinforce and develop mentors' understanding of the different aspects of their role, as well as exploring issues that mentees encounter in the course of learning to teach. The books have two main foci: first, challenging mentors to reflect critically on theory, research and evidence, on their own knowledge, their approaches to mentoring and how they work with beginning teachers in order to move their practice forward; and second, supporting mentors to effectively facilitate the development of beginning teachers. Although the basic structure of all the books is similar, each book is different to reflect the needs of mentors in relation to the unique nature of each subject or age phase. Elements of appropriate theory, research and/or evidence introduce each topic or issue, with emphasis placed on the practical application of material. The chapter authors in each book have been engaged with mentoring over a long period of time and share research, evidence and their experience.

We hope that this series of books supports you in developing into an effective, reflective mentor as you support the development of the next generation of teachers.

For more information about this series, please visit: https://www.routledge.com/Mentoring-Trainee-and-Early-Career-Teachers/book-series/MTNQT

Titles in the series

Mentoring History Teachers in the Secondary School
Terry Haydn, Victoria Crooks and Laura London

Mentoring Mathematics Teachers in the Secondary School: A Practical Guide
Edited by Rosa Archer, Sian Morgan, David Swanson, Claire Clemmet and Stef Sullivan

Mentoring Languages Teachers in the Secondary School: A Practical Guide
Edited by Laura Molway and Anna Lise Gordon

Mentoring Music Teachers in the Secondary School: A Practical Guide
Edited by Motje Wolf, Nikki Booth, and Sarah Younie

MENTORING MUSIC TEACHERS IN THE SECONDARY SCHOOL

A Practical Guide

Edited by Motje Wolf, Nikki Booth, and Sarah Younie

LONDON AND NEW YORK

Designed cover image: © Getty Images

First published 2026
by Routledge
4 Park Square, Milton Park, Abingdon, Oxon, OX14 4RN

and by Routledge
605 Third Avenue, New York, NY 10158

Routledge is an imprint of the Taylor & Francis Group, an informa business

© 2026 selection and editorial matter, Motje Wolf, Nikki Booth, and Sarah Younie; individual chapters, the contributors

The right of Motje Wolf, Nikki Booth, and Sarah Younie to be identified as the authors of the editorial material, and of the authors for their individual chapters, has been asserted in accordance with sections 77 and 78 of the Copyright, Designs and Patents Act 1988.

All rights reserved. No part of this book may be reprinted or reproduced or utilised in any form or by any electronic, mechanical, or other means, now known or hereafter invented, including photocopying and recording, or in any information storage or retrieval system, without permission in writing from the publishers.

Trademark notice: Product or corporate names may be trademarks or registered trademarks, and are used only for identification and explanation without intent to infringe.

British Library Cataloguing-in-Publication Data
A catalogue record for this book is available from the British Library

Library of Congress Cataloging-in-Publication Data
Names: Wolf, Motje, 1982- editor. | Booth, Nikki, 1984- editor. | Younie, Sarah, 1967- editor.
Title: Mentoring music teachers in the secondary school : a practical guide / edited by Motje Wolf, Nikki Booth, and Sarah Younie.
Description: First edition. | Abingdon, Oxon ; New York : Routledge, 2025. | Series: Mentoring trainee and early career teachers | Includes bibliographical references and index.
Identifiers: LCCN 2025008811 (print) | LCCN 2025008812 (ebook) | ISBN 9780367435684 (hardback) | ISBN 9780367435691 (paperback) | ISBN 9781003004196 (ebook)
Subjects: LCSH: Music teachers--Training of. | Music teachers--In-service training. | Mentoring in education. | Teachers--Professional relationships. | School music--Instruction and study. | Music--Instruction and study.
Classification: LCC MT1 .M445 2025 (print) | LCC MT1 (ebook) | DDC 780.71--dc23/eng/20250321
LC record available at https://lccn.loc.gov/2025008811
LC ebook record available at https://lccn.loc.gov/2025008812

ISBN: 978-0-367-43568-4 (hbk)
ISBN: 978-0-367-43569-1 (pbk)
ISBN: 978-1-003-00419-6 (ebk)

DOI: 10.4324/9781003004196

Typeset in Interstate
by KnowledgeWorks Global Ltd.

CONTENTS

List of figures ix
List of tables xi
List of tasks xii
Author Biographies xv
An Introduction to the Series: Mentoring Trainee and Early Career Teachers xvii

Introduction: A practical guide to mentoring beginning music teachers in the secondary school 1
Motje Wolf, Nikki Booth, and Sarah Younie

SECTION I
What do we mean by mentoring? 3

1 **Models of mentoring** 5
   Gill Golder, Alison Keyworth, and Clare Shaw

   Definitions of mentoring 6
   The context in which you are working which underpins your mentoring practice 7
   Effective mentoring models 8

SECTION II
About the mentor 17

2 **Understanding yourself: Exploring beliefs and experiences** 19
   Kelly Davey Nicklin and Gary Spruce

   Examining your own beliefs 20
   Exploring beginning music teacher beliefs 22
   Musician or music teacher: tensions and reconciliations 24
   Teacher identity, context, and the exercise of agency 27
   The cultivation of agency 28

3 Understanding your approach in relation to advocacy, pedagogy, and professional development 31
Rebecca Lundberg

    The advocacy debate and why music should matter 32
    Creating a culture where music is valued and worthwhile music teaching 34
    Professional development and subject knowledge 37

4 Evaluating my impact as a music mentor 41
Motje Wolf and Helmut Schaumberger

    My impact as a mentor 41
    Preparing to be a mentor 42
    Preparation of the beginning music teacher 43
    The impact of the different roles of the music teacher 44

SECTION III
About what a mentor does 55

5 Performance curation – mentoring beginning music teachers in performance projects 57
Narelle Yeo

    Background and rationale 58
    Building a community of practice and recognising existing mastery across the cohort 59
    Repurposing Kolb's experiential learning cycle (1984) into a circular mentoring cycle for performance 62
    Circular mentoring 65

6 Developing a mentor-mentee relationship 69
Bethany Carter-Sherlock

    Developing a collaborative and supportive environment 70
    Active, empathetic, and generative listening 73
    Effective verbal and non-verbal communication 74
    The GROWTH model 78

7 Supporting the mentee: Working at the sharp end 81
Esther Cavett

    What is stress? 82
    What interventions might you use to support your beginning music teacher? 83
    What are your ethical responsibilities when dealing with someone who appears to be suffering from stress? 90
    What steps can you take to look after your own wellbeing 91

SECTION IV
Supporting specific aspects of beginning music teachers' knowledge, skills, and understanding — 93

8 What are the building blocks? Thinking about musical skills, knowledge, and understanding — 95
Anthony Anderson

What are skills, knowledge, and understanding? 95
Thinking about skills, knowledge, and understanding in differing contexts 102
Implications for practice 105

9 Mirror, mirror on the wall... supporting beginning music teachers to become reflective practitioners — 108
Martin Fautley and Ian Axtell

Reflection in and on action 110
Cognitive load theory 111
Classroom management 112
Observing 113
From teaching to learning 114

10 Mentoring for curriculum design — 120
Anthony Anderson

Music mentoring and curriculum design 120
Music curriculum meanings 121
Thinking about music curriculum structures 122
Unpacking the ice floe: mentoring for curriculum design 125
Music teachers as curriculum designers 127
Implications for practice 130

11 Preparing beginning music teachers for delivering lessons focussing on student performance — 133
Terezija Štimec and Motje Wolf

Offering support for teaching classroom performance 134
Offering support in setting the right expectations for classroom performance 134
Understanding different music assessment criteria 137
Encouraging the use of effective feedback for classroom performance 139

12 Observing a lesson — 143
Austin Griffiths

Has this happened to you? 143
What are you looking for in your observation? 144
The observation process 149

13 Supporting pupils' learning   154
Ian Axtell and Martin Fautley

Musical learning as an active process   154
Supporting learning through responsive pedagogy: teaching for learning   158
Pedagogic priorities for social justice: teaching as learning   161

14 Facilitating and leading effective discussions with beginning music teachers   166
Nikki Booth

Facilitating effective discussions through understanding and supporting the phases of development for the beginning music teacher   166
Facilitating effective discussions through developing early reflection skills   169
Using activity theory to lead and facilitate effective, deep, and critically reflective discussions   172
Leading effective discussions with beginning music teachers in more difficult circumstances   178

SECTION V
About moving beginning music teachers on   183

15 Using formative assessment effectively to see the wider picture   185
Nikki Booth

Seeing assessment as a process not just a product   185
Seeing a variety of starting points for pupils not just one   188
Seeing lesson planning as a means for what pupils are going to learn not just do   194
Seeing musical progress as something which happens over a period of time not just in a lesson   198
Seeing learning through the eyes of the pupils not just the teacher   200

16 Music teacher health and wellbeing: A practical survival guide for mentor and mentee   205
Jennifer Rowley

Background and context   206
Literature and theoretical framework   207
Implications for mentoring practice   215

References   217
Author index   233
Subject index   237

LIST OF FIGURES

1.1	Adapted from Clutterbuck's model of Developmental Mentoring (2004, p. 9)	13
5.1	Yeo et al.'s (2022) revised model of circular mentoring in collaborative creative practice, after Kolb (1984)	63
6.1	Annotated example of ISMART goal	78
8.1	Skills, knowledge, and understanding planning activity	101
8.2	The interaction of musical skills, knowledge, and understanding	102
9.1	Learning and doing (Fautley and Savage, 2011, p. 64)	116
10.1	Representative example of a programme of study	124
10.2	Ice floe model of colliding curriculum domains	125
10.3	Stratified curriculum mentoring	128
11.1	Shulman's (1987) teacher knowledge	133
14.1	Activity Theory model (adapted from Vygotsky [1978])	172
14.2	Engeström's (1987) activity system model (adapted)	173
15.1	Assessment *after* the teaching and learning cycle (taken from Booth, 2019, p. 412, and used with permission)	186
15.2	Assessment *within* the teaching and learning cycle (taken from Booth, 2019, p. 413, and used with permission)	187
15.3	Pupil 1 example Year 10 entrance ticket, used with permission	189
15.4	Pupil 2 example Year 10 entrance ticket, used with permission	190
15.5	Pupil 3 example Year 10 entrance ticket, used with permission	190
15.6	Example of progressive questions for different starting points, used with permission	191
15.7	Pupil 4 example exit ticket after a Year 9 group composing lesson, used with permission	192
15.8	Pupil 5 example exit ticket after a Year 9 group composing lesson, used with permission	193
15.9	Pupil 6 example exit ticket after a Year 10 solo performing lesson, used with permission	193
15.10	Pupil 7 example exit ticket after a Year 10 solo performing lesson, used with permission	194
15.11	Separating *learning* and *doing* within learning intentions (Fautley and Savage, 2007, p. 34, used with permission)	196

15.12	A spiral of musical progression (Daubney and Fautley, 2015, p. 6, and used with permission)	199
15.13	How musical skills can be integrated from a composing or improvising stem	199
16.1	Framework for enhancing student mental wellbeing (adapted from Baik et al., 2017)	208

LIST OF TABLES

1.1	Key external drivers influencing mentoring work	9
4.1	The roles of a mentor categorised in domains	44
4.2	Typology of beginning music teachers	45
6.1	Potential challenges faced by beginning music teachers	72
6.2	The GROWTH model	79
7.1	Effects of stress	83
7.2	The PRACTICE model	86
8.1	SKU comparison table	106
11.1	Gathering pupils' data 1	136
11.2	Using pupils' data	136
11.3	Potential issues and proposed actions regarding assessment criteria	138
11.4	Various examples of different assessment criteria used in music teaching	139
11.5	Gathering pupils' data 2	140
11.6	Constructive vs destructive feedback	141
13.1	An example of a lower secondary school scheme/unit of work	157
13.2	Pre-generative scaffolding	158
13.3	Understanding performances	162
14.1	Outcomes of different levels of challenge and support	167
14.2	Stages of development model	168
14.3	Clarified activity theory terminology for use in educational contexts	174
14.4	Starting-point reflective questions using the activity theory framework	176
15.1	Examples of confused and clarified learning intentions	197
15.2	Pupil voice pre-observation questions used at Wolgarston High School, Staffordshire, used with permission	201

LIST OF TASKS

1.1	Mentor reflection: reflecting on your understanding of mentoring	6
1.2	Mentor reflection: understanding the term mentoring	7
1.3	The context in which you carry out your mentoring duties	8
1.4	Three different mentoring models	11
1.5	Responsibilities of the mentor and beginning teacher at each stage of Katz's stages of development model (1995)	12
1.6	Helping a beginning teacher to learn using Clutterbuck's (2004) model	13
1.7	Attributes of an effective mentor	14
1.8	Mentor reflection: reflecting on your mentoring practice	14
2.1	Exploring musical identities	21
2.2	Reflecting upon ideological discourses	22
2.3	Musical enculturation	22
2.4	Values, experiences, and beliefs of beginning music teachers	23
2.5	Self-reflection: your own experiences as a beginning music teacher	24
2.6	Encouraging the musical skills of beginning music teachers	26
2.7	Beginning music teachers within your music department	27
2.8	Agency of beginning music teachers within your department	28
3.1	Considering your own claims for why music matters and music advocacy	32
3.2	Strategies for dealing with advocacy and considering your values of music education	34
3.3	Promoting the development of musicianship	37
3.4	Considering professional development	40
4.1	Reflecting on what your impact as a mentor is	42
4.2	Reflecting on your skills and impact as a mentor	43
4.3	Reflecting on transitions into teaching	46
4.4	Thinking about you as trainer	46
4.5	Thinking about experts that shaped your work	47
4.6	Reflecting on assessment	48
4.7	Reflecting on observation	49
4.8	Reflecting on 'helpful relationships'	50
4.9	Enabling a growth mindset	51
4.10	Reflecting on your systems to manage workload	52

4.11	Reflecting on your role as peer	53
4.12	Reflecting on your past experiences	53
5.1	Self-reflection about performance experiences and mentoring	59
5.2	How can we include multiple voices in the mentoring process?	61
5.3	Thinking about cultural and musical curation	66
6.1	Brainstorming your understanding of the mentoring relationship	70
6.2	Case studies: understanding the beginning music teacher	71
6.3	Approaches to listening	74
6.4	Identifying your own teaching perspectives	75
6.5	Identifying and expanding on positive communication	76
6.6	Practising non-verbal behaviours in a conversational setting	77
7.1	Mentor reflection	82
7.2	Scenario for mentor reflection	90
7.3	Concluding reflection for mentor	91
8.1	Musical skills modelling	97
8.2	Musical knowledge and assessment	99
8.3	Reflecting on musical understanding	100
8.4	Skills, knowledge, and understanding planning activity	101
8.5	Reflecting on the interaction of SKU	102
8.6	SKU in lesson planning (for non-music specialist mentors)	104
9.1	What form does reflection take?	109
9.2	Range of music activities in recent lesson	110
9.3	Questions for mentors	111
9.4	Classroom management	114
9.5	Moving the focus from teaching to learning	115
9.6	Supporting pupil learning	117
9.7	Digging deeper into learning	117
10.1	Defining music curriculum	122
10.2	Thinking about the purpose of planning	124
10.3	What is your pedagogy?	126
10.4	Thinking about hindrances in curriculum design	127
10.5	Comparing curricula	130
11.1	Mentor reflection on offering support to set appropriate expectations	137
11.2	Mentor reflection on guiding understanding of the use of different Assessment Criteria for classroom performance	138
11.3	Reflection on encouraging the use of effective questioning for classroom performance	142
12.1	Points for Mr Sloane	144
12.2	Reflective practice exercise	146
13.1	Your priorities for music education	155
13.2	Identifying musical vocabulary	156
13.3	Contextualising *knowing how* and *knowing that*	156
13.4	Identifying musical learning	157
13.5	Pupils' music thinking	158

13.6	Composing notepads	160
13.7	Beginning composing	161
13.8	Teaching composing	161
13.9	Questions to promote thinking	163
14.1a	Discussing and planning for growth of a beginning music teacher	167
14.1b	Reflecting and planning for growth as a mentor	167
14.2	Identifying the current phase of development and planning for support	169
14.3	Discussing beliefs about music education	170
14.4	Supporting a beginning music teacher's reflective practice	171
14.5a	Supporting the beginning music teacher with a video reflection	171
14.5b	Mentor reflection for supporting the beginning music teacher with a video reflection	172
14.6a	Using the activity theory framework for a deep and critical pre-lesson discussion with the beginning music teacher	178
14.6b	Using the activity theory framework for a deep and critical post-lesson discussion with the beginning music teacher	178
14.7	Reflecting on leading discussions in challenging circumstances	180
15.1	Understanding assessment in music	186
15.2	Reflecting on the effective use of assessment in music	188
15.3	Eliciting and using meaningful evidence to plan next steps in teaching and learning	194
15.4	Writing clear learning intentions	197
15.5	Seeing and planning for holistic musical progression	200
15.6a	A group-based pupil voice discussion with the mentor	203
15.6b	A group-based pupil voice discussion with the beginning music teacher	203
16.1	Reflecting on your understanding of mentoring	206
16.2	Understanding the barriers for beginning teacher retention and what can be done to address this	207
16.3	One example of practice	211
16.4	Different strategies to support beginning music teachers	212
16.5	Responsibilities of the mentor and mentee according to the *Framework for Enhancing Student Mental Wellbeing* (Baik et al., 2017)	215
Vignette 15.1	Reflections about pupil voice from an observer's perspective	202
Vignette 15.2	Reflections about pupil voice from a beginning teacher's perspective	202

AUTHOR BIOGRAPHIES

Dr Anthony Anderson is a Research Assistant in Music Education at Birmingham City University, UK. His research interests centre on music curriculum design in schools. He is a member of the editorial board for the *British Journal of Music Education* and taught in secondary schools as a Head of Music and Performing Arts for 16 years.

Dr Ian James Axtell is a Senior Lecturer in Education Leadership in the School of Education and Social Work, part of the Health, Education and Life Sciences faculty at Birmingham City University. Ian teaches on education master's courses, with a particular interest in how education professionals research their own practice.

Dr Nikki Booth is Head of Assessment Development at the National Examination Board in Occupational Safety and Health (NEBOSH) and both Research Assistant in Music Education and Visiting Lecturer in Education at Birmingham City University. He recently completed his PhD focusing on formative assessment within lower-secondary school group composing.

Esther Cavett is a Senior Research Fellow in Music at King's College London and College Lecturer in Music at Somerville, Jesus, and Lincoln Colleges, where she specialises in teaching the analysis of Western classical music from the 18th to 20th centuries. Her research interests are in music theory and analysis, widening access to music education, music pedagogy, mentoring, and music autoethnography. She works and performs the piano with various musical charities dedicated to improving access to and broadening appreciation of music.

Kelly Davey Nicklin is a Senior Lecturer in Music Education at Birmingham City University and the Course Leader for all PGCE Secondary routes. Kelly was a secondary school music teacher for 10 years and Head of Faculty for Performing Arts before moving into teacher education. Kelly also undertakes roles as an external examiner, exam moderator and school governor.

Professor Martin Fautley is an Emeritus Professor at Birmingham City University. Having previously been a classroom music teacher for many years, Martin now researches and publishes on many aspects of music education in schools, alongside teaching and supervising masters and doctoral students.

Dr Austin Griffiths is a Senior Teaching Fellow on the MA in Music Education of the Institute of Education (University College London) and a Teach First Subject Tutor for secondary music. After graduation from St Chad's College Durham with a degree in

Church History and Theology, he has had an extensive teaching career in secondary schools. He holds an MA in Education from Birmingham City University and a PhD from Warwick University which he completed in 2015. During his post as Senior Lecturer at De Montfort University, Ahe began to develop his interest in Music Education research. His research encompasses elite school music education, gender and race in the repertoire and resistance to change.

Rebecca Lundberg is a Senior Lecturer in Initial Teacher Education at the University of Huddersfield, teaching on the PGCE and BMus Courses. Rebecca gained the majority of her teaching experience working as a music teacher in Secondary Education, predominantly as a Head of Department. Rebecca is a published composer and her teaching and research interests include teaching and learning in music education and composition.

Dr Jennifer Rowley is an Associate Professor in Music Education with special interests in the areas of learning and teaching; identity development, gifted education, and eLearning (its design and use for engagement); and the use of ePortfolio for enhancing student learning. As a teacher-educator training musicians to be music teachers, she has a particular interest in the way that professional identity formation contributes to the documenting and curation of student learning, professional practice, and research.

Helmut Schaumberger is professor of music education at the Gustav Mahler Private University for Music in Klagenfurt, Austria. His main research interests are: teacher training, interdisciplinarity in music education, singing in music education, philosophy of music education, assessment and competence-oriented music education.

Dr Gary Spruce is a visiting lecturer in music education at Birmingham City University. For 16 years he was head of music in a state secondary school. He has written and published widely on music education particularly around the areas of secondary music education, teacher professional development and the relationship between music education and social justice.

Terezija Štimec is a Music Teacher and currently works as Subject Leader for Music at a secondary school in London. She holds an MA in Musicology from Royal Birmingham Conservatoire and a PGCE with QTS from Birmingham City University, where she received a Jane Crawford Award. She truly believes that music can change people's lives and that music education is an important factor in improving society and making this world a better place.

Dr Motje Wolf holds the position of Senior Lecturer in Education at De Montfort University Leicester (UK) where she teaches and researches Music Education. Her main research interests are: vocal pedagogy, choir pedagogy, teacher development, sound-based music, music and wellbeing, and philosophy of music education.

Dr Narelle Yeo is Senior Lecturer in Voice and Stagecraft and the University of Sydney, Sydney Conservatorium of Music. Her research focuses on mentoring for creatives, inclusion, voice production over genres and complex adaptive systems in the arts.

Dr Sarah Younie is a Professor in Education Innovation at De Montfort University and visiting Professor at Chichester University, having been a classroom teacher in schools.

AN INTRODUCTION TO THE SERIES: MENTORING TRAINEE AND EARLY CAREER TEACHERS

Mentoring is a very important and exciting role. What could be better than supporting the development of the next generation of subject teachers? A mentor is almost certainly an effective teacher, but this doesn't automatically guarantee that he or she will be a good mentor, despite similarities in the two roles. This series of practical workbooks books covers mentoring a range of subjects in the secondary curriculum and mentoring in primary schools. They are designed specifically to reinforce mentors' understanding of different aspects of their role, for mentors to learn about and reflect on their role, to provide support for mentors in aspects of their development and enable them to analyse their success in supporting the development of beginning teachers (defined as trainee, newly qualified and early career teachers). This book has two main foci: first, the focus is on challenging mentors to reflect critically on theory, research, evidence, on their own knowledge, how they work with beginning teachers, how they work with more experienced teachers and on their approaches to mentoring in order to move their practice forward. Second, the focus is on supporting mentors to effectively facilitate the development of beginning teachers. Thus, some of the practical activities in the books are designed to encourage reflection, whilst others ask mentors to undertake activities with beginning teachers.

This book can be used alongside generic and subject books designed for student and newly qualified teachers. These books include *Learning to Teach in the Secondary School: A Companion to School Experience*, 9th edition (Capel, Leask, Younie, Hidson, and Lawrence, 2022) which deals with aspects of teaching and learning applicable to all subjects. Further, the generic books are complemented by two series: *Learning to Teach (subject) in the Secondary School: A Companion to School Experience*; and *A Practical Guide to Teaching (subject) in the Secondary School*; as well as *Learning to Teach in the Primary School*. These books are designed for student teachers on different types of initial teacher education programmes (and indeed a beginning teacher you are working with may have used/currently be using them). However, these books are proving equally useful to tutors and mentors in their work with student teachers, both in relation to the knowledge, skills and understanding the student teacher is developing and some tasks which mentors might find useful to support a beginning teacher to do.

It is also supported by a book designed for newly qualified teachers, *Surviving and Thriving in the Secondary School: The NQT's Essential Companion* (Capel, Lawrence, Leask, and Younie, 2019). These titles cover material not generally needed by student teachers on an initial teacher education course, but which is needed by newly qualified teachers in their school work and early career.

The information in this book should link with the information in the generic text and relevant subject book in the series or book for primary student teachers in a number of ways. For example, mentors might want to refer a beginning teacher to read about specific knowledge, understanding and skills they are focusing on developing, or to undertake tasks in the book, either alone or with their support, then discus the tasks. It is recommended that you have copies of these books available so that you can cross-reference when needed.

In turn, the books complement a range of resources on which mentors can draw (including other mentors of beginning teachers in the same or other subjects or age phase, other teachers and a range of other resources including books, research articles and websites).

The positive feedback on *Learning to Teach* and the related books above, particularly the way they have supported the learning of student teachers in their development into effective, reflective teachers, encouraged us to retain the main features of that book in this series. Like teaching, mentoring should be informed by theory, research and evidence. Thus, this series of books introduce theoretical, research and evidence-based advice and guidance to support mentors as they develop their mentoring to support beginning teachers' development. The main focus is the practical application of material. Elements of appropriate theory, research and/or evidence introduce each topic or issue, and recent research into mentoring and/or teaching and learning is integral to the presentation. Tasks are provided to help mentors identify key features of the topic or issue and reflect on and/or apply them to their own practice as they mentor beginning teachers. Although the basic structure of all the books is similar, each book is different to reflect the needs of mentors in relation to the unique nature of each subject.

The chapter authors in the books have been engaged with mentoring over a long period of time and are aiming to share theory, research, evidence and their experience. We, as series editors, are pleased to extend the work in initial teacher education to the work of mentors of beginning teachers. We hope that this series of books supports you in developing into an effective, reflective mentor as you support the development of the next generation of subject teachers.

Susan Capel, Julia Lawrence and Sarah Younie,
December 2024

Introduction: A practical guide to mentoring beginning music teachers in the secondary school

Motje Wolf, Nikki Booth, and Sarah Younie

Mentoring beginning music teachers is a subject close to our hearts. Strengthening music teaching in schools is critical at this time of music being reduced in importance in the curriculum. However, research has shown repeatedly that engaging in music has many benefits from increasing creativity, health and wellbeing, and attainment (Clift, 2012; Hallam and Himonedes, 2022).

About you

This book is aimed equally at the experienced music teacher who is mentoring a less experienced colleague and at the non-musical experienced teacher who mentors a music teacher. Music teaching has many elements that are different to usual classroom teaching. Starting with preconceived ideas about music teaching some teachers have, for example that talent is the only component leading to musical success – which we know is not true – to the practicalities of handling musical instruments during the lesson, these are conceptual and practical elements that need to be addressed in addition to the 'usual elements' of teaching. Throughout the book, practical tasks have been added aiming to help you reflect on the different aspects being considered in each chapter.

About this book

We understand that teaching is one of the most rewarding but equally time-consuming professions and that it is difficult to carve out the time from the busy daily schedule to read a full book. We have, therefore, designed the book so that it fulfils two functions: You may read this as a preparation for your role as a mentor and work through each chapter. However, you might also have discovered this book whilst your mentorship is already established. Thus, you can look through the table of contents and look at the chapters most relevant for you. Each chapter functions as a stand-alone piece of writing.

Content of the book

This book is split into five sections.

Section 1: what do we mean by mentoring?

This section introduces in the meaning of mentoring beginning teachers generally.

Section 2: about the mentor

The three chapters in this section help you to reflect on you as the mentor by looking deeper into beliefs and experiences in mentoring, effective relationships, and the impact of mentoring.

Section 3: about what a mentor does

Three chapters investigate the role of the mentor from the angles of performance curation, and different aspects on offering effective support for your beginning music teacher.

Section 4: supporting specific aspects of beginning music teachers' knowledge, skills, and understanding

Seven chapters offer insights into the nuts and bolts of mentoring. Starting from making a plan, to observing and offering feedback, classic tasks of a mentor are covered here with music teaching in mind.

Section 5: about moving beginning music teachers on

Two chapters are closing the book by discussing seeing the wider picture and important aspects of health and wellbeing in music teaching.

While a book is a one-way communication tool, we, as the editors, would really like to open up the dialogue about the mentoring process. Dialogue has been stated to be one of the most important tools in mentoring (Searby, 2016). We encourage you therefore to share this book and the tasks within the chapters with your colleagues and perhaps - where appropriate - with your beginning music teacher.

Motje Wolf
Nikki Booth
Sarah Younie
January 2025

SECTION I
What do we mean by mentoring?

1 Models of mentoring

Gill Golder, Alison Keyworth, and Clare Shaw

Introduction

Your job as a mentor is to develop a positive working relationship with a beginning teacher to enable them to grow and develop both professionally and personally. How you go about this will be influenced by a number of factors, such as your own experience of being mentored in the past and your common-sense opinions of the role. These are important starting points, but you are likely to grow as an effective mentor when you also base your approaches on evidence. This chapter is generic to all of the books in the series, but in this book, we will be focusing on music teaching. Each chapter focuses on generic and subject-specific issues relating to teaching in a subject that is predominately practical in nature. The chapters are designed to support you in considering the evidence to underpin your practice.

This chapter starts by looking at different definitions of mentoring. It then looks at the importance of the context in which you are working as a mentor, highlighting a number of documents from England and other countries, which impact on your mentoring practice. The chapter then considers three mentoring models which a mentor could adopt to inform their practice. These models underpin various roles you undertake and hence the other chapters in this book.

Objectives

At the end of this chapter, you should be able to:

- Have a greater understanding of what is meant by the term 'mentoring' for a beginning teacher.
- Have an appreciation of the key context in which you work that may influence the manner in which you act as a mentor in school.
- Have an awareness of the plethora of mentoring models that exist.
- Compare and contrast three developmental mentoring models and how these could be used to support your role as a mentor.

Before reading further, undertake Task 1.1.

> **Task 1.1 Mentor reflection: reflecting on your understanding of mentoring**
>
> Reflect on what you understand by mentoring by considering the following questions:
>
> - How would you define mentoring?
> - How does your definition inform your practice as a mentor?
> - How do the various policy and guidance documents relevant to your context influence your mentoring practice?
> - Do you base your mentoring practice on personal experience or on a model(s) of mentoring? If a model, which one(s)? Why?

Definitions of mentoring

Mentoring is widely used in many contexts for the purpose of helping people to learn and develop, both professionally and personally. There are numerous and frequently contradictory definitions of mentoring, with accompanying models of how mentoring is best approached (Haggard et al., 2011). Whilst different models might utilise different terminology and vary in emphasis regarding the role of a mentor, what remains consistent is the view that mentoring is a supportive, learning relationship. The mentor, with their more extensive experience, is there to support the learner's development. The quality of the relationship between mentor and mentee is extremely important.

The terms mentoring and coaching are at times used interchangeably. Both aim to develop the professional or professional competencies of the client or colleague. Although mentoring and coaching have much in common, an important difference between the two is the focus of developmental activities. In mentoring, the focus is on development at significant career transitions whereas in coaching the focus is on the development of a specific aspect of a professional learner's practice (CUREE, 2005).

Montgomery (2017) suggested that definitions of mentoring often involve the concept that advice and guidance to a novice, or person with limited experience, is given by an experienced person. In this way, mentoring can be seen to be hierarchical; a top-down approach largely based on a one-way flow of information.

> Mentoring involves the use of the same models and skills of questioning, listening, clarifying and reframing associated with coaching. Traditionally, however, mentoring in the workplace has tended to describe a relationship in which a more experienced colleague uses his or her greater knowledge and understanding of the work or workplace to support the development of a more junior or inexperienced member of staff.
>
> Chartered Institute of Personnel and Development (CIPD, 2012, p. 1).

In contrast, other definitions of mentoring follow a less hierarchical structure. These include peer mentoring (Driscoll et al., 2009) and group mentoring (Kroll, 2016). In these approaches to mentoring, the flow of information is more bidirectional. Montgomery (2017) suggested they are more personalised as mentoring is adapted to an individual mentee's goals and needs more effectively. Higgins and Thomas (2001) suggested that top-down mentoring had a greater impact on short-term career outcomes and individually driven mentoring supported long-term career development more effectively. Whether the focus is on short- or long-term tailored development of a mentee, there are common aspect to all forms of mentoring. CIDP (2012, p. 1) identified four characteristics of mentoring:

- It is essentially a supportive form of development.
- It focuses on helping a person manage their career and improve skills.
- Personal issues can be discussed productively.
- Mentoring activities have both organisational and individual goals.

In education, school-based mentors play a vital role in the development of student teachers and induction of newly qualified teachers. They also support other staff at points of career development. As with mentoring in other contexts, there is a focus on learning, development and the provision of appropriate support and encouragement. The definition of a mentor outlined in the *National Standards for School-based Initial Teacher Training (ITT) Mentors* in England (Department for Education (DfE), 2016b, p. 11) is someone who 'is a suitably experienced teacher who has formal responsibility to work collaboratively within the ITT partnership to help ensure the trainee receives the highest quality training'. However, in initial teacher education in many countries, including England, assessment of the beginning teacher is integral to the mentor's role. This is supported by Pollard (2014) who suggested that the role of the mentor in ITT has developed because of three aspects, the complexity of the capabilities teachers need to meet, the focus on high professional standards in school and the transfer of knowledge from one generation to another. Before reading any further, undertake Task 1.2.

Task 1.2 Mentor reflection: understanding the term mentoring

1. Research the terms 'mentoring' and 'coaching'.
2. List a variety of terms that you associate with coaching and mentoring.
3. Make a list of common and unique characteristics for both.

The context in which you are working which underpins your mentoring practice

Mentoring is increasingly important in a range of fields, both in the UK and internationally, as a tool to support recruitment into a profession, retention in that profession, professional learning, networking and career development. In teaching, it is widely recognised that there is a strong relationship between professional learning, teaching knowledge and practices, educational leadership and pupil results (Cordingly et al., 2015). As such, there has been an increase in the development of policy and guidance documents as well as frameworks, toolkits and factsheets produced over the past few years to support educators and others in fulfilling their roles as mentors.

As a mentor, it is important to recognise and embed current policy and statutory guidance into your mentoring practice. There are a number of key documents that underpin the mentoring process in initial teacher education and beyond in England and elsewhere. These constitute the key external drivers in shaping mentoring practice in school. Being aware of these is important, but knowing how to use them to support your work with a beginning teacher can add purpose and validity to what you do (there are examples of how to do this in other chapters in this book). They also enable you to recognise the value of being a mentor in school, as 'effective professional development for teachers is a core part of securing effective teaching' (DfE, 2016c, p. 3).

Table 1.1 highlights policy and guidance documents that influence the work you do in school with a beginning teacher in England but also signposts you to examples of international equivalence documents to enable you to make comparisons internationally.

Now complete Task 1.3.

Task 1.3 The context in which you carry out your mentoring duties

Reflect on the context in which you carry out your mentoring duties. Ensure you are familiar with the relevant documents above (or, if you are working outside England, documents specific to your context). What aspects of these documents do you identify as being of most use to your work and why? Are there any implications specific to mentoring beginning music teachers?

Effective mentoring models

As alluded to above, there are a number of mentoring models which a mentor could adopt in order to support the growth and development of a beginning teacher. Attempts have been made to categorise different approaches to mentoring, for example, Maynard and Furlong (1995) suggested that there are three categories of mentoring, the apprentice model, the competence model and the reflective model. The apprenticeship model argues that the skills of being a teacher are best learned by supervised practice, with guidance from or imitation of experienced practitioners. The competence model suggests that learning to teach requires learning a predefined list of competences (the current Teachers Standards in England (DfE, 2011) could be described as a competence model). In this model, the mentor becomes a systematic trainer supporting a beginning teacher to meet the competences. In the reflective model, the promotion of reflective practice through mentoring is key. This requires a beginning teacher to have some mastery of the skills of teaching to be able to reflect upon their own practice and for the mentor to be a co-enquirer and facilitator rather than instructor. Task 1.4 asks you to look at three different mentoring models.

Table 1.1 Key external drivers influencing mentoring work

	Policy/guidance document	Author and date introduced	Key purpose
Teacher Standards Documents	Teachers' Standards (England)	DfE (2011)	Used to assess all student teachers working towards qualified teacher status (QTS) as well as newly qualified teachers completing their statutory induction period. 'Providers of ITT should assess trainees against the standards in a way that is consistent with what could reasonably be expected of a trainee teacher prior to the award of QTS' (DfE, 2011, p. 6).
	The Australian Professional Standards for teachers (Australia)	Australian Institute for Teaching and School Leadership (AITSL) (2011)	The Standards are designed so that teachers know what they should be aiming to achieve at every stage of their career; to enable them to improve their practice inside and outside of the classroom. 'The Standards do this by providing a framework which makes clear the knowledge, practice and professional engagement required across teachers' careers' (AITSL, 2011, p. 2)
Core Content Requirements for Initial Teacher Education	Framework of Core Content for Initial Teacher Training (England)	DfE (2016a)	The aim of this framework is to improve the consistency and quality of ITT courses by supporting those involved in training teachers and student teachers themselves to have a better understanding of the key elements of good ITT content.
	Differentiated Primary and Lower Secondary Teacher Education Programmes for Years 1-7 and Years 5-10 (Norway)	Ministry of Education and Research (2010)	These regulations apply to universities and university colleges that provide primary and lower secondary teacher education. They aim to ensure that teacher education institutions provide integrated, professionally oriented and research-based primary and lower secondary teacher education programmes of high academic quality.
National or Regional Standards for Educators acting as mentors	National Standards for School-based Initial Teacher Training (ITT) Mentors (England)	DfE (2016b)	The standards were developed to bring greater coherence and consistency to school-based mentoring arrangements for student teachers. They set out the minimum level of practice expected of mentors. They are used to foster consistency in the practice of mentors, raise the profile of mentoring and build a culture of mentoring in schools
	The New York State Mentoring Standards Albany (USA)	The State Education Department/The University of The State Of New York (2011)	A set of standards that guide the design and implementation of teacher mentoring programmes in New York State through teacher induction.

(Continued)

Table 1.1 (Continued)

Policy/guidance document	Author and date introduced	Key purpose
National or Regional guidelines for general coaching and mentoring practice		
National framework for mentoring and coaching (England)	Centre for the Use of Resource and Evidence in Education (CUREE) (2005)	The framework was developed in order to help schools implement mentoring and coaching to assist with continuing professional development and other activities. It sets out ten principles based on evidence from research and consultation which are recommended to inform mentoring and coaching programmes in schools. The framework provides a tool for reflection on existing practice and further development and assists a mentor in self-regulation and monitoring of their own practice.
NTC Continuum of Mentoring Practice (USA)	New Teacher Centre (NTC) (2011)	Designed to assist programme leaders as they seek to implement mentoring to support induction programmes that are capable of accelerating the development of beginning teacher effectiveness, improving teacher retention, strengthening teacher leadership and increasing pupil learning. 'It presents a holistic view of mentoring, based on six professional standards……The continuum of mentoring practice describes three levels of development, labelled Exploring/Emerging, Applying, Integrating/Innovating' (NTC, 2011, p. 2).
Professional Development expectations for teachers		
Standards for teachers' professional development (England)	DfE (2016c)	This is intended for 'all those working in and with, schools in order to raise expectations for professional development, to focus on achieving the best improvement in pupil outcomes and also to develop teachers as respected members of the profession' (DfE, 2016c, p. 4). There is an emphasis on using the standards to support regular reflection on existing practice and discussion between all members of the teaching community. There are five parts to the standard which, when acted upon together, ensure effective professional development.
Ohio Standards for Professional Development (USA)	Ohio Department for Education (2015)	These define the essential elements of a strong professional learning system which is one way that school systems can support all educators and encourage improved teaching and learning.

> **Task 1.4 Three different mentoring models**
>
> - What are the features of practice for each of these models; apprentice, competence and reflective?
> - Which features of these models do you use/want to use in our mentoring?
> - When do/would you use each model of mentoring?

Maynard and Furlong (1995, p. 18) acknowledged that these three models exist but suggested that they should be taken together, in order to contribute to 'a view of mentoring that responds to the changing needs of trainees'. It is this recognition that mentoring practices and approaches evolve as a beginning teacher develops and the need for an examination of different stages of development that lead us to exploring three models of mentoring in more detail. We explore three well-known models (Clutterbuck, 2004; Daloz, 2012; Katz, 1995), all of which focus on the need for the mentor to be flexible in their style and approach to best fit the needs of a beginning teacher at any given stage of their development, in initial teacher education and/or their teaching career.

Daloz's (2012) developmental model identifies two key aspects that need to be present in order for optimal learning to take place: **challenge** and **support**. The challenge aspect refers to your ability as a mentor to question a beginning teacher to enable them to reflect critically on their own beliefs, behaviours and attitudes. The support aspect relies on you being able to offer an empathetic ear, actively listen and encourage a beginning teacher to find solutions in order to continue to develop and progress.

Daloz (2012) argues that a combination of high challenge and high support needs to be offered by you as the mentor for a beginning teacher to learn effectively and to **'grow'** (High challenge + high support = **growth**). At the opposite end of this spectrum is what Daloz refers to as **'stasis'**. A beginning teacher's learning in this zone is very limited indeed as a result of their mentor offering low levels of challenge and support (Low challenge + low support = **stasis**). Where challenge is high but support is low, a beginning teacher is likely to **'retreat'** from development (High challenge + low support = **retreat**). However, where challenge is low but support is high, a beginning teacher is unlikely to move beyond their present situation despite their potential for growth being on the increase. Daloz refers to this as **'confirmation'** (Low challenge + high support = **confirmation**). You therefore need to be aware of both the level of challenge you offer and the level of support needed by the beginning teacher.

The second model is Katz's stages of development model (1995) which describes a model for professional growth in four stages (see also chapter 14):

1. Survival stage,
2. Consolidation stage,
3. Renewal stage, and
4. Maturity stage.

During the first stage, **'Survival'**, a beginning teacher is likely to show signs of being very self-focussed and just 'getting by' or coping from day-to-day. They are likely to experience their practice from a position of doubt and be asking questions like 'can I get to the end of the week?' or 'can I really do this day after day?'. During this initial stage, a beginning teacher may show a reluctance to take responsibility for things and, instead, look to blame others, for example, the pupils, colleagues, the school. As a mentor, observing a beginning teacher during the survival stage, you are likely to see elements of confusion and a lack of any clear rules and routines in their lessons. The beginning teacher may also demonstrate little, if any, consistency in their approach to managing behaviour. Their teaching style is often very teacher-centric and they show a reluctance to deviate from their 'script' in any way.

By the second stage, '**Consolidation**', it is likely that a beginning teacher will have begun to implement clearer rules and routines into their classrooms. There is evidence of them starting to question their own practice and being more open to alternative ways of doing things. Whilst observing a beginning teacher at this stage, you are likely to notice that their classes are generally well-managed and that the needs of the average pupil are predominantly well-catered for. In addition, the beginning teacher is likely to demonstrate a greater awareness of individual pupils and their learning needs. However, they are unlikely to have gained a true grasp of how to support and cater for the needs of pupils within specific sub-groups, for example, special educational needs and disability (SEND), English as an Additional Language (EAL) and Gifted and Talented (GandT).

The '**renewal**' stage is the point at which a beginning teacher becoming much more self-aware and self-critical. They have generally mastered the basics and are now striving for ways in which they can improve their practice. They are looking for strategies and ideas of how to introduce more creative and innovative activities into their lessons. As a general rule of thumb, at the 'renewal' stage beginning teachers are often at their most self-motivated and are eager to contribute to departmental discussions, offer suggestions, design additional resources and/or become involved in the running of lunch time and after-school clubs.

The final stage of Katz's model, '**maturity**', is where a beginning teacher is demonstrating signs of developing their own beliefs, teaching style and strategies. They are regularly asking themselves a number of questions which support deeper levels of reflection, both in and on practice (Schön, 1983). They are still looking to improve their practice and are still interested in new ideas and resources. However, their focus has shifted from an inwards perspective to a much broader one. They are now very much interested in the impact of their teaching on their pupils' learning and progress. Task 1.5 focuses on the responsibilities of the mentor and beginning teacher at each stage of Katz's stages of development model (1995).

Task 1.5 Responsibilities of the mentor and beginning teacher at each stage of Katz's stages of development model (1995)

In each of Katz's stages, there are responsibilities for both the mentor and beginning teacher. Identify what you would do to support a beginning teacher at each stage.

And finally, Clutterbuck's (2004) model of developmental mentoring suggests that an effective mentor wants to draw on all four of the 'helping to learn' styles (guiding, coaching, counselling and networking) (see Figure 1.1). Figure 1.1 shows that in any given mentoring

Models of Mentoring   13

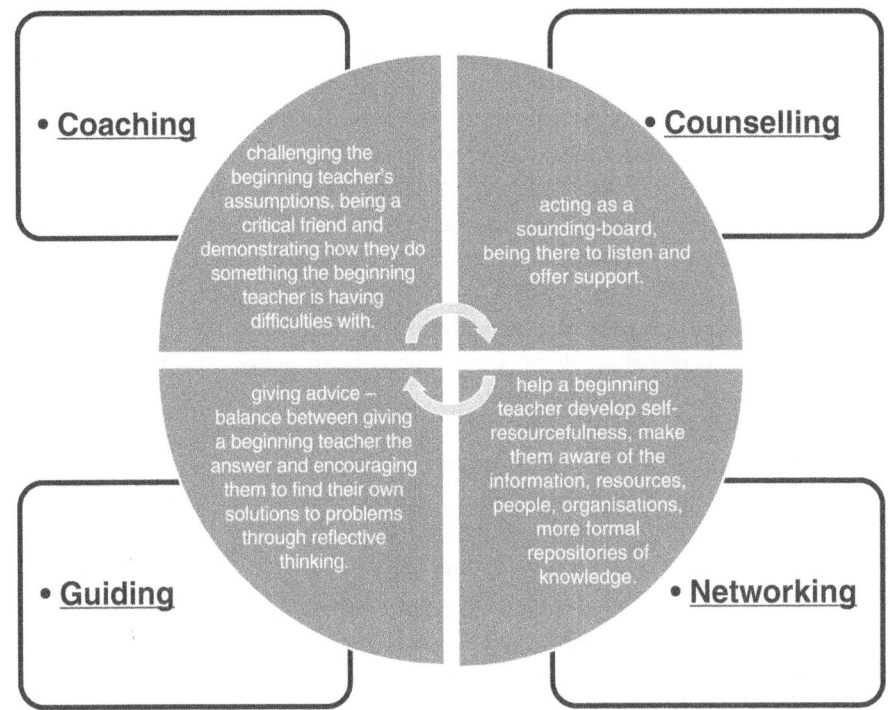

Figure 1.1 Adapted from Clutterbuck's model of Developmental Mentoring (2004, p. 9)

relationship, a mentor may need to adopt a different style and/or approach to challenge and support a beginning teacher at various stages of their development. In developmental mentoring, the beginning teacher sets the agenda based on their own development needs and the mentor provides insight and guidance to support the beginning teacher to achieve the desired goals. A more expert mentor will be able to select the right 'helping to learn' style for a beginning teacher's needs.

Now complete Task 1.6 which looks at Clutterbuck's model.

Task 1.6 Helping a beginning teacher to learn using Clutterbuck's (2004) model

- Consider which of the four 'helping to learn' styles you feel most comfortable with and why.
- Which do you use the least often and/or feel the least comfortable with and why?
- What could they do to overcome this?

Your ability to assess and identify the developmental stage in which a beginning teacher is operating at any given point is a significant aspect of your role in becoming an effective mentor and ensuring growth takes place. Of equal importance, however, is your skill in adapting your own approach to fit the developmental needs of a beginning teacher. It is worth remembering that none of the three models (Clutterbuck, 2004; Daloz, 2012; Katz, 1995) are linear in structure and, therefore, it is likely that a beginning teacher will move 'to and fro' between stages/zones, e.g., if teaching different aspects of the curriculum in which they have greater or lesser knowledge and/or confidence or starting at a new school. With each of the models considered above, it is possible to see elements of all three approaches to mentoring described by Maynard and Furlong (1995). Regardless of the mentoring model on which you prefer to base your practice, the attributes of the mentor play a crucial role in making decisions about the approach to mentoring.

There have been a number of attempts to characterise attributes of mentors. For example, Child and Merrill (2005) sought to generate an understanding of the attributes of a mentor in initial teacher education. Cho *et al.* (2011) described personal qualities that lie at the core of the mentor's identity and professional traits that relate to success in work-related activities. The DfE (2016) described four separate, but related, areas in the *National Standards for School-based Initial Teacher Training (ITT) mentors*, i.e., personal qualities, teaching, professionalism and self-development and working in partnership. Ragins (2016) described the attributes of a mentor as an antecedent to high-quality mentoring; as something that needs to be in place before a mentor–mentee relationship begins. Task 1.7 asks you to consider the attributes of an effective mentor (see also Chapter 2).

Task 1.7 Attributes of an effective mentor

1. Considering the context and models of mentoring outlined in this chapter, reflect upon what you think the attributes of an effective mentor are. Attach a level of significance to each attribute, using three categories of significance: *essential*, *desirable* and *highly desirable*.
2. Having identified the attributes and the levels of significance, place five of the attributes in a prioritised list that best captures the ideal profile of a mentor of a beginning teacher.
3. Reflect on your own practice as a mentor and how you might develop the attributes that you have prioritised.

Finally, Task 1.8 asks you to reflect again on your mentoring practice after having read this chapter.

Task 1.8 Mentor reflection: reflecting on your mentoring practice

After having read this chapter, reflect how your understanding of definitions of mentoring, relevant policy and guidance documents and models of mentoring have/will impact on your practice.

Summary and keypoints

Effective mentoring is a complex and demanding task, but, as with any role that enables you to have a positive impact on the development of others, it is hugely rewarding. In this chapter, we have considered the importance of:

- being aware of different definitions of mentoring,
- understanding the content in which you are carrying out your role and what moral, political, or theoretical drivers might influence the education system that you work in and/or your work as a mentor, and
- having a broad understanding of different models, or approaches to, mentoring in order to make decisions about how to carry out your role as a mentor.

Further resources

Chapters of this book list here further reading relating to design and technology but there isn't a range to list. The ones below are useful and will support your thinking when reading the chapters of this book.

Maynard, T. and Furlong, J. (1995) 'Learning to teach and models of mentoring', *in* T. Kerry and A. Shelton-Mayes (eds.) *Issues in mentoring.* London: Routledge, pp. 10-14.

This chapter should help to deepen your knowledge of the three categories of mentoring, the apprentice model, the competence model and the reflective models.

Cordingley, P., Higgins, S., Greany, T., et al. (2015) *Developing great teaching: Lessons from the international reviews into effective professional development.* London: Teacher Development Trust.

This should help you to gain an understanding of how mentoring fits into current ideas of effective continued professional development and learning.

SECTION II
About the mentor

2 Understanding yourself: Exploring beliefs and experiences

Kelly Davey Nicklin and Gary Spruce

Introduction

Beginning music teachers typically bring to courses of initial teacher education a broad range of experiences as musicians and of music education as learners and sometimes teachers. These experiences will have been gained both within and beyond formal education contexts such as schools. Such experiences will play a crucial role in the formation of their identities as musicians and educators. These identities are multiple and dynamic. Underpinning these identities will likely be strongly held beliefs about the nature of music and what constitutes important musical knowledge and skills (epistemological conceptions), and about what it is to be a musician and to be a music teacher (ontological conceptions) (Philpott and Spruce, 2021).

Beijaard (2019) contends that 'Learning to teach is an identity making process' which 'concern[s] teachers' overall conception of who they are as teachers, who they believe they are, and who they want to be as teacher [and that] teacher learning, therefore, can and should be conceptualised as teacher identity learning' (p. 1). If this is the case, then those working with beginning music teachers have a crucial role to play in supporting the development of their *music* teacher identities. An important part of this process is for mentors to work with beginner teachers to help them interrogate and reflect critically on the epistemological and ontological conceptions they hold, and secondly to explore the extent to which these conceptions provide a sufficiently robust and secure foundation for teaching music to the diverse range of young people they will meet in contemporary music classrooms.

This chapter focuses primarily on the mentoring of music teachers who, either prior to or as part of their teaching courses, have studied music to degree or equivalent level; mentoring non-specialist music teachers present particular sets of challenges and opportunities which there is not space here to cover. It begins by asking you, as a mentor, to explore both your own beliefs as a musician and teacher and the impact of these on your identity as a music teacher and on the decisions and choices you make. Moving on, the chapter considers ways in which you can support a beginning teacher to identify and explore their own musical beliefs and values and to perhaps broaden their conception of what music is both for themselves and for the pupils they teach. Finally, we consider the context of the school as the place within which teacher identities are formed and developed and explore the potential and possibilities for the exercise of beginner teacher agency.

DOI: 10.4324/9781003004196-5

Objectives

At the end of this chapter, you should be able to:

- Examine your own musical beliefs and values and understand how these impact on your practice as a music teacher and mentor.
- Support beginning music teachers in examining their own musical backgrounds, beliefs, and understand how these underpin their beliefs and approaches as music teachers.
- Understand some of the key issues around teacher identity and how these can inform effective mentoring practices.

Examining your own beliefs

In his book 'Teaching Music Musically', Swanwick (1999) contends that a 'particular teaching method is nowhere near so important as our perception of what music is and what it does' (p. 45). Similarly, Spruce (2002) writes that '…the way in which music is perceived – the understanding of its nature and purpose – is critical to the way in which it impacts upon curriculum design, what we teach and the way we teach it' (p. 4). The point that both writers make is that one's values and beliefs about the nature of music as a phenomenon has a significant influence on what one believes:

- it is to *be* a musician and to *be* musical (ontological conceptions);
- to be important musical knowledge and skills (epistemological conceptions).

These ontological and epistemological conceptions are typically experienced as self-evident and universal. They are unspoken, implicit, unquestioned, and uninterrogated. They are, thus, for the most part 'ideological', where an ideology is understood as being formed of common-sense assumptions which contribute towards making the status quo seem natural and beyond question. These common-sense assumptions about what music is and what it does are grounded in one's musical *enculturation* (the music and musical practices one experiences naturally as part of the social networks and cultural groupings of which one is part) and *socialisation*, the more deliberate inducting into the musical values most prized by society, and typically promoted in formal educational contexts such as schools.

These conceptions form the bedrock of beginning teachers' identities as musicians. It is these 'musician identities' which research demonstrates (e.g., Pellegrino, 2009) underpins their nascent identities as teachers (teacher ontologies) and informs their emerging beliefs about:

- what should be included in a 'music education' ('important' musical knowledge and skills);
- the pedagogies that are likely to be most effective in realising its aims (e.g., curriculum and lesson content and choices of repertoire as well as assessment processes and strategies).

Before reading further, undertake Task 2.1.

Task 2.1 Exploring musical identities

If you were asked to describe what it is to be a musician and to act musically, what would you say?

Reflect upon your own musical enculturation and musical socialisation and consider how these have had an impact on your values and beliefs as a music teacher. Which had the most powerful impact on your identity as a musician and a teacher, why?

Your response to this task should be visualised in the format of a Venn diagram of two circles – the first representing your identity as a musician and the second representing your identity as a music teacher. Where the two circles intersect, you should reflect upon any shared values and beliefs across both identities.

As you work with your beginning music teacher, reflect on how your values and beliefs as a musician and music teacher compare to theirs – you could encourage your beginning music teacher to also respond to the same task. Revisit your response at the end of the chapter to see if your views have changed. This is a useful exercise to return to with your beginning music teacher at the end of their teacher education programme – how do both of your responses compare? It would be very useful for a beginning music teacher to critically reflect upon why there may have been changes to their values and beliefs within these identities.

Western classical music: a case study in music ideology

Although over the last 20 years or so there has been a significant diversification in the range of post-compulsory and higher education qualifications in music, including degrees in jazz, popular, non-western musics and music technologies, it remains the case that the majority of teachers on pre-service music teacher education courses are primarily educated in the western classical tradition (e.g., Dwyer, 2016). The 'common-sense' assumptions that they bring with them about music is likely then to reflect the values, processes, and practices of this music.

The impact of the ideologies of western art music on western music education have been well rehearsed (e.g., Bull, 2019; Green, 2003; Small, 1987; Spruce with Matthews, 2012) and can be summarised as follows:

- A tendency to conceive music as an object (reification) rather than primarily as something that people do (a social practice).
- A belief that 'good' music is characterised by its autonomy, i.e., that its 'meaning' is entirely contained with its materials and that it exists independently of any social context.
- The sharp delineation of the roles of 'composer', 'performer', and 'audience' all with their distinct responsibilities to the musical object.
- A belief in a musical canon (musical works of the classical tradition to which all children should be introduced).

The strength of the ideological discourses which support this conception of music is, as Spruce (2017) has pointed out, evident in the everyday language used to talk about music – 'pieces of music' and 'musical works and compositions' – and the tendency to consider the notated/objectified form of the music to be synonymous with the music itself – 'don't forget to bring your music to rehearsal'. A reified conception of music has led directly to western music education's emphasis on the building bricks of music: from the focus on the 'musical elements' in the early stages of schooling to the analysis of set works in external examinations; the separation of musical theory from musical practice and sound; the broad division of music curricular (particularly at examination level) into performing, composing, and listening. However, as Philpott (2010) points out, this is not the way in which young people (and particularly teenagers) typically experience music beyond school. Rather, they experience music in a much more integrated way, with performing, creating, and listening being brought together and as a social practice – music as a practice. Many young people experience a tension between their enculturated musical selves (and music as they experience it outside of school) and the musical values, practices, and ways of learning music that are promoted within schools, leading consequently to alienation from formal music education.

Before reading further, undertake Task 2.2.

Task 2.2 Reflecting upon ideological discourses

- Do you agree with the analysis presented above, particularly in relation to the impact described as having on young people's attitudes to formal music education?
- Looking back to your response to Task 2.1, to what extent do you feel that your beliefs about music are or were governed by the musical ideology described above?

Exploring beginning music teacher beliefs

It is likely that for those achieving a place on a teacher education course, their formal music education will have met their needs, or they will have successfully negotiated the barriers that it put in their way (they will have successfully 'played the game'). One of the challenges for you, the mentor, is to work with beginning music teachers to help them recognise that whilst their music education may have worked for them it might not have done so for many of their peers.

Before reading further, undertake Task 2.3.

Task 2.3 Musical enculturation

If music teachers are unable to reflect critically on their own musical enculturation and socialisation then there is a risk that they simply impose the way in which they were taught and learnt unknowingly and undifferentially onto the young people that they teach.

- Discuss with your beginning music teacher their own musical enculturation and socialisation by imagining their musical journey as a river with significant 'landmarks' along the way that have shaped them into the musician they are now. Ask them to reflect on how their enculturation and socialisation have impacted on their values and beliefs as a musician and on their vision for the kind of music teacher they wish to be.
- Now ask them to think back to their music education from the perspective of their peers. Did their music education provide equal opportunities for everyone to flourish musically? If not, why not? If it did, how did the teacher achieve this? What does this reflection tell them about what it is to be an 'inclusive teacher'?

Where beginning music teachers do not come from western classical music backgrounds some issues should be noted:

- They are likely to have experienced the practices and procedures of western music as the dominant music ideology within their musical socialisation.
- They may consider their lack of experience, knowledge, and skills in western art music to be a 'deficiency' whilst not valuing what they bring from their own traditions.
- They are still likely to carry with them implicit musical values and beliefs which require unpicking.

Encouraging all beginning music teachers to bring to the fore of their thinking what in Bordieuan terms might be described as their *habitus* – their 'socially acquired systems of beliefs and values' (Dwyer, 2016, p. 6) - can lead to the interrogation of and reflection on hitherto unquestioned and uninterrogated personal musical values and beliefs and the potential limitations of the identities that they bring to preservice teacher education courses.

Before reading further, undertake Task 2.4.

Task 2.4 Values, experiences, and beliefs of beginning music teachers

Consider the individual profiles for the beginning music teachers shown below. What might you assume about the values, experiences, and beliefs of these beginning music teachers?

- **Profile 1:** A guitarist with a pop/rock background who has studied vocational music qualifications;
- **Profile 2:** An instrumental teacher with 10 years of experience of private instrumental teaching wanting to move into a classroom setting;

- **Profile 3:** A music technology graduate who specialises in composing with technology; and
- **Profile 4:** A music college graduate who specialises in woodwind performance.

Consider the profile of a beginning music teacher that you are working with. Did you make any assumptions about their values, beliefs, and experiences that were proved to be incorrect?

Schools and particularly music mentors, therefore, play a key role in supporting beginning music teachers to 'confront' their identities and in doing so to subject their own beliefs to scrutiny. Finney and Philpott (2010) suggest, '[e]xcavating what is thought to have been suppressed yet having latent potential involves the creation of challenge leading to dissonance and the possibility of working through this in a productive way' (p. 17). This 'working through' will involve approaches to mentoring which involve the co-excavation of beginning music teachers' *and* mentors' habitus and unconscious ideologies rooted in unexamined epistemological and ontological conceptions. This can be a particularly fruitful exercise where there is a perceived dissonance between the musical beliefs and values of the beginning music teacher and their mentor.

Before reading further, undertake Task 2.5.

Task 2.5 Self-reflection: your own experiences as a beginning music teacher

Reflect upon your own experiences as a beginning music teacher. What support and actions from your own mentor(s) were the most useful in helping you to develop your identity as a music teacher and to explore your unquestioned assumptions and beliefs? Who else was involved in helping you to shape your own identity as a beginning music teacher?

Beauchamp and Thomas (2011) state that 'student teachers undergo a shift in identity due to the range of experiences they gain in the process of becoming a teacher' (p. 175). How did your identity as a musician and a teacher change during the time of your own pre-service teacher education? How has this identity developed and changed during the course of your teaching career to date?

Musician or music teacher: tensions and reconciliations

It is perhaps evident from the issues already explored that a major challenge for those embarking on courses of pre-service teacher education is reconciling the relationship and any potential tension between their deeply felt and embedded identities as musicians (often developed through many years of high-level study particularly as a performer) and their nascent and emerging identities as music teachers. Supporting beginning music teachers to reconcile the tensions between these two macro-identities is one of your most important roles, not least because, as Ballantyne and Zhukov (2017) point out: 'a contributor to praxis shock and burnout in music teachers is the nexus between their perceptions of themselves as musicians and as educators' (p. 242). Although such burn out may occur later in a career, pre-service teacher education and mentoring provide one of the few, but important, opportunities in which such tensions might be reconciled.

Although tensions between the 'discipline specialist' identity (Pellegrino, 2009) and teacher identity is present in all subjects, it is arguably particularly acute in music because, as Regelski (2009) notes, music teachers are

> often unique among most of the other teachers in schools who do not typically 'do' the subjects they teach (art teachers sometimes are an exception). Unlike music teachers who, independently of their teaching, are trained musicians, most teachers are not trained physicists, chemists, historians, or the like, but have mastered their subject to the degree needed to teach it...
>
> (p. 3)

Echoing what we have noted already he writes that 'self-regard as music professionals usually has a bearing on what and how they teach' (p. 3).

Ballantyne et al. (2012) note that – initially at least – whether beginning music teachers identify as musicians or teachers is governed by their experience prior to beginning teacher education courses and is significantly influenced by their 'musical self-efficacy', that is: 'how a teacher perceives their own musical abilities' (p. 213). Musical self-efficacy is, as we have noted, likely to be linked to a particular set of music practices, values, and beliefs and the beliefs and values inherent in them. Therefore, where musical efficacy is particularly strong, it can work against inclusive musical practices that require a broader conception of 'what music is and what it does' (Swanwick, 1999). Moreover, as Bernard (2005) has pointed out, a strongly held identity as a musician over that of a teacher can create a barrier to learning the pedagogical skills that are often required of a teacher in a music classroom.

However, given that, as Regelski (2009) points out, many music teachers continue to be practising musicians and that within secondary schools (ages 11-18), music teachers are expected to support the development of choirs, bands, orchestras, music theatre productions, and other groups. Music teaching can legitimately be conceived of as 'a function of being a musician' (Wagoner, 2012). It is therefore not realistic – were it even desirable – for the 'musician identity' to be entirely subservient to that of the 'teacher identity' (Wagoner, 2012, n.p.). Rather, both need to exist in a context-dependent, dynamic relationship with each other that allows identity-fluidity. As Pellegrino (2009) notes, '...music teachers are, ideally, integrated people who bring meaningful music experiences with them into classrooms' (p. 50). Similarly, Bernard (2005) describing the 'artist-teacher' emphasises the importance of acknowledging 'the centrality of experiences of making music in the ways that music educators understand themselves and their work' (p. 28).

It is the notion of 'meaningful music experiences' and the 'centrality of making music' that the identity of the 'teacher-artist' has the potential for greatest educational benefits. Earlier in this chapter we cited Swanwick's (1999) contention that the 'particular teaching method is nowhere near so important as our perception of what music is and what it does' (p. 45). Swanwick (1999) continues as follows:

> Running along any system or way of working will be the ultimate question - is this really *musical*? Is there a feeling for expressive character and a sense of structure in what is done and said? To watch an effective music teacher at work (rather than a 'trainer' or 'instructor') is to observe this strong sense of musical intention linked to educational purposes: skills are used for musical ends, factual knowledge informs musical understanding.
>
> (p. 45)

Ironically, perhaps given what the research says about beginning music teachers privileging their identities as musicians, they are sometimes unwilling to draw on their musical skills in the classroom and use these to model musical processes and potential outcomes.

Before reading further, undertake Task 2.6.

Task 2.6 Encouraging the musical skills of beginning music teachers

Crestwood School in Dudley (an area in the English Midlands) is part of the Invictus Trust of Schools. When beginning music teachers need encouraging to use their own musical skills or to focus on musical sound as the primary medium of communication, the music mentor, Rob Sweeney, asks them to teach a 'silent lesson'. This is not what it might initially appear to be - a lesson with no sound; rather a lesson where no talking is allowed by either the teacher or the pupils. All communications take place either through signals by the teacher (for organisational/management issues only) or through musical sound/music making. The pupils are used to this happening on occasions and respond well, producing musical work of high quality. The beginner teachers find it a really useful exercise - if a rather unnerving one!

Work with your beginning music teacher to devise a lesson or part of lesson in which their own musical skills take centre stage. Depending on their confidence, this might take the form of a 'silent lesson'. Begin by giving them the planned learning outcomes for the lesson and ask them to teach these outcomes primarily or exclusively drawing on their own skills as a musician and using musical sound.

Following the lesson, encourage your beginning music teacher to reflect critically on the impact of their lesson. Questions for your beginning music teacher to consider could include:

- What was the impact on the pupils' musical learning?
- How did this lesson compare to other lessons that you have taught?
- What were some of the challenges that you had to work through when planning and teaching the lesson?

Teacher identity, context, and the exercise of agency

In a review of literature around teacher identity, Beauchamp and Thomas (2009) identify a range of factors that contribute to the construction of teacher identity both within teacher education courses and beyond. Recurring themes are: the relationship between identity and the sense of self (we touched upon this in discussing the relationship between the identities of musician and teacher); identity as a dynamic phenomenon which 'shifts over time under the influence of a range of factors both internal...and external to the individual' (p. 177); how individuals exhibit multiple identities; and identities as context-bound or context-specific. This last theme is particularly important in that it suggests that that identity does not have an autonomous existence independent of a context (i.e., exists simply within an individual) but exists only in relation to contexts.

Perhaps unsurprisingly then, Beauchamp and Thomas (2009) identify the context of the school as a key factor in the formation of a beginning teacher's identity: 'The school environment, the nature of the learner population, the impact of colleagues and of school administrators can all be influential in shaping a student or new teacher identity...' (p. 184). Significantly for music education, with its multiplicities of pedagogies and approaches, they also note that the subject discipline and the teaching cultures associated with it also constitutes an important context for the mediation of beginning teachers' emerging identities as music teachers. They suggest that both the context of the school and the subject discipline within schools can provide 'important confrontations with one's identity as a teacher' (Beauchamp and Thomas, 2009) and cite literature that argues for 'the importance of placing students in teaching contexts that provoke tensions to challenge their identities, and thus allow for questioning of themselves and their beliefs' (p. 185).

Wagoner (2012), writing of the relationship between musician identity and teacher identity, notes that for music teachers (and prospective music teachers) there are a 'different set of anticipatory social expectations than those associated with teacher preparation in non-music content areas'. Anticipatory social expectations (or anticipatory socialisations) being the values and dispositions that individuals need to learn and adopt in order to become accepted members of a group.

Before reading further, undertake Task 2.7.

Task 2.7 Beginning music teachers within your music department

Consider what are the 'anticipatory social expectations' (Wagoner, 2012) for a beginning music teacher coming to work in your department. How do you think they differ from those of other subjects? What are the reasons for these expectations? Will some beginning music teachers be able to demonstrate these more easily than others? If so, why?

Using the profiles of the beginning music teachers in Task 2.4, consider the initial challenges that each beginning music teacher may face in the context of working in your own music department or setting.

What challenges might you face as a mentor if the values and beliefs of your mentee are very different to your own? What challenges might you or your mentee face if your values and beliefs are very similar?

The cultivation of agency

Bernstein (1996) argues that schools, and particularly classrooms, are fields within which knowledge is recontextualised through the 'pedagogic device' and made suitable for teaching. Traditionally, these spaces for recontextualising knowledge provided opportunities for (music) teachers to exercise personal and professional agency. However, increasing accountability measure at both macro (national) and meso (school) level have limited such opportunities. As Fautley (2017), amongst others, has pointed out, this has resulted in music teachers often being compelled to adopt pedagogical and assessment paradigms that are not always appropriate to developing young people's musical understanding in ways that are musical. At the time of writing this chapter, in England, the epistemological basis of music education is a contested area. A commitment to experiential approaches to music pedagogy and the notion of the primacy of embodied knowledge (musical knowledge and understanding demonstrated through making music) is being challenged by policy makers under the banner of 'knowledge-rich' curricular which privileges declarative/factual knowledge over the procedural and embodied (e.g., Spruce et al., 2021).

An important part of beginning teachers' (and indeed all teachers') sense of identity is their capacity to exercise agency over their practice and workplace in order to transcend the discourses of compliance that arguably characterises the contemporary education context in many countries. Priestley et al. (2015) argue that teachers' potential for agency is dependent on their capacity to imagine alternative ways of acting and of being within the classroom and that a key determining factor here is 'their roots in past cultures and structures which have played a role in the socialisation of teachers which shape the agency of teachers as they engage with present day contexts' (cited in Philpott and Spruce, 2021, p. 296). It is to acknowledge that teachers (beginners and otherwise) are not at the mercy of their socialisation. As Dalladay (2016, n.p.) writes:

> ...there is little that one can do to alter our life-histories, [but] we can be agents in recognising and, if necessary, changing our biographies as they are formed and recognising how far the experiences of the past need to impinge on the activity of the now and future.

Ballantyne et al. (2012) highlight the importance of pre-service teacher education in 'guiding students towards viewing themselves as shapers of their own identities and professional destinies' (p. 30). An important issue for mentors, then, is the extent to which they provide a supportive framework within which beginning music teachers can exercise a degree of agency over their own practice.

Before reading further, undertake Task 2.8.

Task 2.8 Agency of beginning music teachers within your department

Consider the agency that would be afforded to a beginning music teacher working in your own music department. How much agency might the beginner music teacher have in developing their own teaching practices? Consider if this sense of agency might vary from the departmental perspective to the whole school/institution perspective.

Conclusion

In this chapter, we have argued for the importance of exploring your own beliefs as a mentor and supporting beginning music teachers in examining their own identities, beliefs, and values. Engaging reflexively with values and beliefs can enable beginning music teachers and mentors to move beyond, as Larivee (2000) suggests, mere surface reflection on 'strategies used to achieve predetermined goals' (p. x) to moral and ethical considerations, including the purposes of music education. Such co-excavations require a dialogical approach to mentoring 'where development occurs as a consequence of shifts between different identity positions that map onto the topography of a teacher identity system' (Henry, 2019, p. 264). Here, both beginning music teachers and mentors examine and question their own musical beliefs and values and hold these up for scrutiny. The challenges to such an approach should not be underestimated for both mentor and beginning music teacher. Nevertheless, the potential prize is the development of a music education workforce and music pedagogy which is more inclusive and unalienating for pupils and where music teachers develop a greater sense of agency over their practice.

COVID-19 had a huge impact on schools and music education. It resulted in challenges for mentors and how they could support their beginning music teachers. Two of the main challenges for mentors were:

- Music teachers in the school environment had to adapt their approaches due to COVID-19 restrictions and, as a result, some teachers were not able to adopt the pedagogical and *musical* approaches they would have wished to. A dialogue with beginning music teachers about how teaching and learning was adapted and the impact this had on musical learning could be considered crucial for beginning music teachers' understanding.
- COVID-19 restrictions also had an impact on the support and feedback that mentors provided for beginning music teachers, particularly in circumstances where online learning was required for extended periods of time. Being able to make the tacit explicit when discussing teaching and learning in the music classroom is a trait of mentors who are able to nurture and develop successful beginning music teachers.

Summary and key points

- Those working with beginning music teachers have a crucial role to play in supporting the development of their identities as a music teacher.
- Mentors should support beginning music teachers in interrogating and reflecting critically upon the epistemological and ontological conceptions they hold.
- The majority of teachers on pre-service music teacher education courses are primarily educated in the western classical tradition and 'common-sense' assumptions that they

bring with them about music is likely to reflect the values, processes, and practices of this music.
- Working successfully with a diverse range of young people in an inclusive music classroom that does not alienate pupils from formal music education requires beginning music teachers to explore their own epistemological and ontological conceptions about music and music education.
- *Teacher identity* and *musician identity* exist in a context-dependent, dynamic relationship with each other that allows identity-fluidity, and these identities will likely change over the course of one's music teaching career.
- An important part of the beginning music teacher's sense of identity is their capacity to exercise agency over their practice and workplace. This can be limited in an increasingly regulated and accountability-led education system.

Resources

Ballantyne, J. and Zhukov, K. (2017) 'A good news story: Early-career music teachers' accounts of their "flourishing" professional identities', *Teaching and Teacher Education*, 68, pp. 241-251.

This article explores beginning teachers understanding of their own professional identities and the factors and issues that impact on their professional lives.

Dalladay, C. (2016) *Music teacher biography and its impact on teaching practice.* Available at: https://www.semanticscholar.org/paper/Music-teacher-biography-and-its-impact-on-teaching-Dalladay/434bf9eb289fdf1206ccbca7caf33dabe6aef71a [accessed: 3 August 2022].

In this paper, Chris Dalladay explores the impact of music teachers' biographies on their teaching approaches and practices.

Garnett, J. (2014) 'Musician and teacher: Employability and identity', *Music Education Research*, 16(2), pp. 127-143.

In this chapter, we discussed how music teacher identity is context-dependent. In this article, Garnett develops this idea further demonstrates how teachers need to construct a 'narrative of employability' which resonates with the particular context or setting within which they are to work.

3 Understanding your approach in relation to advocacy, pedagogy, and professional development

Rebecca Lundberg

Introduction

This chapter discusses the relationship between music education advocacy, music teacher beliefs in how music should be taught, and the impact of subject knowledge on pedagogical choices. As a starting point, it encourages consideration of advocacy claims, the questions that they can raise and how you, as a mentor, can support beginning music teachers in dealing with this successfully. The chapter then considers how having the correct approach to teaching the subject is vital in promoting the subject in the long-term, in regard to pedagogy and musicianship. It will reflect on the mentor's role in supporting beginning music teachers in developing their understanding of creating a culture where music education is valued through worthwhile music teaching. Finally, there is consideration of your own professional development as a musician and teacher, the impact this can have on the pedagogical choices you make, and the significance of your role as a mentor in providing a convincing model for beginning music teachers in their own development.

Objectives

At the end of this chapter, you should be able to:

- Develop an awareness of your role as a mentor in articulating the relationship between common advocacy claims in music education and their potential impact on appreciation of the subject;
- Have an understanding of what underpins your pedagogical choices and your role as a mentor in developing this understanding with beginning music teachers; and
- Develop an understanding of the importance of continued musical development as a mentor and teacher.

Before reading further, undertake Task 3.1.

> **Task 3.1 Considering your own claims for why music matters and music advocacy**
>
> 1. Briefly consider and reflect on your values of music education.
> 2. When do you feel that advocacy is necessary? List the reasons that you use to advocate for music education.
> 3. How are your values of music education different to your advocacy claims?

The advocacy debate and why music should matter

Advocating for music education has increasingly become a requirement of the music teacher role (Elpus, 2007), although it is often misunderstood by music teachers (Mark, 2005). The benefits of the subject often need little explanation to musicians, therefore, considering how to articulate the justification for music education can provide challenges for music teachers, particularly when dealing with a lack of understanding from school leaders (Zeserson et al., 2014). Bowman (2005) describes advocacy as a political endeavour; however, the reference to advocacy in this chapter is not to encourage policy change, but a case of how you, as a music teacher and mentor, deal with advocacy in your own school environment, the relationship between advocacy arguments and misconceptions of curriculum music, and the impact that this can have on pupils and beginning music teachers under your guidance. Advocacy messages should stem from your values of music education (West and Clauhs, 2015), but the philosophical reasons behind these values are not necessarily successful in promoting the subject (Bowman, 2005). Therefore, understanding these contradictions can be important for beginning music teachers, not only in defining their own advocacy approach as music teachers, but more significantly, in encouraging them to (re)consider the values of why and how music should be delivered in the curriculum.

Common arguments in defence of music education can often focus on benefits that are not musical, factors which Bowman (2014) refers to as 'extrinsic'. The 'State of the Nation' report (Daubney et al., 2019) opens with the positive impact the study of music can have on the economy and concludes with the suggestion that subjects such as music are vital in preparing for future employability. The report also focuses on other instrumental benefits, including making links between the study of music and cognitive development and physical and mental health. The 'State of Play' report (Savage and Barnard, 2019) refers to links between music education and improved language skills and begins with a statement highlighting the relationship between learning an instrument and academic development. Hallam (2010) discusses the correlation between studying music and academic achievement in other areas and the impact on transferrable skills, creativity, and wellbeing. A simple internet or social media search also demonstrates how commonplace these arguments have become. Musical reasons for studying music in school are rarely the main aims given and in searching for support with how to justify the subject, this is potentially the wrong message.

Understanding Your Approach 33

The intrinsic/extrinsic argument is a long-standing debate in music education (Bowman, 2014), with the inherently musical reasons for teaching the subject hard to articulate (Reimer, 2005) and the subsidiary motives creating a potentially dangerous situation where we are promoting teaching music for non-musical benefits (Pitts, 2017). Whilst these reasons may indeed have degrees of validity, they do highlight the ambiguity of the collective message and in turn, the relevance to you as a teacher and mentor of understanding the advocacy debate. Elliott and Silverman (2015) make some key points for mentors in relation to this discussion. Beginning music teachers should be wary of all advocacy arguments and their potential to undermine the subject and dishearten music teachers. They should also be supported not only in articulating the correct message, but in understanding that the best way of promoting music education is to provide the opportunity for pupils to experience meaningful musical experiences. It is part of your role as a mentor to make this explicit. Consequently, being prepared to discuss with beginning music teachers the reasons for why you teach music and how these connect with the musical choices you make in lessons, is an important part of their preparing for the music teacher role, not only in dealing with advocacy appropriately and the issues it can bring, but also in regard to their own teaching.

There are benefits to having a range of different advocacy tools; however, there must be an understanding that the claims that are made regarding the reasons behind music education, whether extrinsic or intrinsic, are as Bowman (2014) describes 'contingent', in that they will depend, amongst other factors, on how music is experienced and therefore taught. This premise is also highlighted by Hallam (2010) who suggests the positive impact of music education is reliant on rewarding and successful experiences. Therefore, how and why we teach music will have an impact on pupils receiving the benefits which is an important and powerful message that should be an ever-present consideration for you as a mentor and part of the dialogue with beginning music teachers.

The obvious danger of unrealistic or misjudged advocacy claims is that music education is seen as irrelevant if they are proved to be unfounded (West and Clauhs, 2015), so it is important that advocates are resolute about those factors that are unique to music (Eisner, 2001), regardless of the other offerings associated with the teaching of the subject. However, another risk is that advocacy tends to focus on the benefits of music rather than the teaching methods (Westerlund, 2008). Therefore, perhaps the greater topic of discussion is if these claims are used to defend what we are currently doing in music teaching. Various authors refer to the term 'status quo' in regard to music teaching (Bowman, 2005, 2010, 2014; Conkling, 2007; Hesterman, 2012; Reimer, 2005; Williams, 2019), suggesting that music teachers may use advocacy claims to defend how music is and has been taught, rather than considering the success of how music is delivered. As Reimer states: 'We advocate for what we do when the question begging to be asked is whether what we do is validly and optimally connected to what we claim' (2005, p. 140).

Pitts (2012) proposes what we value often is borne out of our own musical learning experience, and therefore, it is not uncommon for music teachers to teach how they were taught in terms of their pedagogical choices (Thompson, 2007). As a mentor, it is important that you are aware of the potential to use your own music education as a barometer for the decisions you make in relation to content, strategies, and materials, not only in evaluating your own practice effectively, but also in understanding how beginning music teachers shape their own development. Austin and Reinhardt (1999) found that beginning music teachers' beliefs on the subject were very similar both before and after their training, with Schmidt (2012) emphasising that values and beliefs will then influence the training experience. Pajares (1992) concurs, highlighting the difficulty with predetermined ideas in teachers, due to their familiarity with school, suggesting that they have to be strongly challenged by new ideas. Equally, Pitts (2012) proposes having a role model that inspires beginning music teachers to change or reconsider their view, therefore highlighting a significant mentor responsibility. Thompson (2007) also stresses the importance of challenging assumptions with ongoing opportunities for reflection and analysis of their beliefs in relation to their teaching. These issues not only highlight the complex nature of discussing and developing teacher beliefs and choices, but also the importance of your role as a mentor in promoting change at an early stage.

Bowman (2005) proposes that if the curriculum being delivered is good enough, advocacy becomes less of an issue. Discussions around the benefits of music education are not necessary if the next generation is inspired by the worthwhile qualities of music education. This is where it becomes more relevant to you as a mentor in promoting this message with beginning music teachers. As Westerlund states, justifying by how we teach music rather than the reasons for music in itself should start with the following question: 'Under what conditions is the learner likely to experience the personal positive value of his or her music education' (2008, p. 80). Therefore, considering how we teach music in relation to what is worthwhile for the learner is an excellent starting point for music teachers.

Before reading further, undertake Task 3.2.

Task 3.2 Strategies for dealing with advocacy and considering your values of music education

Consider the relationship between your advocacy claims and your values of music teaching.

1. How do you deal with the advocacy claims above? What strategies can you share with beginning music teachers?
2. Consider the specific educational choices you make because of what you value. How have your teaching beliefs and choices been influenced by your own music education?
3. How are your values of music education evident in your mentoring role and teaching practice?

Creating a culture where music is valued and worthwhile music teaching

Research by the Music Commission (2019) has stipulated the need for improved progress in music education, in reference to musical knowledge, understanding, and skills development. It also highlights the difficulty in quantifying how pupils make progress due to the different ways this occurs. This is not just a recent concern, with OFSTED (2012) highlighting the mixed outlook in regard to progression in secondary music teaching, with teachers not focusing on how skills develop over time, instead looking at topics in schemes of work that often lack detail. Blakeslee encourages more of a focus on meeting minimum standards, arguing for 'the same clear goals for student achievement that we expect for other areas of the wider curriculum' (2004, p. 34). In searching for these standards, it is imperative that the statutory national guidance is used to offer the outline of the educational value that is needed (Bate, 2020; Elpus, 2007). The introduction of the Model Music Curriculum (DfE, 2021) also indicates the importance of progression and the need for support for teachers in planning for this. Although non-statutory, it is designed to offer guidance in delivering a sequenced curriculum within the statutory requirements.

The Music Commission refer to the 'core fundamentals' (2019, p. 24) for pupils, in what music lessons should provide, but more importantly express the importance of them being able to 'do something with it' (Music Commission, 2019). This potentially aligns with Pitts' (2012) research which focuses on music in the classroom providing an opportunity for lifelong learning and appreciation of music, arguing that teachers have a responsibility for pupils' musical attitudes and engagement, both during school and long term. Ultimately, if pupils are making progress, have the understanding to continue to engage with music after compulsory education, and perhaps more importantly have the interest to do so, music education can be considered as successful and worthwhile. Therefore, one of the first considerations for you as a mentor and teacher should be what pupils are to take away from compulsory music education, with the aim of long-lasting engagement. Elliott and Silverman state that achieving lifelong engagement of pupils is dependent on music education developing depth of musical understanding and being seen as 'achievable, accessible and applicable' (2015, p. 461). Eisner (2001) suggests that how pupils experience the curriculum is of equal importance, with the Music Commission (2019) also highlighting how they are taught is vital. Zeserson et al. (2014) concur, citing the issues created by the lack of pedagogical agreement in the delivery of music education. As a mentor, encouraging a critical discussion around the reasons behind your choice of strategies and approach is also highly relevant to the development of beginning music teachers, particularly when they can observe and reflect on how they work in practice.

The discussions around pedagogy in music education over the last two decades have often focused on the formal and informal learning dichotomy with a shift in focus from how to teach, to what and how pupils learn (Folkestad, 2006). Green's (2008) research into how popular musicians learn has been an important part of the dialogue and the Musical Futures organisation has promoted informal learning with some success (Hallam et al., 2017). However, considering the misunderstandings of the approach and the subtleties of how it aligns with other pedagogical research highlights the potential difficulty in correctly interpreting pedagogies and therefore the importance of the mentor in supporting understanding in this area.

One of the aims of informal approaches is to promote autonomy for the musical learner, including the principles that skills and knowledge development is less structured and learning starts with music that pupils have chosen and is mainly self-directed with the teacher as facilitator. Elliott and Silverman (2015) are critical of school music when pupils are treated as passive audiences in their own learning. Pitts (2012) also argues that assumptions cannot be made about where teacher choices fit in the experience of pupils with Folkestad (2006), stating that the musical experiences of pupils should always be the starting point for what comes next. Swanwick (1988) discusses the importance of teacher choice regarding the level of formality in lessons, also highlighting the difficulty with defining specific objectives due to the potentially unstructured nature of musical development. Whilst ensuring that pupils feel involved in their musical development is important in creating engagement and relevancy, this level of autonomy needs to be carefully managed.

Misconceptions of the informal learning approach include the use of popular music in lessons, on the premise that this will automatically be relevant to pupils (Green, 2006) or teachers misinterpreting the facilitator role resulting in inadequate musical guidance and support (OFSTED, 2012). OFSTED (2021) also highlight the challenge of managing student repertoire choices within a planned curriculum and the importance of appropriate guidance for novices, which may appear to contradict the principles of this approach. However, the term 'self-directed learning' is perhaps problematic as it suggests a lack of teacher involvement (Allsup, 2008), when arguably, for this to be successful, it potentially involves a high level of musical understanding from teachers in considering how pupils will develop the skills needed to cultivate their musicianship. In this way, the music teacher should have a clear understanding of musical skills to be developed over time, although pupils may have an element of unplanned choice in that they learn these skills as they are needed, in turn creating motivation. As Sexton (2012) states, pupils will deal with the theory and skills as they need to know them. When referring to development of musical understanding, Elliott and Silverman (2015) propose the amount of challenge for pupils needs to be just past their level of understanding, suggesting that this process of engaging learners in increasingly challenging musical problems encourages them to problem find and problem solve. This in turn motivates learners to set their own new goals, which will automatically require a higher level of understanding and although this can come with risks of pupils feeling frustrated, it can be counteracted by pupils being allowed to experiment and potentially, at times, fail (Elliott and Silverman, 2015). Consequently, responding to and fostering the potentially haphazard nature of pupils' musical understanding and musicianship is an important skill that you as a mentor can help beginning music teachers to develop through the opportunity for practice and critical discussion.

The discussion here is to encourage consideration of your choice of pedagogy as a music teacher and mentor and the principles behind these approaches which are generally or individually relevant and beneficial for your pupils. Folkestad suggests that music education is the 'meeting place for formal and informal learning' (2006, p. 139) and overall should encourage a focus on allowing pupils to make music. As a mentor you need to be able to discuss and provide examples of what a mix of pedagogies can look like in practice and how music lessons can promote these principles. What should be integral to any approach is the focus on making music and being musical. Swanwick (1999) refers to music teachers considering what it means to teach musically, Small's concept of 'musicking' (1998, p. 9) highlights the importance of being involved in music through performing and listening and Elliott and Silverman promote the idea of a practical, apprenticeship-like approach to pupils learning music: 'When musical goals and standards are clear, and when teachers and students know they are meeting important musical challenges, the curriculum-as-practicum is charged with enjoyment and growth' (2015, p. 444).

Music teachers need to structure the opportunity for pupils to develop their musicianship, as giving pupils the tools to become better musicians through making music, will foster long-lasting enjoyment in the subject. This is only possible with the appropriate direction from music teachers. Part of the role is to promote, encourage, recognise, and identify the skills of musicianship as they develop in pupils. What Green (2008) defines as facilitating, Elliott and Silverman (2015) describe as ensuring quality and appropriate teacher feedback. Allowing opportunities for beginning music teachers to develop appropriate responses to pupil work is an important part of the mentor role; however, this level of feedback in relation to musicianship, modelling and correct musical choices, also relies on good musicians with an appropriate level of subject knowledge.

Task 3.3 asks you to consider your expectations of musical progression and how this is reflected in your teaching and mentoring role.

Task 3.3 Promoting the development of musicianship

1. What are your musical expectations for pupils at the end of their compulsory music education? What do you consider to be the 'core fundamentals' of musicianship and how do you foster these?
2. What are the general assumptions that are made regarding pupils' musical interests and how do these impact on your choices?
3. How do your responses to the above feed into your work as a mentor?

Professional development and subject knowledge

The Carter Review (2015) specifies the importance of teachers having strong subject-specific pedagogy and appropriate subject knowledge development. It can, however, be difficult for music teachers to feel confident in all aspects of subject knowledge, due to the nature of musical development in one area of expertise, with Swanwick (1999), suggesting that music teachers are in the uncomfortable position of having to work outside of their specialism. Consequently, the needs of music teachers in relation to professional development can be diverse. Mentoring provides a professional development opportunity in encouraging reflection of your own practice (Carter, 2015); however, shaping and directing the required subject knowledge of beginning music teachers is also important in their development. Part of your role as a mentor is to provide a convincing model for beginning music teachers in this area, not only in promoting the importance of developing your own subject knowledge and pedagogy understanding but also in encouraging beginning music teachers to have the right priorities. The transition to music teacher can be difficult (Conway et al., 2004) with preservice teachers under pressure to deal with the new school and classroom environments, resulting in the need to focus on general teaching skills (Welch et al., 2011), perhaps at the expense of their own musical development. It is important to encourage beginning music teachers to continue to consider themselves as musicians, as this is potentially a key part of their identity (Ballantyne and Grootenboer, 2012), which in turn will bring much needed confidence and expertise.

Pellegrino (2011) discusses music-making as professional development, highlighting a range of teacher and pupil benefits including learning new music, styles, and strategies for teaching, maintaining a high level of musicianship and pupils seeing a musical role model. More importantly, seeing music-making in this way promotes the connections between being a musician and a music teacher. Schmidt and Robbins also discuss the role of the musician in driving the teacher as this 'blends personal and professional growth and leads to renewal and wellbeing' (2011, p. 98). As discussed earlier, making music is a fundamental part of teaching music. It is vital that this is mirrored in the practice of music teachers and continues to be an inherent part of your own ethos as a teacher and mentor. Jorgensen (2010) promotes involvement with wider scholarship, suggesting that reflection on what music teachers should be doing and reading on music education is important but often neglected through time constraints. It is also well documented that music teachers often feel professionally isolated (Music Commission, 2019; OFSTED, 2009; Thompson, 2007; Welch et al., 2011), so encouraging an interest in the wider professional field is paramount. Moreover, beginning music teachers value the opportunity for collaboration and professional discussions (Bautista and Wong, 2019), therefore promoting this as part of the mentor-beginning teacher relationship is key, as this may be a rare opportunity of working with another in-school specialist. Encouraging engagement with a network of other teaching professionals will help with this (Schmidt and Robbins, 2011; Welch et al., 2011), particularly by promoting and providing opportunities for dialogue in an informal capacity with Conway (2008) finding that teachers felt this to be particularly effective in terms of professional development. Therefore, making time for beginning music teachers to connect with the wider profession and consider good quality teaching through engaging with reading and interaction with other music educators will promote an accessible and effective form of professional development throughout their careers.

It is also important that teachers understand how they need to develop. Hesterman (2012) argues of the dangers of continuing with preconceived ideas in music teaching, suggesting that making the effort to adapt and change with culture and society is significant in teacher development. Therefore, your professional development as a teacher and mentor should be driven by what is required to improve your teaching practice in relation to what is relevant to pupils. Johnson argues that to do this, the way musicianship is taught needs to 'fit the musical realities of our time' (2010, p. 24), highlighting how popular music has changed perceptions of what musicianship is and therefore what is required in music education. He suggests that the musical practices of today are less prescribed and 'more aural than visual' (Johnson, 2010, p. 23), although the support of notation can also be beneficial in the right situation. However, teaching aural development and with more freedom may be particularly challenging for some beginning music teachers. Whilst more classroom music teachers have developed in the Western classical tradition (Hargreaves et al., 2007) than those brought up through more informal styles, most music teachers will still potentially have a tendency towards one pedagogy, making it a huge challenge for teachers to be comfortable in teaching a different way. Jorgensen (2010) highlights the lack of opportunity for beginning music teachers to discuss pedagogical decisions, due to the variety of other considerations and pressures, and potentially, the reluctance to change approach could be down to a lack of confidence in what they know or how to make changes. Your role as a mentor is potentially crucial in this regard in modelling approaches, clarifying priorities and providing opportunities for discussion and reflection.

These issues around pedagogical development and lack of confidence in subject expertise highlight the complex nature of supporting subject knowledge development in music. Elliott and Silverman (2015) emphasise the importance of the teacher's musicianship, suggesting that the greater this is, the more they can promote this in their pupils, also underlining that subject knowledge will understandably influence teacher choices. Making pedagogical decisions based only on the capabilities of the teacher does not put the needs of pupils at the forefront of music education. Therefore, it is important for you as a mentor to encourage and facilitate the development of subject knowledge that is outside the comfort zone of beginning music teachers. Crucially, Elliott and Silverman also acknowledge the importance of the 'teaching-learning context' (2015, p. 403), suggesting that some issues will only be apparent once a lesson has started, and therefore, expertise is developing a 'working understanding' (Elliott and Silverman, 2015) of these situations. This suggests that mentors are uniquely placed to be able to promote discussion around subject knowledge development in relation to pupil understanding in lessons. Conway et al. (2005) also state the opportunity for reflection and an element of choice is more powerful than a prescriptive approach, highlighting the impact on engagement and motivation if teachers are in control of their own learning. Whilst these conversations are potentially complex due to the range of prior knowledge and experience of beginning music teachers, ensuring they are aware of their strengths and areas of development and that this aligns with the developing needs and interests of their pupils is important.

As Bowman suggests, there is 'no one true way' (2010, p. 11) for music education and music teaching should involve constant reflection on finding the right approach in the moment. In doing this, the starting point has to be good subject knowledge. OFSTED describe this in relation to pupil progression as teachers 'knowing how pupils make musical progress' (2009, p. 48), also suggesting that this is one of the weaker areas of secondary music teaching. The Music Commission (2019) defines progress as the acquisition of musical knowledge and technical skills over time, the application of these skills in an increasing range of contexts and the development of individuality and independence as a musician. With this in mind, it is imperative that mentors help to build the picture with beginning music teachers of what progression looks like and how to draw on their expertise to give appropriate musical advice in a classroom situation. Elliott and Silverman (2015) discuss the effectiveness of pupils being guided by teachers who are musically proficient, highlighting the level of motivation this can create. This guidance also underpins pupils' musical development.

The premise behind worthwhile professional development must start with music teachers having excellent subject knowledge. Beginning music teachers need to find a balance between considering themselves as musicians and taking confidence in what they can do, at the same time as having a professional and refreshing approach to continually develop in other areas. For you, as a mentor, professional development should include the necessary strategies to keep your musicianship relevant to your teaching, whilst fostering the right values and attitudes in beginning music teachers to develop and reflect on their practice. The considerations and discussions around why you make the choices you make is vital as is your responsibility as a musical role model who reflects the nature of current music teaching. Having this approach will empower you with the confidence and expertise needed to inspire the next generation.

Before reading further, undertake Task 3.4.

> **Task 3.4 Considering professional development**
>
> 1. In what ways do you engage in professional development? What are your main considerations in this area?
> 2. How would you describe the pedagogies that you use? What are the difficulties for you in working with different pedagogies? How can you develop subject knowledge in this area?
> 3. Identify how you could support a beginning music teacher in developing a stronger awareness of appropriate guidance in regard to developing musicianship.

Summary and key points

A fundamental responsibility of a music teacher's role is to enthuse the next generation in the enjoyment of making and responding to music. Uninformed advocacy claims can be a barrier to this and it is important that in creating a culture where music is valued, teachers strive to inspire pupils through worthwhile music teaching rather than focusing on articulating the benefits of the subject. In making music education relevant, lessons should promote enjoyment and progression. Teachers should have a positive attitude towards evolving their practice, with the aim of developing their own musicianship and that of their pupils through appropriate choices in relation to pedagogy and musical feedback. As a mentor, this has implications for your own practice, but importantly, you also have a pivotal role in promoting this message with beginning music teachers. The following points from this chapter are important in this discussion:

- The relationship between advocacy claims and music educational values;
- How teacher choices and feedback relate to progression and enjoyment; and
- The role of subject knowledge and professional development in teaching worthwhile lessons.

Further resources

The resources listed below are useful in supporting and extending the discussions and considerations within this chapter.

Elliott, D. J. and Silverman, M. (2015) *Music matters: A philosophy of music education*. 2nd edn. New York: Oxford University Press.

Chapter 2 has a more detailed discussion around the advocacy debate and Chapter 13 should help you consider the concept of developing musicianship.

Pitts, S. (2012) *Chances and choices: Exploring the impact of music education*. New York: Oxford University Press.

This encourages consideration of how music lessons can have an impact on pupils and encourage a lifelong interest in music.

4 Evaluating my impact as a music mentor

Motje Wolf and Helmut Schaumberger

Introduction

In this chapter, we will explore your impact as a music mentor. To understand how deep your impact is, we analyse the highly complex role of a mentor and suggest the impact will be stronger if expectations are met. To improve the impact, it will be important to understand how to evaluate it. The chapter will also look into beginning teachers' expectations of a mentor and vice versa. One way of ensuring expectations are met is to negotiate expectations. You, as a mentor, are not solely responsible for the successful start of a beginning music teacher's career as other experts, peers and mentee self-reflection play an important role in an 'interlocking system of support' (European Commission (EC), 2010, p. 21), too. However, '[…] the mentor should act as a guide through the milestones of teacher education where the ultimate aim is to eliminate the need for the mentor in the process' (Farrell, 2018, p. 227).

Mentors, as well as peers and other experts, can provide support on three levels: the professional, the personal/emotional, and the social level. You, as an experienced, suitably trained teacher, are a key actor in this support system. Your main tasks as a mentor are coaching, training, advising, and discussing as well as coordinating the regulations at school level. Reflecting on the goals of mentoring (stimulating professional learning, creating a safe environment for learning, and socialisation into the school community) (EC, 2010), will help you to improve your impact as a mentor.

Objectives

At the end of this chapter, you should be able to:

- Define the role as mentor for yourself/formulate what the role as a mentor means for you;
- Be aware of your expectations as a mentor;
- Negotiate expectations with the beginning music teacher; and
- Evaluate the impact of your relationship with the beginning music teacher.

My impact as a mentor

Before reading further, undertake Task 4.1.

DOI: 10.4324/9781003004196-7

> **Task 4.1 Reflecting on what your impact as a mentor is**
>
> Read the following scenario and reflect on the positive and negative aspects of it.
>
> Mentor A has five years of music teaching experience and is new to mentoring. Therefore, Mentor A prepares thoroughly for their new role planning to tell the beginning music teacher B the important aspects about the school in their first two meetings. A reserves two hours for the meeting and summarises the most important points in a script. B should be informed as early as possible about the school context and above all about the disciplinary problems in one of the music classes. At the first meeting, A presents their script and goes through it point by point. After two hours, A has the feeling that B has got a good impression of the new classes, especially the disturbing behaviour of the boys in one of the music classes. A's biggest concern: B should not make the same mistakes as A did as a beginning teacher.
>
> After the first meeting, B feels overwhelmed: The school seems to be a minefield where young teachers are exposed to very uncomfortable situations. It takes B a lot of effort to find motivation for the first lesson observation the next morning.

The scenario shows that many factors play a role in a mentor-mentee relationship and that well-intended advice from the mentor can also result in the opposite. It becomes clear that the mentor's role model and their advice, in particular, impact significantly on the beginning music teacher. Wong (2004) defines the mentor as important 'perhaps the most important component of an induction programme' (Wong, 2004 referenced after EC, 2010, p. 22). If mentoring is to be a positive process for the mentor and the beginning music teacher, regular discussions and, above all, a stable professional and appreciative relationship is required. To achieve a positive impact of the mentoring process, it is important to ensure the qualities and competencies of a mentor: '[...] seniority and hierarchical criteria are less important than qualities such as inter-personal skills, communication and knowledge about the learning of (beginning) teachers' (EC, 2010, p. 24).

To reflect on the impact a mentor can have on the beginning music teacher, the role of the mentor needs to be defined well. The example in Task 4.1 highlights a potential problem: Mentor A did mean well but did not act in their expected role as nurturing and supporting. Therefore, in the following, the multifaceted role of the mentor and their impact will be investigated.

Preparing to be a mentor

To maximise impact, the quality of mentor training is important. However, this is not always given (Carter Review, 2015). If you do not have adequate training as a mentor yet, we would like to encourage you to find a mentoring course that teaches the basic skills mentioned throughout this book and offers time for reflection on your work as a mentor, too.

Defining your role and responsibilities as a mentor is crucial. In addition, you should ask yourself what goals you pursue as a teacher in mentoring a beginning teacher. What beliefs do you hold when you think of mentoring a beginning teacher? In addition, every time you are assigned a new mentee, ask yourself what exactly this mentee needs to develop in the best way possible. Preparing for successful mentoring also includes having a pool of materials. As a mentor, you would be expected to keep records throughout the whole process. We encourage you to keep as many written records as possible of all the meetings and work appointments during the year – this might exceed the requirement in your respective country. In particular, this includes notes from the induction meeting, in which the goals, expectations, fears, and hopes of the beginning music teacher are discussed, as well as a mentoring diary in which you write down any observations during the class or questions about topics arising in the course of the mentoring. Such records are very helpful at the end of your mentee's first year as it is then you need to make an informed judgement.

Furthermore, in order to prepare becoming a mentor, it would be useful to reflect on your skills and impact as a mentor. Before reading further, undertake Task 4.2.

Task 4.2 Reflecting on your skills and impact as a mentor

This task encourages you to think about how and in which areas you could develop your skills as a mentor. Try to answer the following questions to increase your impact.

- How could you create the necessary professional distance with your mentee without building barriers at the same time?
- Who would you like to be as a mentor? 'Parent'? 'Good colleague'? 'Friend'? Which role might be more appropriate? Which is not appropriate?
- How do you manage difficult situations and processes?
- How do you deal with conflict situations?

Now try and think about the beginning of your teacher career and ask yourself what you would have liked to gain from your mentor.

Preparation of the beginning music teacher

Beginning music teachers need to be prepared for several aspects that Isbell (2015) and Malmberg (2018) have identified. Isbell points out that placing more emphasis on performance, rather than skills like teaching over other skills 'appears to complicate the occupational identity shift to professional educator' (Isbell, 2015, p. 10). This is confirmed by Malmberg (2018, p. 45) who states that becoming a music teacher is in 'public perception… a step down' from being a performing musician. Isbell (2015, p. 10) adds that beginning music teachers may start their teacher training with a 'strong identity as musicians due to the limited opportunities to "try on" a teacher identity'. Malmberg (2018, p. 42) confirms that 'music teacher novices experience an identify transition'. Time will need to be given to explore this shift from performer to music educator, from a highly specialised musician to an accomplished teacher. Reflecting on this can become an essential aspect of the professionalisation of beginning music teachers.

The impact of the different roles of the music teacher

There are many ways of identifying the different roles of the mentor. As outlined above, the EC separates mentoring into professional, personal/emotional, and social domains (EC, 2010). Farrell (2018), in a model, applied to mentors of English language teachers, proposed the following roles: language teacher, trainer, facilitator, counsellor/guide, expert, impartial observer, diagnostician and assessor, workload [manager], and peer. In the following, we investigate each domain further by sorting the different roles of Farrell's model into the domains of the EC paper. Music teaching, as opposed to language teaching, includes additional aspects, starting from the administrative work to coordinate performances and peripatetic teachers to the actual musical work within the classroom and ensembles. Therefore, Farrell's model also has been adapted to the needs of beginning music teachers. Furthermore, we added the role 'past mentee/beginning music teacher' as your past experiences as a beginning (music) teacher and a past mentee will impact your own mentoring. For the remainder of this chapter, we will discuss each domain and with this the different roles being a mentor can bring. For an overview, please see Table 4.1.

1. Professional domain

The roles of music teacher, trainer, expert, diagnostician/assessor, and impartial observer help to fulfil the key requirements that the EC defines for the professional domain: 'access to knowledge through exchange between new/experienced teachers; further courses or classes, consultations' (EC, 2010, p.18).

Impact of the role as a (music) teacher

The Carter Review highlights effective mentors are strong role models of the Teachers' Standards (Carter Review, 2015). The first role, held by mentors, is that of a (music) teacher. The word *music* has been put in brackets as the authors of this chapter are aware there may be occurrences where a mentor is not a music teacher themselves. Therefore, we highlight that music teachers do not only teach music, but they are also musicians. Hence, they

Table 4.1 The roles of a mentor categorised in domains

Domain	Role
1. Professional domain	Music teacher
	Trainer
	Expert
	Diagnostician/assessor
	Impartial observer
2. Personal/emotional domain	Councillor/guide
	Facilitator
	Advisor on managing workload
3. Social domain	Role as peer
	Role as past mentee/beginning (music) teacher

possess not only a general interest in music but also very specific expertise in some genres of music. When entering school, a beginning music teacher is expected to be a universal expert ranging from knowing about classical to pop music to being a multi-instrumentalist and singer for ensemble work or a technician when teaching music technology. The role as a music teacher is therefore complex and beginning music teachers will feel the shift of performer to educator strongly: Roberts (1991a, 1991b, 1993 cited after Isbell, 2015, p. 7) pointed out that music education major students feel 'stigmatized by being labelled as teachers and struggled within a Faculty of Music culture that awards social status on the basis of musicianship rather than teaching expertise'. While this research was based in the USA, this has also been shown by Malmberg (2017) for Austrian music education students suggesting this is an ongoing and international issue. Malmberg (2017) states music students are seen by society as upholding culture but going into schools to teach music is perceived as entering a lower status. This is a dichotomy which is difficult for beginning music teachers as they are grappling with their identities as a musician and music educator. Isbell (2015, p. 10) highlights that 'a culture emphasizing and rewarding [musical] performance over other skills, including teaching, appears to complicate the occupational identity shift to professional educator'.

Malmberg (2017, p. 48) identified four different types of students starting their teacher training: the educator type, the travelling artist type, the integration type and the open-ended type (see Table 4.1). She explains the different types of students come into their training with different experiences, life goals, and job expectations. Malmberg (2017) does not propose different mentoring strategies for each type of beginning music teacher. However, the typology can be helpful when meeting your beginning music teacher for the first time; it portrays not only the different aspirations for their careers but also the underlying (teaching) philosophies and self-concepts as musician and educator. We have provided a synopsis of the typology in Table 4.2.

The mentor can help the beginning music teacher to mediate the difficulties between understanding themselves primarily as a performer or as an educator. The music mentor has a function as a role model, modelling good teaching and musicianship. Even if you are not a music teacher, being aware of the conflict between being a performer or education will help you in the process of mentoring.

Table 4.2 Typology of beginning music teachers

Type	Educator	Traveling artist	Integration	Open-ended
Definition	views 'music as one possible medium to foster children' (Malmberg, 2017, p. 49)	Views 'Music Education as a starting point to somewhere else' (Malmberg, 2017, p. 49)	Manages to 'integrate both the artistic and the pedagogical practice' (Malmberg, 2017, p. 50)	'is deeply ambivalent as to how he/she will use the experiences' of their beginning career and if they would stay in school. (Malmberg, 2017, p. 50)

Source: Malmberg (2017, pp. 49–50).

Before reading further, undertake Task 4.3.

> **Task 4.3 Reflecting on transitions into teaching**
>
> 1. Reflect on your own transition from musician to music educator. What challenges did you face from peers, your school/organisation, and wider communities? How did you negotiate them?
> 2. Looking at Malmberg's typology of beginning music teachers (Table 4.2), where would you locate yourself? Ask the beginning music teacher to do the same.
> 3. Reflect with your beginning music teacher on how they understand themselves as a music teacher. What were their musical and educational influences? From where does their motivation stem?

Impact of the role as a trainer

Farrell (2018) understands the role of the trainer as focusing specifically on the pedagogic skills, as a trainer of key classroom competencies. Two types of knowledge come into play here: pedagogic knowledge and pedagogic content knowledge (as defined by Shulman, 1987). While pedagogic knowledge does not require specific musical knowledge and hence can be trained through a teacher who is outside the subject area of music, specific music pedagogy knowledge (pedagogic content knowledge), however, is best trained through a music educator. If music is not your background, maybe there are colleagues at a local music hub or a subject association, who might be able to assist here further. The Carter Review (2015, p. 39) specifies that beginning music teachers should have the opportunity 'to observe good and outstanding practice', however, we appreciate the difficulties this can pose for schools with small music departments.

Looking back at the typology of beginning music teachers, it is the pedagogic aspects that are the newest to the beginning music teacher. It is important that you are honest about your skillset. If you are open to a discussion with the beginning music teacher, both your experiences as an educator and as a musician will provide a space of reflection on the development of pedagogic content knowledge. This might be aided through regular observations and opportunities for reflection.

Before reading further, undertake Task 4.4.

> **Task 4.4 Thinking about you as trainer**
>
> Think about the following questions:
>
> What are your personal classroom pedagogic approaches and management strategies?
>
> What might be the best way of discussing those with the beginning music teacher?
>
> How comfortable are you with the role as trainer?
>
> Do you feel comfortable being observed? Why/why not?
>
> Are you open to learn new teaching approaches from your mentee/other teachers?

Impact of the role as an expert

A beginning teacher expects their mentor to be an expert (Farrell, 2018). In this section, we will examine this in more detail as this highlights the question: an expert in what? Does this mean a mentor has to be an expert in teaching? Or in music teaching? And, in which type of music teaching? All of it? It is unlikely that all mentors who are working with beginning music teachers will be musicians themselves. Does that mean they cannot mentor on an expert level? We would strongly question this. Instead, we suggest that expertise lies in the knowledge of pedagogy. We discussed in the previous section that beginning music teachers need advice on pedagogic content knowledge. However, if there is missing musical expertise this might be mitigated by using well-defined questions and by keeping an open mind on both sides. Even if the mentor is a musician themselves, they might not share the same pedagogic content knowledge. So, the mentor's expertise that might be expected from the beginning music teacher must lie rather in being a good mentor and being a good teacher. This fits with the Carter Review (2015, p. 41) which states that 'effective mentors are outstanding teachers who are also skilled in deconstructing and explaining their practice - outstanding practitioners are not automatically outstanding mentors'.

The impact of this role is difficult to determine as it relies very much on how 'expert' is defined. Of course, if a beginning music teacher can observe an expert music educator enthuse children about music and develop their skills, that impact will be sizeable. However, this expert role can also be fulfilled in other ways. It is possible to jointly watch the contributions of music educators on social media or in conferences and workshops. Hence, the impact that a mentor can bring lies mainly in the skill of analysis and explanation of teacher practice.

Before reading further, undertake Task 4.5.

Task 4.5 Thinking about experts that shaped your work

Carry out the following task together with your beginning music teacher. Compare notes.

Think of somebody within music education (or somebody from your own field if you're not a music educator) who has impressed you. Were you working with them as a colleague? As a pupil yourself? What of these elements have you or would you like add to your own teaching? Why those?

Impact of the role as a diagnostician and assessor

According to Farrell (2018), this category interlinks with the roles of Impartial Observer and Expert. This role can have a considerable impact on the beginning music teacher and holds the potential for deep reflection within the process of mentoring. As a diagnostician and assessor, your role will be linked to formally or informally evaluate and feedback on the work of the beginning music teacher. This role contradicts the role of the peer because, at the moment of assessment, the hierarchy between mentor and mentee will change (Farrell, 2018).

The Carter Review (2015) has outlined six principles of feedback based on Coe et al. (2014) which might be useful to inform this role:

1. the focus is kept clearly on improving student outcomes;
2. feedback is related to clear, specific and challenging goals for the recipient;
3. attention is on the learning rather than to the person or to comparisons with others;
4. teachers are encouraged to be continual independent learners;
5. feedback is mediated by a mentor in an environment of trust and support;
6. an environment of professional learning and support is promoted by the school's leadership.

Carter Review (2015, pp. 44-45)

What criteria drive your assessment of the beginning music teacher? Linking back to the country-specific teacher standards will help to determine those. This is also suggested by the Carter Review (2015, p. 41):

> The most effective mentors have a secure understanding of the Teachers' Standards, including a range of methods for assessing against the standards, in a way that goes beyond the minimum requirements for meeting them.

Whenever there is an assessment involved, questions regarding reliability and validity will be raised. It is therefore important with the assessment to make sure that it is fair and transparent. Do keep in mind that you are assessing a fellow education specialist - even though they hold fewer years of experience. Using this assessment to model good assessment strategies to the beginning music teacher will have a great impact on their own future assessment practices. The first year of a beginning music teacher in school is part of a lifelong process of development. Hence, it cannot be stressed enough that the result at the end of this year is not a final statement about the performance of a teacher of their entire teaching career.

Before reading further, undertake Task 4.6.

Task 4.6 Reflecting on assessment

Reflect on a situation when you were assessed in your life. Why do you think of this situation? You will think of this situation possibly because it made a lasting impression on you and your career. Was this positive? Was it negative?

Following this, think about what assessment of the beginning music teacher means for you? What does it mean for the beginning music teacher? Think about what kind of assessor you would like to be? How can you support a beginning music teacher by providing positive and constructive feedback?

Impact of the role as an impartial observer

Farrell (2018) points out that '[t]he mentor's role in this process is one of encouraging and aiding reflection to raise the mentee's awareness of "where they are and where they should be" in terms of teaching proficiency' (Farrell, 2018, p. 232). Many of the different roles described above fulfil this function. However, this role is equally important to the previously described role. Without being an impartial observer, it will be difficult to assess the beginning music teacher. The mentor's task is to provide the framework for reflection through feeding back their observations.

In terms of impact, you will be able to provide invaluable support by giving honest and fair feedback to the beginning music teacher. This can help with all aspects of teaching. In this role, you can support good strategies of planning or lesson delivery as well as identify and address areas that might need more development.

Before reading further, undertake Task 4.7.

Task 4.7 Reflecting on observation

Think back to the first time you were observed. Who observed you and what was their agenda? Were they able to be impartial? What helped you to feel comfortable? What did not? Following this, try to identify the aspects that helped you to feel comfortable to be observed. Discuss those aspects with the beginning music teacher.

2. *Personal/emotional domain*

According to the EC (2010, p. 18), the aims of the personal/emotional domain are to 'develop identity as teacher, reinforce competences, boost self-confidence, reduce stress and anxiety, motivate, avoid drop out'. The key requirements to reach these aims are 'safe, non-judgemental environment, reduce workload, team teaching, co-teaching' (EC, 2010). Therefore, this section will investigate the impact of the roles as counsellor/guide, facilitator, and advisor on managing workloads as those roles will contribute to establish this.

Impact of the role as a counsellor/guide

Bodoczky and Malderez (1996, referenced after Farrell, 2018, p. 231) refer to this role as developing 'helpful relationships'. While the role of the mentor is not to help beginning music teachers with mental ill-health, there are specific anxieties shared amongst beginning music teachers. It is the aim of this 'helpful relationship' to enable beginning music teachers to develop best practice.

School entry phases for beginning teachers are phases of transition. People in transition are in constant motion between previous ideas and concepts as well as those currently being developed (Malmberg, 2018). Malmberg links this process of transition to the idea of *Multiple Status Passage* by Glaser and Strauss (1971). The transition process is perceived by the beginning teachers as complex, extremely challenging in terms of physical and mental strength, and sometimes feels uncontrollable (Malmberg, 2018). Participants questioned their identity: 'How does being a teacher fit me? [...] I am no longer a musician' (Malmberg, 2018, p. 299). Therefore, a beginning music teacher should provide a space to explore these juxtapositions of old and new roles and identities.

The 'helpful relationship' will also be useful in managing the other juxtaposition of being trained to be a musician at a conservatoire or a music department to then enter a different, school-based teaching profession. Teaching is culturally not as highly valued as being an artist as reported by Malmberg (2017). While Malmberg (2017, 2018) looked at this issue for Austrian music students and beginning music teachers, this will presumably be similar in other countries. In England, music teachers usually study their instrument, composition, or musicology first. Then, they add one year of initial teacher training, either university or school-based, to this. This initial teacher training might help the beginning music teachers to manage their expectations and to prepare them for this juxtaposition of being a musician versus being a music teacher. Nevertheless, it will be the task of the mentor to accompany this process further through mediating carefully between musical and pedagogic expectations. Further problems have been pointed out with music teachers being often isolated in schools (Wolf and Younie, 2018) and suddenly having to take on various roles they were not prepared for. For example, where music technology is required to be taught as well, there is a whole set of pedagogic content knowledge related to teaching music with technology that will be required (Wolf and Younie, 2019). While all of this can be learned, the different types of knowledge and expectations to be an expert in these can be overwhelming. At times, where the subject of music constantly needs to be defended, it will also be a task for a beginning music teacher to become an activist for the arts at school.

In order to avoid being overwhelmed by the juxtaposition of practices and the manifold expectations of a beginning music teacher, it is important to provide space and strategies for discussing this beyond a single lesson reflection. Stepping back from the immediate daily routine and thinking about the wider picture will enable the beginning music teacher to anchor themselves within the profession of being a music teacher while developing a lifelong reflective practice.

Before reading further, undertake Task 4.8.

Task 4.8 Reflecting on 'helpful relationships'

1. Make a list of the most important topics to discuss with the beginning music teacher. You could also create this list jointly. Topics could be subject-specific: e.g., musical development, performance anxiety, overwhelm from planning lessons, rehearsals and performances, general anxieties around being assessed, behaviour management in the class, etc., school-specific matters could include hierarchies, surviving staff expectations, being a part of a team, areas of responsibility in the school, etc.. Create a schedule, thinking carefully (perhaps together with your beginning music teacher) about what will be discussed best at which point. The golden rule should be, less is more. Reflect back at the scenario at the beginning of this chapter (Task 4.1) and keep in mind how much advice a beginning music teacher can take in at any one time.
2. The role of the counsellor is different from the role of the music teacher or the expert. Where do you draw the line answering questions from the beginning music teacher? How can you protect yourself from being overwhelmed by too many (sometimes personal) topics?
3. To what extent can you increase your impact in any role by choosing the meeting format, the meeting location, and the time of the meeting? Where do you meet with your beginning music teacher? This might be the music room after school, but meeting in a cafe away from the school might also create healthy distance.

Impact of the role as a facilitator

Here, Farrell (2018, p. 231) points out that the mentor takes on the role of a coach asking, 'the right questions and help[ing] to allow the mentee enough time and space to become the teacher that they want to be'. This is in line with Conway (2015a), who specifically looked into mentoring beginning music teachers. She points out that the mentee needs to be proactive in finding answers to questions. Providing the space for the beginning music teacher to find these answers is a key role for the mentor. Kolman *et al.* (2017, p. 94) speak of 'learner-centred mentoring' which 'begins with the knowledge and skills the teacher candidate brings to the classroom, and learning occurs through experiences in the classroom' enabled through the mentor. This space of reflection is important for beginning music teachers.

Referring to Dweck's work on growth mindset (2008), Kolman *et al.* (2017, p. 111) point out that new teachers can experience a fixed mindset 'as they struggle during their first years of teaching and beyond in different school contexts'. Nurturing a growth mindset for beginning music teachers should hence be a priority for the mentoring process. This in turn will help the beginning music teacher as the importance of nurturing a growth mindset in pupils has been noted in the literature (for example, Adams, 2019; Davis, 2017). Especially, Davis (2017) highlights the importance of allowing for error within the classroom music-making, which is something the mentor in their role as a facilitator could apply also for the relationship with the beginning music teacher. A growth mindset will help to cope with errors, difficulties, and struggle as the beginning music teacher neither thinks of themselves as a perfect teacher nor a failure but knows there are areas in-between. A growth mindset facilitates learning and continuous development. Enabling a beginning music teacher to develop such a mindset will have an invaluable impact on the future career of the individual.

Before reading further, undertake Task 4.9.

Task 4.9 Enabling a growth mindset

List beliefs the beginning music teacher may hold about themselves. Examples could be:

- I cannot teach large groups.
- I don't know what to do with X.
- I haven't got enough time for X.
- I won't be able to bring the choir to a performance.
- Dissect each belief: Is it true? What might be a strategy to overcome it?

Impact on helping to manage the workload

Music teachers' responsibilities often go further than 'only' classroom teaching. There will be the management of the peripatetic instrumental teachers, ensemble work (which includes looking for sheet music, arrangements, ordering music, managing, maintaining and buying instruments, etc.), visits to and participation in local concerts and events, etc.. Additionally, where the performance level allows, there may be also taking part in choir competitions, concert tours, etc. This requires knowledge of music event-specific health and safety and dedicated risk assessments. Music teachers might also work for more than one school, which adds to the complication of dealing with different administration systems, colleagues, and pupils as well as their parents. High workloads combined with the isolation music teachers often experience have been mentioned as a stressor for music teachers (Sindberg, 2011).

It will help beginning music teachers to create achievable projects and to have realistic expectations of what can and cannot be done. However, especially when you do not come from a music teaching background, you as the mentor have to develop a good understanding of the workload of a music teacher to do this. Learning early in the teaching process how to distinguish urgent and important tasks and how to not firefight but be in control of the workload is important. Sharing your own systems of how to manage the workload and also how to deal with the demands, will have a great impact on the beginning music teacher.

Before reading further, undertake Task 4.10.

Task 4.10 Reflecting on your systems to manage workload

What are your systems that help you to manage your workload?

How have you developed those? Why do they work?

Can you provide an opportunity for the beginning music teacher to think about their systems?

---

3. Social domain

According to the EC (2010, p. 18), the aims of professional support on the social level are 'socialisation into school and profession, promote cooperation, promote collaborative learning, promote involvement in and from school community'. The key requirements to reach these aims are 'collaborative work, co-teaching, team teaching, teamwork, project groups' (EC, 2010, p. 18). In the following, we will discuss the impact of the roles as peer and past mentee.

Impact of the role as a peer

The role and also the impact as a peer is important; often music departments are very small, which means colleagues will need to stick together and support each other. If music does not hold a high status within the school, the music teachers at the school will need to collaborate and defend the subject within their school. Being a peer in this case goes both ways as mentor and mentee learn from each other (Farrel, 2018). Farrel (2018, p. 233) further points out the importance of showing 'some vulnerability and [allowing] the mentee to mentor them in certain areas'.

The power of music for creating a social bond (Hallam, 2010) should not be underestimated. Over time, professional boundaries may blur and friendships might develop during the mentor-mentee relationship. Here, the mentor needs to keep in mind the other roles, such as that of an assessor, to keep professional conduct in place, even if there is a great concert to celebrate or the school's ensembles are on a concert tour. Professional boundaries need to be upheld as long as the mentorship is in place.

Understanding yourself as a peer to the beginning music teacher will help to establish a trustworthy relationship. While the teaching team within the school might be hierarchically organised, the mentor's role as a peer will help to provide the beginning music teacher with a person who is approachable when needed.

Before reading further, undertake Task 4.11.

Task 4.11 Reflecting on your role as peer

Remember the last time you had a meaningful conversation with a colleague about teaching. What did you value about this? Was it the advice or the fact your colleague understood the situation? What are aspects you can adopt for your own practice as a mentor?

Impact of the role as past mentee/beginning music teacher

One last role needs highlighting which might not be on the forefront of the mind of a new mentor: you have gathered experiences both as a beginning music teacher yourself and potentially also as a past mentee. What you have experienced and learned during that time will shape you as the mentor and teacher you are now. Therefore, certain situations, positive and negative, will resonate with you stronger. Being aware of this will prevent unspoken expectations of the beginning music teacher.

Before reading further, undertake Task 4.12.

Task 4.12 Reflecting on your past experiences

Think about the following questions and reflect on how the answers might be influenced by your previous experience:

Which of the previous roles were easy for you and which ones did you find difficult?

What expectations do you have of the beginning music teacher?

What are concerns you have for your beginning music teacher?

Summary and key points

- In this chapter, we have shown that there are many aspects to the mentor's role that may generate different levels of impact. This was demonstrated by looking at the different roles of the mentor and investigating the impact of each of the roles.
- The roles were sorted into three domains: professional, personal/emotional, and social domains following the European Commission Report on Mentoring (EC, 2010).

- This chapter and the accompanying tasks you did were to help you reflect on the different impact your roles have in the regular exchanges you have with the beginning music teacher as well as at important stages, such as assessment points.

Further resources

Carter Review of initial teacher training

Department of Education (2015) *Carter Review of initial teacher training*. Available at: https://assets.publishing.service.gov.uk/government/uploads/system/uploads/attachment_data/file/399957/Carter_Review.pdf [accessed 19 November 2021].

This is a helpful document of Initial Teacher Training in England.

Farrell, C. (2018) 'The role of the mentor', in Dikilitas, K. et al. (eds.) *Mentorship strategies in teacher education*. Hershey, PA: IGI Global, pp. 225-234.

This is the original model of the roles of the mentor that has been adapted for this chapter.

Conway, C. (2015a) 'Beginning music teacher mentor practices: Reflections on the past and suggestions for the future', *Journal of Music Teacher Education*, 24(2), pp. 88-102.

Conway has dedicated a lot of her work to researching the experiences of beginning music teachers and how to mentor them best.

SECTION III
About what a mentor does

5 Performance curation – mentoring beginning music teachers in performance projects

Narelle Yeo

Introduction

This chapter explores the possibilities for circular mentoring (participants mentoring and being mentored in constantly evolving roles during rehearsals) in discrete performance projects during beginning teacher training. It provides a practical model for building the idea of circular mentoring as a positive and collaborative creative practice (Yeo and Rowley, 2018). Music teachers often work not only in the classroom but also offer a high number of extra-curricular activities. These portfolio elements of the music teacher's career are reframed as core practice, rather than an extra-curricular burden. By providing this unique, positive approach, beginning music teachers can build a professional and personal identity that values their own, and their pupils, teaching and learning, musicianship, and cultural citizenship.

Traditional mentoring models address the need for beginning teachers to have an experienced guide (Benson, 2008; Hudson, 2012). Very little has been written on mentoring beginning teachers, who have the added burden of performance curation in schools. Ballantyne (2007) found that this element may be the reason for higher burnout rates affecting beginning music teachers, due to the excess time burdens. How can this inevitable stretching of the school day be positively oriented and enable this danger to be overcome? Research shows that being involved in a performance project framed using circular mentoring builds self-efficacy, organisational, and production skills and develops effective rehearsal practices as well (Yeo and Rowley, 2017). Positive engagement in real-world performances with pupils, breeds positive self-efficacies for all participants, and may stem the obvious dangers of extra-curricular based burn-out.

Objectives

At the end of this chapter, you should be able to:

- Expand the definition of musical mentoring to a circular mentoring model, which allows for collaborative creativity and fluid roles in experiential learning.
- Understand the importance of real-time performance mentoring for beginning music teachers in building self-efficacy and recognition of their own unique musical and/or organisational skills and talents.

DOI: 10.4324/9781003004196-9

- Devise and develop performance projects facilitating positive ensemble and group behaviours, musical skills, extra-musical skills, and personal resilience in time-dependent rehearsal and performance contexts.
- Explain how to provide effective reflective practice for beginning music teachers in producing musical content of quality and educative value.

Background and rationale

A beginning music teacher requires proficiency in a range of distinct skills, including music production, time management, project management, and artistic direction. These skills, often overlooked in initial teacher training, can easily be learnt in a discrete performance mentoring context, rather than being acquired de-facto and treated as an extra-curricular burden.

However, the standard for mentoring beginning teachers has traditionally been 'top-down' – an experienced teacher imparting knowledge and skills to a beginning music teacher. While this is vital, the beginning music teacher also needs safe-to-fail experimentation in performance contexts, as burn-out is highly correlated with extra-curricular work (Ballantyne, 2007).

For these reasons, a circular mentoring program, The Inclusion Project, was devised (Yeo and Rowley, 2018) to provide music teachers with the necessary exposure to the value of ensemble performance as community collaboration. This was a high-stakes professional performance through an intensive rehearsal process, with participants placed in the role of mentor/mentee through various exercises during the production period. The goal was a high-level performance outcome and the building of self-efficacy in all participants, particularly in beginning music teachers. It provided an experiential learning setting for beginning teachers to reflect on how a time- and outcome-dependent complex adaptive process could lead to positive outcomes for participants, upskilling in a range of areas as well as delivering creative musical content of value and import. The unique element of this project is found in the circular nature of the mentoring model, which serves to build efficacy and capacity in beginning music teachers as they experience, in real-time, their dual roles as mentors and mentees.

Yeo and Rowley's (2018) research into beginning music teacher training mimics the high-stakes outcomes in a professional performance, within a positively framed *circular mentoring* model. *Circular mentoring* democratises the performance rehearsal experience, finding ways in which *all* participants can mentor others during rehearsal. All parties to the musical experience have special knowledge and space is given in rehearsal to foster this sharing of specific knowledge. In Yeo and Rowley (2018), professional musicians, teachers, mentors, and performing pupils participated in an intensive touring production experience, with the goal of establishing the myriad roles of music mentor in a practical context, using a revised model of Kolb's Experiential Learning Cycle (1984). The study had three important foci:

1. Mentors are actively circulated throughout the ensemble while leaning into the presumption that beginning music teachers have competencies that can be immediately tapped into and shared;
2. Beginning music teachers learn the value of an adaptive system based on ethical musical leadership and 'collaborative creativity'; and
3. Self-efficacy and ensemble efficacy is practiced for beginning music teachers in a professional performance.

Performance-based mentoring projects provide beginning music teachers with a real-world collaborative performance outcome while constantly flipping and dynamically changing the role of mentor and mentee. The community value of collaborative music-making and time-specific high-level outcomes are expressed by two previous participants:

> We were able to start replacing the self-centred, competitive mindset in the performing arts industry with mentoring and sharing.

> I learnt the importance of shaping the industry through mentoring, serving and encouragement.

Before reading further, undertake Task 5.1.

Task 5.1 Self-reflection about performance experiences and mentoring

Answer the following questions before you continue:

- When was the last time you performed on stage?
- When was the last time you felt strongly positive about being part of a creative ensemble? Can you think of one reason why you felt this way?
- How important is it for you as more experienced teacher to be mentored in your own performing?
- How important is it for you as more experienced teacher to be mentored in performing with school ensembles?

Building a community of practice and recognising existing mastery across the cohort

While mentoring for teachers is vital (Hudson, 2012), Benson (2008) found that mentoring programs were perceived as less relevant to beginning music teachers as other classroom teachers, because of their unique emotional and structural needs. Beginning music teachers often already possess a level of mastery in music performance, or they likely would not have chosen this career. Viewing themselves as complex competent creatives and teachers justifies the importance of performance projects for their own wellbeing, as well as that of their pupils (see also Chapter 4). What if these skills could be harnessed into an immersive performance project, using a circular mentoring framework that could truly reflect the reality, aspirations and desire for personal and professional self-efficacy of the beginning music teacher?

There is a need of beginning music teachers to have a structured community of practice, an ensemble that recognises their unique emotional and logistical needs, as well as their own personal mastery of an instrument or voice, with creative experimentation such as role play, and hybrid training in online environments (Berg and Rickels, 2018; Van Driel and Berry, 2012). A mutual community of performance practice is as vital to any beginning teacher as is their classroom management and curriculum teaching practice (Blair, 2008).

Public performance is experiential learning. Kolb's (1984) experiential learning cycle identified concrete experience, reflective observation, abstract conceptualisation, and active experimentation as four essential pillars of experiential learning. This is different to the apprenticeship cycle which has dominated one-on-one musical mentoring (skills acquisition through repetition and imitation of a master's practice). Yeo and Rowley (2018) expanded and redefined Kolb's cycle to apply to musical mentoring of a diverse cohort of pupils and teachers:

1. Doing (concrete experience);
2. Undoing (reflective observation);
3. Reframing (abstract conceptualisation); and
4. Group defined, improvisatory mis-en-scene (active experimentation and performance in situ).

Most mentoring models are pictorially represented as circles of influence but are in fact top-down authoritative models, where master teachers impart their knowledge using competency or apprenticeship structures. This elevates retention rates (Buchan et al., 2013) but ignores another burn-out risk: the stress of curating performances alongside teaching.

A case study

The aim for this case study is to demonstrate the model of circular mentoring in action whilst giving ideas on which elements can be applied in a mentoring context in the English ECT mentoring system.

In an action research project, beginning music teachers participated in an intensive rehearsal process leading to professional performance. They were mentored in a range of ways in a unique circular mentoring program. Circular mentoring is learning facilitated through a hierarchical interchange of roles through rehearsal and reflection (Yeo and Rowley, 2020). Mentors were professional performers, conductors and directors, beginning music teachers and amateurs. While all were involved in the performance itself, each beginning music teacher was mentored in an area matched to their skill set. They in turn mentored others in the programme in an area of relative competence in reference to the group.

In this case study, mentors and beginning music teachers were trained in other collaborative elements of putting on a project, whether that be backstage or production crew or public relations, to expand the skills and experience of all participants and the possibilities for unexpected webs of collaboration within the ensemble. The youngest and least experienced members of the ensemble were instructed to mentor more experienced members of the cast, including the professional performers. They did so in an area where they, the mentors, had expert knowledge, for example, conditions in the local area, relating to a particular element of the narrative as a child, for example.

Even though it might appear like this at first sight, this way of mentoring is not an equal playing field; where any member of the ensemble has expertise, they are given the mentoring or leading role in that moment, only to relinquish it into the group when the level of expertise changes. The community is built around the specific rehearsal and performance conditions and incorporates some elements of complexity theory to build the unique conditions that fuel rehearsal and performance in the content at hand. The process is formally structured and revolves around a series of 'safe to fail' experiments in communication between all members of the ensemble.

Before you continue, please complete Task 5.2.

Task 5.2 How can we include multiple voices in the mentoring process?

As pointed out above, mentoring in the English system is a top-down process. Furthermore, going beyond established hierarchy might be a scary process. What might be ways for you as an experienced teacher and mentor to include other voices into the mentoring process?

Together with your beginning music teacher reflect on fields of expertise and make a plan on how to include the different voices:

- What field of expertise do you have as a mentor?
- What is the field of expertise of your beginning music teacher?
- What field of expertise do the pupils hold?

The how-to...

- **Get a local professional company on board**

    Ideally, you can work with the beginning music teacher to organise this together as this will enable beginning music teachers, you, as an experienced teacher and the pupils in your school to learn from each other through the circular mentoring system. By involving other professionals into the mentoring circle, you will not only add other voices to the mentoring process, but also start building professional contacts with your local arts providers, something that can be useful for inspiring pupils.

    Start by asking them if you could use their venue but if that is too difficult with administrative burdens on you, invite the people to come and work with you and your pupils in your school. Having professional performers involved in the project will inspire pupils. In the case study above, the project was the production of a one-act opera as part of a professional season in the regional centre of Wollongong in New South Wales, Australia. The Sydney Conservatorium targeted beginning music teachers to participate in the project, which was built around the preparation and performance of a one-act opera, with intensive rehearsals for a week on tour bringing both regional singers and beginning music teachers together in situ. The project targeted working professional singers, beginning music teachers and undergraduate singers and instrumentalists along with youth singers from the broader regional community. As such, the project also had an outreach focus, bringing a range of performers into the project and acting as a conduit for young talented singers to access Conservatorium projects that may not be available in rural areas. The entire budget was $10,000.

- **Find willing professionals to bolster the process (you only need two or three for impact)**
  The mentors in the case study were professional musicians and educators with a range of skills in performing, producing, directing, and administrating. Each of the assigned mentors possessed at least two of these skills. All participants in the project could engage in performance, backstage, production, direction, costuming, make-up, logistics roles, but all of the performers were responsible for more than one role, and all but one performed in the piece onstage as well. This project engaged four professional performers as well as two performer/educators. There were also professional directors, producers, and production team, with students also undertaking these roles in mentee positions.
- **Have a definite plan and limited time**
  Elbert Hubbard was quoted as saying that there are 'two necessities in doing a great and important work: a definite plan and limited time' (Hubbard, 1912).

  It is vital that there be some pressure introduced, for example, a short rehearsal period. Of course, this needs to be appropriate to the level of your pupils. The pilot project was aimed at older students and involved a tour for seven days, with the outcome of the project a professional public performance to a paying audience as part of a festival. On-time delivery of professional quality work was paramount. In a school environment, the process should probably outweigh the product and expectations on professionality can be relaxed. While keeping the mentoring process focused on the performance is essential, this does not supplant the importance of meeting participants where their needs are, building capacity based on the given conditions and cohort characteristics. Planning these elements with your beginning music teacher together will give them skills in the area of performance planning, which is an expected area of expertise for music teachers in secondary schools.

Repurposing Kolb's experiential learning cycle (1984) into a circular mentoring cycle for performance

To fit Kolb to purpose, a circular structure for rehearsals was developed (Figure 5.1). Kolb's experiential learning cycle shows four pillars of exercise, skills development, analysis, and conscious experimentation. This model uses three of these four pillars of (doing, undoing, reframing) and expands it, using the principles of effective rehearsal and performance. The project was conducted using this model. All participants were instructed to mentor or mentee everyone else in the cohort at different times, and to observe other mentoring taking place from the privileged position of being in the scene, on the stage, or in the orchestra pit, creating circles of influence and engagement in the ensemble.

Concrete experience – the importance of doing

Singers were placed in a real-world professional performance scenario, under time pressure, with a high-stakes performance outcome. Both professional performers and performer-educators were embedded in the cohort. Practical experiential learning was at the core

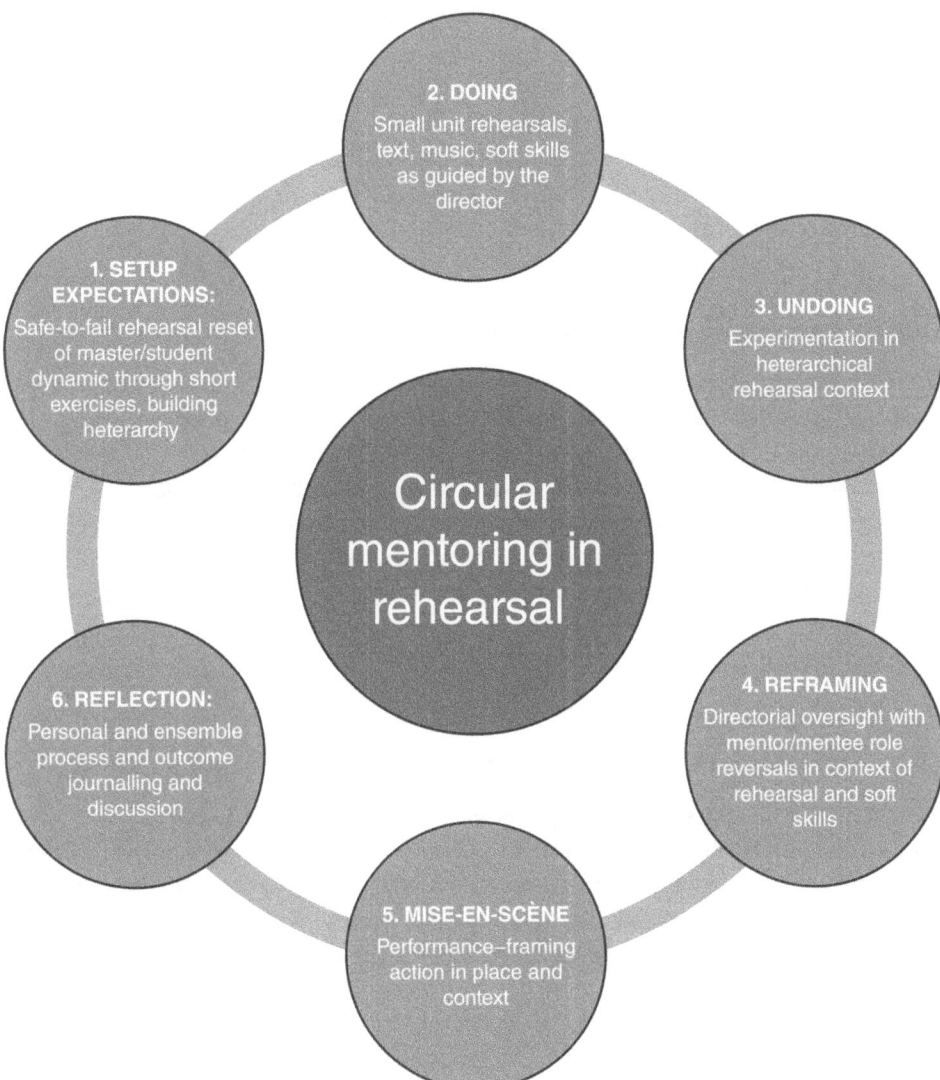

Figure 5.1 Yeo et al.'s (2022) revised model of circular mentoring in collaborative creative practice, after Kolb (1984)

of this project and was fundamental to mastering kinaesthetic skills required to embody a character or role, as well as the confidence and self-efficacy required to be an effective music teacher.

Reflective observation: taking a personal inventory of skills – the undoing

Pre, during, and post-project reflection was a vital tool for everybody in the circle, reflecting on the impact of the project on self-efficacy in real time. In this part of the process, all participants were encouraged, using various team building and reflective activities, to focus on growth mindset tools in recognising their own particular skillset and marking it as relevant to the project (Dweck, 2017). This kind of 'undoing' says that you are already a valued and important member of the cast, with a particular set of skills, but that you individually choose when to step into the mentor role and 'teach' those skills to the ensemble. Using a personal inventory approach, group dynamics are managed so that relative experience is not used as a comparison tool, but that any area of personal competency can be mined to enhance the rehearsal dynamic.

Abstract conceptualisation – the reframing

Participants were provided with the tools, through forms of play and a series of exercises, to conceptualise their learning and their role in process in abstract terms. In *I Pagliacci* by Leoncavallo, there is a Commedia dell'arte play-within-a-play. This was reflected in rehearsal through a series of mirroring and sliding doors metaphor games, into an exposé of real life in front and behind the stage, and the complexity of characters and humans alike as revealed onstage and in the rehearsal spaces behind the set. This reframing was highly useful in both conceptualisation of the project as providing real insights into putting on an opera, to an abstract conceptualisation of the myriad skills, abilities, and improvisatory play required for successful collaborative creativity.

Active experimentation – efficacy building activities – the mise en scène

From the French for 'placement onstage', *mise en scène* is a term co-opted from film, a complex term that, in part, describes the conceptual framing of a scene, including the placement of set, props, scenery, lighting, and actors. In this context, *mise en scène* also places all the contributors in the rehearsal and final performance – the sum of all parts of the collaboration. Only at the end of the project are beginning music teachers aware of the frame and the complexity of their learning experience. The analysis of the utility of this process was undertaken through an e-portfolio model of self-reflection.

In modelling good rehearsal practice, project planning, innovation, flexibility, improvisation, and individual and ensemble capacity building, we create a rehearsal room with circular mentoring that is unique. Yeo's (2017) research into complex adaptive systems in rehearsals showed the benefits of allowing ensemble systems to develop with stated goals of heterarchy and personal and ensemble efficacy. Rehearsals are complex adaptive systems, with both real and shadow systems of power influencing their processes, successes, and failures. Naming the intention of the ensemble to empower *all* participants leads to positive performance and self-efficacy outcomes as a useful learning and teaching tool. The *mise en scène* is perceived by participants as built collaboratively. This creates a buy-in mentality for all participants:

> In the Spiegeltent... I was very impressed with the professionalism and dedication displayed by the cast- quickly adapting to the space.

> The children's experience throughout Pagliacci was nurtured and memorable – being able to have a person to talk to, look up to and assist.

Circular mentoring

In April 2017, 45 participants signed up for a Sydney Conservatorium/Wollongong Conservatorium collaborative Inclusion Project, leading to a professional performance of Leoncavallo's *I Pagliacci* in the Spiegeltent, Wollongong. The cast was drawn from 23 regional learners from the ages of 8-26 and 16 Conservatorium students completing their studies in music education or performance, along with six professional performers. This unique project has been repeated four times under different rehearsal and performance conditions. It is the subject of continued research into the benefits of circular mentoring for beginning music teachers.

The beginning of rehearsal is devoted to removing a sense that experience/higher skill level creates a necessarily higher status in the rehearsal room. This is unfamiliar territory for some participants, who expect strong leadership from the production table, but easily achieved through a number of short acting and singing exercises to build ensemble, one key element being the fostering of unexpected participants in mentor roles. For example, creating short mentoring games upend traditional perceptions of relative value between experienced and inexperienced performers.

The director, principal singer, and conductor all demonstrated fluidity of roles at the beginning of the process, including room set-up. The standard production table was not imposed until late in the project. As a complex adaptive system, there were a few simple rules in place:

- A professional performance outcome is goal. There is a plan to stage the work within a short space of time and the performance will be high quality. All performers and production team have to prepare as if they were already a trained professional.
- A positive ensemble is the underpinning of the experience, created through intense shared experience. The atmosphere in the rehearsal room is of experimentation and mutual respect, from the production table to the youngest performer.
- All performers and mentors and all performers are mentees in some area of the rehearsal process and all deserve respect. It is possible to learn something from each participant:

    The overall atmosphere and attitude towards the production was exciting and professional. This was an eye-opening moment for many...realising that this production is more than just a performance, but a cross-generation mentoring experience.

- All performers and crew are able to assist in another area of interest to build one's own capacity. There is encouragement to seek these experiences:

    I've really learnt professional rehearsal etiquette from the principals in this course. Another thing I have learnt is the importance of teaching the art of opera to young kids and really raising younger kids into the culture.

Participants move through the intense experience, and the *mise en scène* of both the rehearsal process and performance can be transformative. The performance reflects the creative collaboration achieved in the complex adaptive process of creating a functional ensemble. Each member has had an opportunity to be both mentor and mentee and something in-between. The beginning music teacher will have obtained a range of relevant skills, built self-efficacy, and had the opportunity to be both mentor and mentee in this process.

Conservatory respondents gave qualitative responses to the survey ($n = 13$) and e-portfolio task ($n = 5$), with universally positive feedback for the experience, and a high correlation between mentor-mentee experiences and personal efficacy outcomes for the project. Participants noted a range of personal outcomes:

> ...It was incredible to finish staging and running through the full show with the Principal artists- a sense of accomplishment filled the rehearsal room.

> Pagliacci rehearsals provided insight into working and interacting with children, which will benefit my teaching style and outlook on learning as I experience teaching music in the classroom.

Before reading further, undertake Task 5.3.

Task 5.3 Thinking about cultural and musical curation

Finally, because music teaching is also cultural and musical curation in your school context, find a reason to put on a public musical event, then:

- Engage pupils, emerging educators, and professional musicians who all agree to the premise and the process.
- Make the event high stakes and time-dependent outcome driven.
- Work to a deadline and work to a professional standard (this does not need money, just goodwill).
- Allocate roles dependent on suitability. Roles should be cast according to ability, but abilities in other areas should be valued and explored.
- Expect professional performances from the most experienced to your youngest and least experienced participant.
- Create a frame (or *mise en scène*) for the rehearsal process.
- Be flexible and allow adaptive systems to develop within that frame.
- Find a skill that everyone who is collaborating in the process can teach or mentor others on, even if it is not directly on topic (abstract conceptualisation). This develops an ensemble mentality, allows for circular mentoring, and builds capacity.
- Set up a circular mentoring structure which is adaptable.
- Think of music teacher mentoring as not a top-down process but a lively engagement with all levels of the industry and with multiple possible roles.
- Watch beginning music teachers fill with anticipation and excitement at the difference they can make to their school and community.

Summary and key points

Circular mentoring has a positive impact on teacher retention rates, by showing the value of discrete performance projects for beginning music teachers, and by creating a positive mentoring experience for them.

Circular mentoring can add different voices to the mentoring process. It is a way of democratic teaching that allows pupils and teachers to mentor each other on the same level. A beginning music teacher may benefit from hearing the pupils' views.

Collaborative creativity with circular mentoring may be protective for beginning music teachers who have not yet considered the performance elements of the role they are undertaking and how daunting they can be. These short rules may assist in setting up a similar worthwhile mentoring project:

- **The contract – set your rules well**
  All participants agree to positive behaviours in rehearsal, such as a commitment to mentor others or be mentored in the process, to actively build a positive ensemble, and to value and voice the contributions of others in the process.
- **The introduction – warm up the crowd**
  Begin with a series of participatory exercises to help participants engage in the circular mentoring model. Actively foster a positive group mindset and shared outcomes.
- **The play – make something beautiful, something that matters**
  Use all the skill sets to create a professional output.
- **The show day – do something that challenges you**
  The result will be a transformative leap in personal confidence.
- **The reflection – notice the change**

  Provide a reflection and feedback forum:

  We were part of a music experience that involves a cross-generation responsibility of the passing down of knowledge and values of music. The combination of amateur and professional performers not only improved and contributed to the musical sound and overall performance quality, but established an attitude of valuing performance opportunities as a fostering and sharing experience, not just for personal gain and individual promotion. (Participant reflection)

Performance projects *are* efficient tools for up-skilling beginning music teachers and provide positive life satisfaction and teaching retention benefits. Using Kolb's (1984) experiential learning frame, adjusted for musical purpose, mentors can devise circular mentoring performance projects of high value for beginning music teachers. They can see themselves as both mentor and mentee as the project adapts, developing a unique community of practice and minimising the negative impacts of demanding workloads. For musicians and teachers, circular mentoring (Yeo and Rowley, 2018) in a performance context allows for beginning music teachers to learn, teach, mentor, be mentored, be part of an ensemble, create an ensemble, value all contributions, and create an experience for both their pupils and themselves.

Further resources

Brown, B. (2013) Stop giving your power to Critics. Vulnerability and Shame. 99U Conference 2013. *Official Motivation*. 8/8/2022. https://www.youtube.com/watch?v=ouCHEt8DwjE

Part of Brene Brown's thesis on vulnerability and creativity, is asking us to "show up", be seen, and create. Mentors and teachers' roles involve giving others the tools for creating their own learning and teachers have a responsibility for being clear about their own values before they engage in any teaching. Brown suggests courage as a core value. Finally, Brown calls for creatives to get in the "arena" and to only seek feedback from those who are in the "arena" with you.

Deak, J. (2015). Jon Deak's tips for music teachers. *Sibelius Academy University of the Arts Helsinki*. Available at: https://www.youtube.com/watch?v=vxxinc9qWZw.

Jon Deak, composer and academic, has devoted his practice late-in-life to mentoring compositional skills in young learners. His philosophy as eloquently expressed here involves "first listening to the child", recognising the lack of certainty in music, and the myriad possibilities for interpretation and artistry. Deak sees the process leading to performance as creative journey, necessarily impacting and inspiring all areas of a learner's life.

Allsup, R.E. (2016) *Remixing the classroom: Toward an open philosophy of music education*. Bloomington, IN: Indiana University Press.

Allsup grapples with the complex demands on music teachers, with academic, practical and philosophical advice on expanding teaching practice models in music. Allsup recognises the need for flexible thinking and non-judgemental laboratory work from a range of cultural musical traditions. The discussion also includes open and closed forms of practice and describes their differing purposes in educating the whole musician.

6 Developing a mentor-mentee relationship

Bethany Carter-Sherlock

Introduction

A beginning music teacher's placement at a new school can be quite daunting. Additionally to the fears faced by all beginning teachers related to content knowledge, behavioural strategies, involvement in staff activities and understanding school policies and procedures, beginning music teachers may experience different, subject-specific challenges. The school may lack resources, not have a fully qualified music staff or the teacher may be the only teacher of music in that setting and therefore feel isolated. Furthermore, if music is not a school or community priority, funding may be allocated to other subject areas, and therefore, enhancing value for music may be difficult. Increasing the school's value for music may also become challenging when existing timetabling structures only embed the learning of music through annual 'enrichment days', or 'carousel learning' where music is taught on a rotational basis with other subjects and therefore only studied for part of the year (Incorporated Society of Musicians, 2018, p. 8). The beginning music teacher may feel judged by their perceived lack of musicianship, understanding of ensemble, or different instrumental techniques, or they may be concerned about how to make their subject accessible to a mixed ability music class of 20-30 students. Further, they may be confused about how to effectively teach such a practical subject under potentially tight COVID-19 restrictions surrounding voice and wind instruments. For these and many more reasons, it is important to create a trusting, collaborative and supportive mentoring relationship that enhances the beginning music teacher's experience as rewarding and beneficial, and ultimately inspires professional and personal growth.

The skills gained from this chapter are not limited to mentoring beginning music teachers, but can also be adapted to suit leadership, colleague, situational, or formal mentoring of teachers at any stage in their career. In particular, the chapter will firstly look at the significance of creating a collaborative and supportive environment. To do this, the importance of understanding the school context and the context of the beginning music teacher will be examined, and qualities needed to initiate and sustain an effective relationship shall be investigated. Active, empathetic, and generative listening skills will then be considered as important to maintaining an environment within which the beginning music teacher feels comfortable sharing their thoughts and feelings. Finally, effective verbal and non-verbal communication skills will be discussed and the GROWTH model will be suggested as a framework for developing or furthering teaching goals.

DOI: 10.4324/9781003004196-10

Objectives

At the end of this chapter, you should:

- Have a greater appreciation of the importance of knowing your beginning music teacher, their context, and potential challenges as a beginning music teacher, especially within the COVID-19 climate;
- Have a range of strategies to assist you in creating a supportive and collaborative environment;
- Understand the importance of active, empathetic and generative listening skills to the mentoring relationship; and
- Have an increased understanding of non-verbal and verbal communication in the context of the relationship, and appreciate the GROWTH model as a possible framework for mentoring conversations.

Before reading further, undertake Task 6.1.

Task 6.1 Brainstorming your understanding of the mentoring relationship

Reflect on your own experience of embracing a new occupation or path of study and consider the people who mentored you through your induction. Contemplate the following:

- Who would you consider was your best mentor? What qualities did they have to make you come to this decision?
- Did you engage in mentoring conversations? If so, how did these make you feel?
- Did your mentor assist you with developing your own identity relevant to your new context? If so, in what way?

Developing a collaborative and supportive environment

It is important that the relationship you have with the beginning music teacher is grounded in a collaborative and supportive environment. You should mindfully create this environment with the intention of stimulating growth through nurturing (Harrison et al., 2006) to gradually withdraw your support and encourage the beginning music teacher to embrace different and more superior challenges. To begin, you will need to consider creating a trusting environment where the learning and wellbeing of both yourself and the beginning music teacher is enhanced. Below are some introductory ways you can build a supportive relationship based on trust. It is suggested that you also make your own context-specific list (Hobson, 2003):

- Create and adhere to a workable schedule that contains set dates and times for conversations, observations, feedback, etc.
- Immediately involve the beginning music teacher in relevant social events that are suited to their background and culture. Events may include face-to-face or virtual birthday celebrations, staff morning teas, 'start of term drinks', etc.

- Include positive collaborative tasks and encourage active reflection for all staff during faculty, whole school, or key learning area meetings.
- Allow the beginning music teacher time to observe other teachers and team teach with staff who have different experiences and teaching approaches.
- Involve the beginning music teacher in virtual or actual staff music 'jams', or invite them to join external musical groups.
- Supply an introduction pack (with essential documents such as bell times) and give them a tour of the school.

A trusting relationship will enhance the beginning music teacher's willingness to share and participate in developing ways to prevent, manage, and deal with greater challenges with you as they will not feel judged (Hudson, 2016). Trust can be further created by ensuring what you say will happen actually does, engaging in quality mentee-centred communication (Strong and Baron, 2003), being supportive through challenges (Hudson, 2016), celebrating successes, and valuing the beginning music teacher and the contributions they bring to the teaching profession. These will be discussed later in the chapter.

To assist with creating a positive mentoring relationship, it is important for you to know the beginning music teacher. This can be done mostly through conversation, although other means of acquiring information may also suit your context. Personal and professional qualities including personality, age, cultural and social background, and previous educational and occupational experience will influence how you approach the beginning music teacher. To consider how the context of the beginning music teacher may influence the mentoring relationship, undertake Task 6.2.

Task 6.2 Case studies: understanding the beginning music teacher

Read the case studies and consider the questions below.

Julian

Julian is 23 years of age and has been offered a classroom music teacher position at a secondary school approximately six hours from his hometown. His friends advise him to wait for a closer position to become available, but understanding the limited job opportunities in his area, Julian decides to take the position. At university, Julian performed averagely, although he excelled on his primary instrument, the violin. When arriving at the school, Julian realises that he is the only classroom music teacher, there are 400 students and music is compulsory for all students aged 13-15.

Sarah

Sarah is a 35-year-old beginning music teacher. She initially studied journalism and worked for three years as a Community Relations Officer for Orange City Council, after which she gained a position as Media Liaison Officer for the Department of

> Education. Sarah is married and has three daughters, all of whom attend the local primary school. She is well known and respected in the community and has recently been offered the position of classroom music teacher at a local secondary school of 1100 students. There are two other classroom music teachers and one studio teacher currently working at the school.
>
> Identify any potential concerns or difficulties these beginning music teachers may have. Consider both personal and professional challenges, and how you might best support each beginning music teacher with overcoming these difficulties.

Understanding perceived and actual challenges will also assist you with knowing how to approach your relationship. Conway (2015b) mentions that behavioural issues and administration tasks are particularly challenging for all beginning teachers, and you will also find other difficulties experienced specifically by beginning music teachers in Table 6.1. The author suggests that you also create your own list of challenges relevant to your school context.

To assist the beginning music teacher with preparing for and dealing with these challenges, it is important that you are realistic as the beginning music teacher needs to know that even the most experienced educator finds many of the above challenging. Therefore, it is important to share stories from your own experience, particularly those you can laugh about, and quickly support strategies that ease the negative impact of challenges.

Table 6.1 Potential challenges faced by beginning music teachers

Potential challenge	Description
Limited resources and funding (Krueger, 1996)	Teaching with limited resources can seem overwhelming and balancing these resources across several music classes can potentially be difficult.
Parent/community expectations of musicianship perfection. Expectation of increasing amount of performances (Munroe, 2019)	Beginning music teachers may feel threatened by the perceived undervaluing of their abilities as a teacher and musician. They may experience parent or community pressure for increased performances or feel overwhelmed by the administrative tasks involved in organising a performance.
Global crises challenges (de Bruin, 2021)	Beginning music teachers may be confused about how to teach a practical subject whilst abiding by Health Department legislation such as guidelines related to creating COVID-19 safe environments.
Emotional, educational and locational isolation (Krueger, 1996)	A beginning music teacher may perceive they have inadequate content knowledge or no one with whom they can share an emotional connection. They may be situated in a classroom that is distanced from colleagues.
Differentiation (Munroe, 2019)	Teaching students of varied musical abilities could be overwhelming.
Delivering engaging content (Fallin and Royse, 1994)	Engaging students who have little or no appreciation for music may be difficult.
Personal difficulties (Pellegrino et al., 2017)	These include challenges associated with life outside of the school context and may include sleeping patterns, friendships, personality-based issues, community involvement, health, and relationships.
Managing individual aspirations as a musician (DeLorenzo, 1992)	A beginning music teacher may want to further their own performance ability and balancing this with the demands of classroom teaching could be difficult.

Developing a Mentor-Mentee Relationship 73

In addition to understanding the context of the beginning music teacher, discovering similarities should enhance the ease with which collaboration takes place and the beginning music teacher feels supported. Conway (2015a) suggests that in an ideal context, they should be mentored by a music teacher. Furthermore, other ideal similarities between the mentor and beginning music teacher both personally (age and gender) and professionally (working in close proximity and teaching similarly aged students) may enhance understanding. It is also suggested that they are encouraged to network with other music educators in various classroom, studio and ensemble contexts to further build on different musical knowledge and skills, and share concerns.

Finally, it is suggested that you distance yourself from your own identity as a teacher to avoid 'cloning' your beginning music teacher (Hicks et al., 2005). To do this, it is important to be open-minded and engage in mentee-focused positive conversations surrounding their strengths and areas for development (Boreen and Niday, 2000; Harrison et al., 2006). Developing a genuine interest and curiosity in their identity as a music teacher will assist you with focusing on identifying and building these strengths. To support this, Richter et al. (2013) recognise the importance of the constructivist approach to mentoring which considers and builds on the beginning music teacher's existing knowledge of skills and content to promote their professional identity, increase confidence and passion for teaching, enhance self-efficacy, and ultimately further wellbeing and reduce teacher 'burn out'.

Active, empathetic, and generative listening

Harrison et al. (2006) recognise that effective listening skills are important to building and maintaining positive mentoring relationships. Hence, most of your time as a mentor should be spent listening to the concerns, feelings, and thoughts of the beginning music teacher (Campbell and van Nieuwerburgh, 2018). The way you listen can greatly impact the quality of your relationship. To further develop your listening skills, three approaches to listening will be discussed below.

Active listening seeks to gain insight into the other person's thoughts and feelings by being present and attentive to what is conveyed (Campbell and van Nieuwerburgh, 2018). It is based on a trusting relationship where you approach the conversation with curiosity to learn about the beginning music teacher's thoughts and feelings and listen with the intent to discover more about their needs, ideas, and experiences in the classroom. There are many ways to show that you are actively listening to what they are saying. These include questioning, acknowledging feelings and ideas, rephrasing what the beginning music teacher has said, and avoiding distractions. Each of these skills will be further investigated in the communication section of this chapter.

Empathetic listening considers the beginning music teacher's feelings and emotions through seeking clarification with the intention of fully understanding their perspective (Campbell and van Nieuwerburgh, 2018). This level of listening is particularly important to the mentoring relationship as your conversations can be increasingly emotional. Thus, it is important to use phrases such as *I understand how you feel* supported with a nod of acknowledgement. Some workable strategies to enhance your empathetic listening skills include scheduling time for conversations so that emotions are not disregarded due to time constraints, using open-ended questions that promote deeper responses, practising in a variety of contexts, allowing time for silence, and feeling relaxed as a mentor.

Identified by Scharmer (2018) as the deepest level of listening, generative listening focuses on the potential for change and has a growth mindset. It is a listening skill that is required for the GROWTH model (Campbell and van Nieuwerburgh, 2018), a framework investigated later in this chapter, and promotes greater change, newer ideas, and increased satisfaction in the relationship. Generative listening involves the following:

- **Deeper presence:** Putting aside your own perspectives, prejudices and daily concerns to focus on the beginning music teacher's experiences.
- **A mentee-controlled conversation:** Withholding from speaking until they are finished so that you gain a deeper understanding of how they are feeling. This way, you can assist them in the best way possible.
- **Listening to what is not said:** Considering verbal silences and what these might mean in the context of the conversation, and paying attention to subjects and ideas that are either avoided or verbally stumbled over.
- **Being observant:** Identifying changes to body language, tone, posture, etc., as these may convey hidden feelings.

Before reading further, complete Task 6.3

Task 6.3 Approaches to listening

Reflect on the three listening levels mentioned above and address the following:

- Have you ever engaged in a conversation that uses one or more of the above listening approaches (whether as a listener or speaker)? If so, describe the skills used in the conversation.
- Which of the above listening strategies, if any, had you not previously considered?

Effective verbal and non-verbal communication

To maintain a trusting relationship and promote sustainable lifelong learning and growth you should consistently use language that is open, positive, and supportive (Boreen and Niday, 2000; Buell, 2004). In addition to celebrating their achievements, discourse should focus on the beginning teacher's feelings, strengths, and goals or areas for development. There are many factors that can potentially influence the quality of this communication and therefore threaten your relationship. In addition to school-based variables such as the lack of time resulting from having to deal with more pressing issues, contextual influences including cultural and social background, varied perspectives of teaching, personal differences, and various levels of teaching experience can potentially hinder a quality mentoring conversation. Creating a realistic mentoring timetable that is imbedded in your existing timetable and available to executive and classroom staff may prevent colleagues from giving you last minute issues to follow up during mentoring time. Moreover, it is important to identify your own teaching perspectives prior to engaging in mentoring conversations so that you are aware of how these could potentially influence the beginning music teacher's development of their own music teacher identity.

Before reading further, complete Task 6.4

Task 6.4 Identifying your own teaching perspectives

Reflect on your own teaching strategies and consider the following questions:

- You are teaching 'How to Play the Guitar' to a class of 15 students. Five of these are capable musicians and three learn at a slower rate in comparison to the rest of the class. What strategies would you immediately consider using? How might another staff member differentiate for this class?
- You are teaching scales and modes. How would you enhance engagement? What strategies might another staff member use?
- You have a class of 20 fourteen- to fifteen-year-old students. Three girls refuse to complete any work, claiming that they do not need to learn music. What behavioural strategies might you use to address this issue? What might another staff member do?

There are many ways to develop your communication skills so that the relationship with the beginning music teacher is a positive one. Consider the specific verbal communication strategies listed below:

- Avoid using commands for example, you *must firstly brainstorm 'Universal Music' to gauge students' understanding*. Strong and Baron (2003) recognise the importance of using less direct language such as *perhaps., Have you thought about...?* and *I wonder whether...* Ideally, the beginning music teacher should be encouraged to think about their own strategies but if needed, indirect language enhances ownership of ideas and assists the beginning teacher with developing their 'teacher-self'.
- Avoid using 'but', 'although', or 'however' (Campbell and van Nieuwerburgh, 2018). If you begin a sentence by complimenting the beginning music teacher on aspects of an observed lesson and then continue with *but...*, everything you say before 'but' is meaningless. This may hinder the beginning music teacher from relying on their own judgement and may decrease their confidence in their abilities. Campbell and van Nieuwerburgh (2018) suggest using 'and' instead of 'but', 'however', or 'although'.
- Use positive language: Although all feedback must be authentic, humans respond best to positive reinforcement (Buell, 2004).
- Use personal language and give reasons for why you find a particular strategy/idea etc. effective. For example, *I enjoyed the way you introduced the bass and treble clef because you personified them in a way that was recognisable to students. I've never thought about doing it like that before*. This adds value to the relationship as the beginning music teacher realises you have learnt something from them (Boreen and Niday, 2000; Buell, 2004).

- Using humour (Cain, 2007), expressing understanding and validating feelings: For example, after suggesting a strategy for introducing new information in an engaging way, you may laugh and comment *even though sometimes I just want to get the content out*.
- Adopt a conversational style (Strong and Baron, 2003): Although it is important to use a teaching metalanguage, a conversational style of communicating should keep the beginning teacher relaxed and encourage open reflection.
- Avoid 'why' questions in initial 'getting to know you' settings: Campbell and van Nieuwerburgh (2018) recognise that using 'why' questions when you are understanding the context of the beginning music teacher (such as their interests, culture, and generational differences) may be perceived by the beginning music teacher as judgemental. 'What' questions should be used here instead.
- Give time to respond (Campbell and van Nieuwerburgh, 2018): Waiting three to five seconds will achieve more quality responses.

There are a variety of approaches to building a mentoring relationship through communication, some of which will be discussed in this chapter. A positive psychology approach focuses on the wellbeing of the beginning music teacher (van Nieuwerburgh, 2016) and assists with building resilience. Language is encouraging, strengths are developed, and conversations are approached with an open mind in a nurturing environment (Buell, 2004). In reflection of the importance of positive language, complete Task 6.5.

Task 6.5 Identifying and expanding on positive communication

Read the sample mentor comments with the following questions in mind:

- Which key words or phrases are positive in each of the sample comments below?
- Extend each of the comments to further develop the use of positive language.

1. *I was speaking to some students whilst on lunch duty to check whether we had enough students to run an elective music class next year. Bella (a student) said she would choose music if you were teaching the class. If it runs, would you like to take the class?*
2. *(discussing a 'lesson that went wrong'). Yeah, but remember we all have lessons like that. We can never predict when students have had an argument with their parents or may be engaged in peer conflict at lunch, etc. and they bring this to the classroom. As teachers, we think that we are not engaging them or challenging them – we are very quick to blame ourselves for what may have happened outside the classroom.*
3. *I really enjoyed how you introduced texture by using different pieces of fabric.*
4. *I'm about to start teaching Orchestral Instruments to my class. I've taught it before, but I've been finding that the students are increasingly disengaged from the content. Any suggestions for how to make it more interesting?*
5. *How do your 'performance circles' work? Do you group students of varied musical abilities or similar abilities?*

Strengths theory (van Nieuwerburgh, 2016) recognises that people accomplish tasks, discover more ideas, experience feelings at a deeper level, and work more effectively when they are using or explaining knowledge or skills that they are good at. Thus, although it is important to discuss perceived 'classroom catastrophes', it is also essential to be realistic and encouraging (van Nieuwerburgh, 2016) by commending the accomplishments of the beginning music teacher through open dialogue, staff award systems, or faculty celebrations. The cognitive coaching model also recognises their strengths and works towards developing hidden capabilities, deliberate reflection and consideration for the thought processes behind teaching strategies (Strong and Baron, 2003).

In addition to verbal communication, non-verbal behaviours can also affect the relationship you have with the beginning music teacher. The following list contains several positive non-verbal behaviours you can practice to further enhance your relationship during mentoring conversations:

- Absolute attention should be given to the beginning teacher. This involves using eye contact and avoiding distractions such as phones and laptops. Campbell and van Nieuwerburgh (2018) suggest that note-taking can imply attention although for some individuals this may initiate anxiety and it is best to firstly check with the beginning music teacher.
- Creating a safe setting. Conversations should be held in a relaxed yet professional environment away from interruptions from other staff or students (Campbell and van Nieuwerburgh, 2018). Where possible, conversations should occur face-to-face to ease potential stressors and limitations of the virtual environment. Authoritarian positioning should be avoided by sitting next to the beginning teacher at an appropriate distance.
- Voice habits such as speaking too frequently which may result in the beginning teacher perceiving that you are 'controlling' the conversation (Buell, 2004). Speaking too quickly, using monotone, or paying careless attention to diction may imply that you are bored, have more important tasks to do, or care little for the beginning teacher's progress.
- Body language should be encouraging, relaxed, and not extravagant. This includes correct posture (Egan, 2002), small hand gestures, nodding in agreement (Egan, 2002), eye contact (Campbell and van Nieuwerburgh, 2018), smiling and laughing when appropriate, and ensuring facial expressions convey focused listening (Campbell and van Nieuwerburgh, 2018) and not your desire to speak.

Before reading further, undertake Task 6.6.

Task 6.6 Practising non-verbal behaviours in a conversational setting

With a colleague, adopt the role of mentor in a role play mentor-mentee conversation about a particular aspect of teaching. Using positive non-verbal communication, begin by asking about your colleague's approach to, for example, dealing with phone distractions in class. After the conversation, ask your colleague to identify some of your behaviours and how these made them feel.

The GROWTH model

Coaching conversations have been proved to positively benefit the beginning music teacher and mentor emotionally and academically (van Nieuwerburgh, 2016) and can be used to avoid the unintentional dismissal of professional conversations as unimportant or irrelevant to the busy life of the teacher. A framework that focuses on specific targets whilst still encouraging the development of the beginning teacher's own teaching style is the GROWTH approach to conversation. Campbell and van Nieuwerburgh (2018) identify the GROWTH model as effective to the mentoring relationship in encouraging a learning conversation that increases awareness of self and ownership of teaching practices. Thus, the beginning music teacher develops their own identity as a music teacher and is increasingly prepared for achieving future career aspirations (Campbell and van Nieuwerburgh, 2018). Conversations may target areas wished to be developed by the beginning teacher (this may be as vague as *I want to work on my knowledge of content*) and these areas can be refined through quality conversation (Campbell and van Nieuwerburgh, 2018). These conversations should assist you with creating short- and long-term goals that may, as suggested by Campbell and van Nieuwerburgh (2018), follow the ISMART method of inspirational, specific, measurable, achievable, relevant, and timely goals. An annotated example of an ISMART goal has been written below:

Supporting and encouraging the setting of these goals promotes positive emotions such as self-esteem, optimism, and self-efficacy and enhances the beginning teacher's ability to consider alternate and creative strategies to overcoming challenges (van Nieuwerburgh, 2016). The GROWTH model, the stages of which are listed in Table 6.2, can be used to further

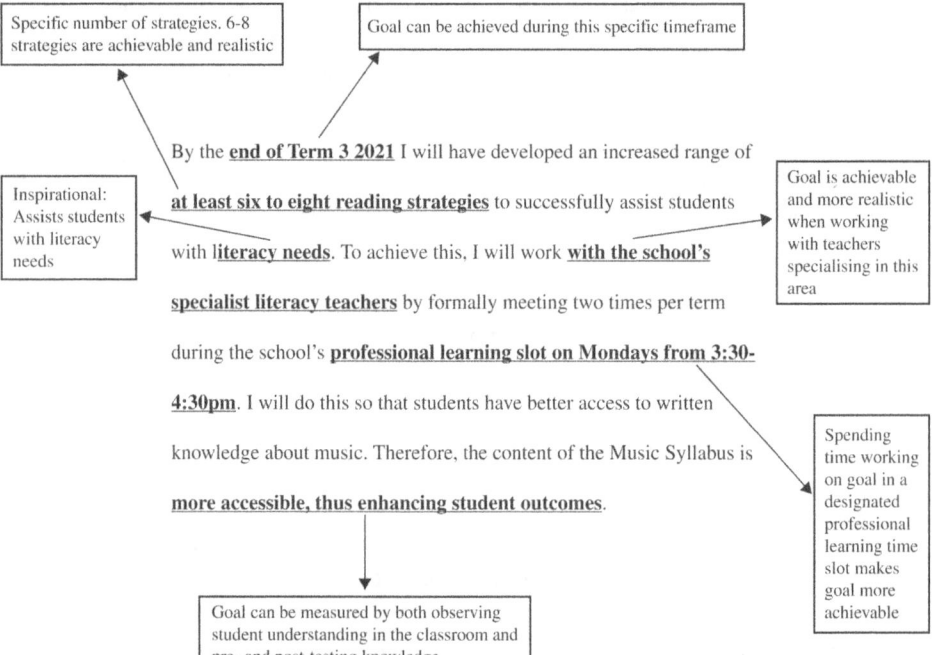

Figure 6.1 Annotated example of ISMART goal

Table 6.2 The GROWTH model

Stage	Explanation	Sample questions
Goals	Goals are important to furthering a strength or developing a desired aspect of teaching practice. Setting and achieving realistic goals will increase wellbeing and value for continued professional development.	• What would you like to achieve? What are you passionate about achieving? • How will you feel when you have achieved this? What will it mean to you? How is it significant? • Do you think it will be achievable within the given timeframe?
Reality	Acknowledges existing supports and skills that may assist with achieving the goal, but also recognises potential for development.	• What resources, procedures, or skills available can assist you with achieving this goal? Are any of these being used currently? Are they working? • What aspects of the goal can you control? What is outside of your control?
Options	Initiates the beginning teacher's consideration for the various ways that the goal could be achieved.	• What resources or strategies could you suggest to someone else with the same goal? What are the advantages and disadvantages of these? • What options could assist you with achieving this goal? Have you seen others use these?
Will	After exploring the benefits and disadvantages of each option, the beginning teacher considers which is most beneficial to their context.	• Which of these options best appeals to you? • Is this option doable in the near future? • What do you believe will occur after you successfully put this strategy in place?
Tactics	The beginning teacher identifies the steps needed to achieve this option and establishes a timeframe.	• Looking in your diary, by what date do you think you will have implemented this option? Is this achievable? • What smaller steps need to take place? When will you do these?
Habits	This conversation should ultimately motivate beginning teachers to habitually and openly self-reflect, and develop professionally (Hudson, 2016).	• What may hinder you from achieving this goal? How can this be managed? • What additional resources are needed to assist you? • How will you feel after you have carried out these actions?

Source: Campbell and van Nieuwerburgh (2018).

progress or create a goal. It is important that these questions are adapted to suit the nurturing mentoring environment and the focus of the conversation. They should be shaped in reflection of your knowledge of the beginning teacher as per earlier in the chapter.

When considering this model, it is important to think about the following: Firstly, the beginning teacher may not know how to achieve their goal and it is therefore important to break it down into smaller steps. For example, if the beginning teacher's goal is behavioural management and they are unsure of how to achieve different strategies in the classroom, you may instead ask *how can you increase your understanding of different behavioural strategies?* Secondly, creating smaller goals with smaller steps will be more achievable for beginning music teachers who are in their first year of teaching. In contrast, when mentoring for leadership, the beginning teacher may wish to achieve larger goals although it is still important that the mentor encourages the use of smaller steps to make goals more achievable. Finally, you may need to guide the beginning music teacher to avoid the creation of a goal that is unachievable in the context of the school and with the beginning music teacher's existing capacities. Therefore, the GROWTH conversation should take place in an increasingly nurturing and understanding environment.

Summary and keypoints

There are many points to consider when you are developing a relationship with your beginning music teacher and although these may seem time-consuming, especially within a busy and varied school context, developing a quality mentor–mentee relationship is extremely valuable to your own professional and personal development. In this chapter, the following have been considered:

- Developing a trusting, collaborative, and supportive environment within which beginning music teachers feel comfortable to share their concerns and develop their teaching practice;
- Utilising active, empathetic, and generative listening to maintain a supportive environment and enhance the beginning teacher's identity as a music teacher;
- Practising effective verbal and non-verbal communication to develop an authentic working relationship, and using the GROWTH model (Campbell and van Nieuwerburgh, 2018) to encourage ownership of practice and active reflection.

Further resources

The resources listed below are useful to further developing your knowledge and skills discussed in this chapter.

Campbell, J. and van Nieuwerburgh, C. (2019) *The leader's guide to coaching in schools: Creating conditions for effective learning.* https://resources.corwin.com/campbellcoaching.

This website provides you with videos of sample coaching conversations that can be used in the context of mentoring beginning teachers and aspiring leaders.

Covey, S. and Merrill, R. (2006) *The speed of trust: The one thing that changes everything.* New York: Free Press.

Covey and Merrill's (2006) text expands on the importance of trust. In particular, the book mentions *13 Behaviours* that are significant to building and maintaining a quality relationship.

Stone, F. (2004) *The mentoring advantage: Creating the next generation of leaders*, Chicago: Dearborn Trade Publishing.

This text further addresses the challenges that may impact the quality of communication you have with the beginning teacher and provides case studies of mentoring conversations.

7 Supporting the mentee: Working at the sharp end

Esther Cavett

Introduction

In my first term, I didn't know how to say "no". I was so busy, I hardly had time to go to the loo let alone think strategically about developing my role as a teacher of music.
private communication between author and her mentee.

This chapter is about supporting the beginning music teacher who feels at the limits of their ability to cope, someone who came into teaching with high expectations of themselves and of teaching as a career and who, without expert guidance and support from their mentor, might burn out and leave the profession. The beginning music teacher, particularly if working in a single person department, can be physically and emotionally isolated and without ready access to a subject-specific supervisor. They may also be expected to provide extra-curricular music for the school and manage external resources, such as peripatetic music teachers and music hubs. Even the most able and highly motivated individual can, under such circumstance, feel their job is virtually impossible. With the advent of COVID-19, difficult situations became even more challenging. Mentees told me, for instance, of having to completely revise face-to-face lesson plans for online learning at one day's notice, or of being told they no longer have their own teaching room with musical instruments but must instead push a trolley full of glockenspiels (their mallets can be easily sanitised) from classroom to classroom in a shopping trolly.

The chapter outlines some interventions that mentors can use to support the wellbeing of beginning music teachers. I have used these interventions as an external coach and mentor engaged to support beginning music teachers working in a variety of different state schools in the UK, but they can be used equally well by a mentor. Reflecting my training and interests, these interventions derive from evidence-based psychology and are used in both counselling and coaching/mentoring contexts. They can help a mentee manage stress, potential burnout and significant workload, they are simple to use, applicable within different educational environments, and can be used to enhance the performance of beginning music teachers so they thrive rather than strive in their role. This chapter concludes with a brief consideration of how a mentor who is not trained as a counsellor or therapist might work with a mentee who is highly stressed, and how you, as mentor, might take care of your own wellbeing when working with a mentee who is facing significant difficulties.

DOI: 10.4324/9781003004196-11

Objectives

At the end of this chapter, you should be able to better understand:

- The 'anatomy' of stress and how it might manifest itself in a beginning music teacher.
- Some psychologically based models you can draw upon as a mentor to support the beginning music teachers you work with.
- Your ethical responsibility as a mentor in relation to a beginning music teacher who might be showing the symptoms of burnout (knowing when to 'refer on').
- The importance of mentor's self-care when dealing with people working in challenging professional environments.

Before reading further, please undertake Task 7.1.

Task 7.1 Mentor reflection

Please reflect on those occasions in your work life when you have felt some or all of the following:

'I'm constantly working yet seem unable to manage my time effectively'.
'I don't feel equipped to manage this situation'.
'I can't live up to other people's expectations of what I'm capable of achieving'.
'I have too much to do, and don't know how much more I can take on without making a horrible mistake'.

Consider what steps you took to manage these issues, from whom you asked for help (or, if you didn't ask for help, why not?), and whether you now think your fears at the time were fully justified.

What is stress?

Stress is a natural reaction to challenge and danger and can keep us motivated and alert. Stress can, however, become problematic and effect people negatively. All of us are likely to have had thoughts such as those set out in Task 7.1, but stress affects each individual differently, due to different character traits, quality of early life experience, genetic make-up, and environmental factors. Some people thrive on stress whilst other people find even ordinary situations difficult. Chronic stress is can be triggered by internal factors (for example, attitudes and beliefs) and external factors (for example, the death of a loved one) and can have a negative impact on performance, and lead to heightened levels of arousal which the individual finds hard to switch off. If stress is not managed it can lead to depression or long-term, persistent anxiety (for further information on the nature and consequences of stress, see Bor *et al.*, 2014 and Palmer and Cooper, 2013).

For beginning music teachers, many factors can lead to stress. They are confronted with an environment they do not fully understand and over which they have little control. They have often entered the profession as a vocation and may find their ideals are

Table 7.1 Effects of stress

Effects of stress on emotions	Effects of stress on the body
Low mood	Tension and restlessness
Anxiety and worry	Muscle aches
Low self-confidence	Headaches and sweating
Fearfulness	Nausea, dizziness, skin problems, indigestion
Lack of interest in life	Problems with sleeping
Frustration	Difficulty concentrating
Agitation	Increased heart rate
Effects of stress on behaviour	**Effects of stress on thinking**
Difficulty with decision making	All or nothing thinking and catastrophising ('this is awful and must never happen again')
Procrastination	
Overreacting to difficult situations	Disqualifying the positive ('last term was awful')
Avoiding problematic situations	Jumping to conclusions ('it is all my fault')
Abuse of alcohol or drugs	Personalisation and blame ('you are useless at your job')
Teeth grinding	Overgeneralisation ('all of my old friends dislike me')
Bad temper	Mind reading (assuming you know what others are thinking about you)
Self-neglect	

Source: Adapted from Bor et al. (2014, pp. 13-16).

not matched by the realities of day-to-day school life: for example, behaviour management may be compromised or struggling students may not be supported due to lack of resource. The beginning music teacher may also need to manage peripatetic instrumental teachers, arrange for broken instruments to be repaired, and sort out after-school rehearsals. A multitude of factors may lead to long days and evenings spent planning lessons and administration, and ultimately to exhaustion.

Negative stress affects our feelings, bodies, behaviours, and thoughts. Some examples are given in Table 7.1.

The four domains referred to in Table 7.1 (emotion, body, behaviour, and thinking) are intrinsically linked. Thus, a beginning music teacher who works on lesson planning until two in the morning and then fails to wake up to the alarm will probably experience a combination of symptoms from the different domains whilst rushing to get to their first lesson: for example, extreme fearfulness, heart palpitations and dry mouth, and negative thoughts about performance.

What interventions might you use to support your beginning music teacher?

The term 'intervention' is used in this chapter to refer to a model or approach used in coaching and mentoring which has been developed from evidence-based research in psychology and, in particular, adult learning (or andragogy, as it is sometimes referred to). Such interventions can focus on the body or a combination of body and mind, such as progressive muscle relaxation techniques, physical exercise, and meditation/mindfulness (some of which are discussed in more detail in Chapter 16), and they may have antecedents in a variety of

84 *Mentoring Music Teachers in the Secondary School*

other contexts, for instance counselling and psychotherapy (Nelson-Jones, 2015), and some religions practices (Cashwell and Young, 2020).

This chapter reviews four interventions designed to refocus and adapt unhelpful thoughts and behaviours, which can be used alongside other interventions referred to in this book. The four interventions are referred to below as 'stress mapping', 'the PRACTICE model', 'ABCDE model', and the 'reflective diary'. Cognitive-behavioural coaching and mentoring assumes that 'the way a person feels is largely determined by the beliefs they hold and their appraisal of a particular situation or problem' (Palmer and Szymanska, 2018, p. 109). As a consequence, it is helpful for the beginning music teacher under stress to develop the skill of 'thought disputation', a skill which underlies each of the interventions described in this chapter. As will be illustrated below, thought disputation involves improving problem-solving skills and developing an awareness of irrationally held beliefs and distorted cognitions. The generation of more rational thoughts about a situation and consideration of alternative solutions will have a corresponding impact on behaviour and emotions, reduce stress, enhance performance, and ultimately empower the beginning music teacher to become their own coach and mentor.

Stress mapping

A beginning music teacher may ask for help with a specific issue or may want more general support. In either case, it is useful for you as mentor (particularly if you are from outside the organisation) to have some sense of the context in which the mentee perceives themself to be working. Equally, it is helpful for the beginning music teacher to develop a view of their overall working environment because, by doing so, they can start to make a balanced assessment of their resources, including people they can turn to for support, people who need their help, and people (and things) who (or which) could make their life easier. A 'stress map' (following Palmer, 1990) can facilitate this process. A stress map is a visual representation of the beginning music teachers' perception of their transactional relationships within their immediate environment. To create a stress map, the beginning music teacher and you as the mentor would ideally sit together at a table, though of course you can interact on Zoom or equivalent if necessary. You then ask them to find a piece of paper and pen (or ideally pencil to allow for changes of mind) and give them the following instructions:

> Write your name in the middle of the paper. Then write the names of the people with whom you work most closely nearby, as if you are the sun and the other people are planets in your solar system. This exercise is all about your perception of your place within your organisation: who is invested in you and who you are invested in. Next, further away from you and your immediate contacts, write the names of people you think are connected with the people you work with, some of whom you will know of only indirectly, such as the school senior management team or school governors. Finally, add in the names of things which are important to your life: the piano in the school hall, the laptops with their specialist music composing software on them, the staff room photocopier, and so on.

As the beginning music teacher fills out the page, you can talk together about the people and things populating it, which again helps create perspective. Once the overall shape of the map is complete, the next instruction is as follows:

Draw a circle round each name on the stress map and draw a pair of parallel lines between each pair of people (or people and things) that are connected. Next put a number next to each line showing, on the lower parallel line, how much stress you are causing the person (for instance, your subject supervisor) or people (for instance, your students) or things (for instance, the photocopier) you interface with and, on the upper parallel line, the amount of stress each is causing you (10 is most stress and 0 is no stress). Do the same for each secondary relationship (that is, relationships which do not involve you directly), for example, the relationship of your most senior line manager with the head of the school, or the head of the school with the school governors. In most cases, you can only make an assumption about the nature of these secondary relationships, which is fine because I'm interested in your perceptions, whether or not they are actually the case.

As a mentor you can then discuss the implications of what the stress map has revealed. Often beginning music teachers are not fully aware of the 'ecology' of their school, and the visual representation can clarify this. It can be enlightening for beginning music teachers to realise that the pressures they are under from their immediate supervisors may often be because their immediate supervisor is under pressure from their line manager due to larger policy decisions made by the senior management team or due to personal relationships within the school.

A stress map can also reveal hidden opportunities. In my experience, as a result of doing this exercise, one beginning music teacher realised he could apply to be the teacher-trustee on the governing body of the school, which gave him invaluable insight into his own role. Another beginning music teacher, who was contracted as a class teacher, realised she could respond to the request from her head of humanities to teach small group instrumental lessons by seeking peripatetic instrumental teacher resource from the local music hub. Another beginning music teacher noted that the IT person who came to repair electrical equipment was always very friendly and decided to get to know him better. This person turned out to be working part-time at the school because he spent the rest of the time developing online music resources, which he was happy to share with the beginning music teacher to assist in lesson planning. Another beginning music teacher realised that the greatest source of stress she faced was never being sure that the photocopier would work in a timely fashion and decided to prioritise getting it fixed. Generally, the greater the discrepancy between the numbers on parallel lines the more likely it is there is some unbalance in the system which needs to be addressed.

The PRACTICE model

The PRACTICE model is one of many problem-solving models which can be used to develop the thought disputation skills of a beginning music teacher (Palmer, 2011; Palmer and Szymanska, 2018). Each letter represents a step in a sequence of questions which the beginning teacher will be asked to explore during the course of a mentoring session, as set out in Table 7.2.

Table 7.2 The PRACTICE model

1. Problem identification.
2. Realistic, relevant goals.
3. Alternative solutions generated.
4. Consideration of consequences.
5. Target most feasible solution(s).
6. Implementation of chosen solution.
7. Evaluation.

Source: Adapted from Palmer (2011, p. 157).

Though there are similarities between this model and the GROWTH model referred to in Chapter 6, which itself derives from the well-established GROWTH model (as in goal, reality, options, will; see Whitmore, 2017), there is arguably more emphasis on the problem *solving* and *solution* focussed aspects in the PRACTICE model. This positive emphasis is in accordance with more recent trends in coaching and mentoring, influenced by the 'positive psychology' movement which identifies and builds on an individual's 'signature strengths' (Peterson and Seligman, 2004) and looks at human cognition in terms of 'prospection' (looking to the future) rather than ruminating on and regretting the past (Seligman et al., 2016).

The Socratic questioning process which lies at the heart of the PRACTICE model is explored in Palmer and Szymanska (2018). Some aspects of the process are illustrated next by considering the sort of exchange which might take place between you and the beginning music teacher referred to earlier in this chapter who oversleeps. Imagine that she comes to her first mentoring session confessing to negative thoughts of the kinds referred to in Task 7.1, castigating herself for getting to school late, and saying she desperately wants help with improving her time management.

Step 1: Problem identification

> You as mentor: What exactly do you think causes you to sleep through your alarm.
> Beginning music teacher: I am always tired. I always have too much to do. I am so overloaded I work late and then I can't sleep.
> You as mentor: You say this as if you have no choice in how you feel or your workload. Could you consider how to reformulate this problem so that you might feel you have some control over it and can make some changes?
> Beginning music teacher: At the moment my school workload is too much, and I need to find ways of containing it. I think if I had less to do, I could stop work earlier in the evening and this would improve my sleeping.

Step 2: Realistic, relevant goal

> You as mentor: what do you think you might change to reduce your commitment at school? Let's try and create some specific, measurable, achievable, relevant, time-limited (SMART) goals.
> Beginning music teacher: I am being asked to become involved in a lot of extra-curricular music-related events. Some of these I understand, like the end of term

wind-band concert, but others are not really anything to do with me, like providing incidental music for the school play. I could start by working really hard at cutting back anything which is not central or closely connected to my contracted role at school. I need to recognise I can't manage everything I would ideally like to do.

Step 3: Alternative solutions generated

At this stage, as the mentor you encourage the beginning music teacher to look at a variety of options for cutting down on workload by brainstorming the situation, and ask her to put forward any thoughts which occur to her, however silly or unrealistic they might sound, making a note of them as she speaks. The solutions include:

1. Refusing to do anything more than timetabled teaching.
2. Saying no to anything which involved evening commitments.
3. Asking her head of department (not a musician) to help rationalise her commitments.
4. Identifying when she is being drawn into a new project and consciously deciding whether or not to accept a role.
5. Considering if someone else can take on some of her existing workload or could share it with her.
6. See if someone else or something else could take on some of her workload entirely or support her.
7. Making a list of everything she has to do, distinguishing between things which are (a) important and time sensitive, (b) important but not time sensitive, (c) not important but time sensitive; (d) not important and not time sensitive. Consider not doing the things within category (c) and (d).
8. Signing out of her social media accounts to save time and avoid distraction
9. Resigning from her job.

Step 4: Consideration of alternatives

As the mentor you now ask the beginning teacher to consider the consequences of taking the various courses of action identified at step 3, scaling each solution from 0 (least realistic) to 10 (most realistic).

She considers options 1 and 2 to be unrealistic given the scope of a sole music teacher's role in the school. She likes the idea of explicitly asking for help from someone more senior than herself, as proposed in option 3, and thinks that could be coupled with being more assertive when asked to take on new projects she does not have time for (at option 4). She thinks her head of department could help her approach people she is already working with to discuss cutting down on existing commitments (see option 5). Option 6 involves more lateral thinking regarding seeking out other resources. She has already completed a stress map and realises that she is not making as much use of outside resources (music hubs, outreach offerings by a local choir and orchestra) as she could. The beginning music teacher likes the freedom introduced option 7 and decided at least for the time being to ignore 'nice to haves' in favour of important matters. She also likes the existential freedom opened up by option 9. The very fact it is written down and visible underlined the fact that she chooses to stay at the school despite all her difficulties, loves teaching, and believes she had a contribution to make. Option 8 is harder to commit to given that social media is her way of staying in touch with friends.

Step 5: Target most feasible solutions

> You as mentor: Of all the options we have discussed which ones might you realistically address first?
>
> Beginning music teacher: I can get my action list sorted out so that I can actively decide not to do the 'nice to haves' rather than worrying about all outstanding items (option 7). I will then go and see my head of department to ask for support in cutting down my role (perhaps she doesn't realise I've got so overloaded). This will involve consideration of options 3, 5, and 6. Finally, I will put a screen time limiter on my phone so I can only look at social media for an hour a day (option 8).

Step 6: Implementation and step 7, evaluation

Further mentoring sessions will look at the outcomes (step 6, implementation) to assess how far the chosen solutions have been implemented, and then evaluate the effectiveness of the intervention. This process of reflection and evaluation (step 7) allows the beginning music teacher to see that a seemingly intractable problem can be broken down into smaller components, each of which can be dealt with in turn and start to feel manageable. This realisation helps the her develop resilience when facing other difficulties in the future.

Different stages of the PRACTICE model can be focussed on, rather than moving through the full sequence in each mentoring session. So, for instance, the beginning music teacher might concentrate on identifying the problem and defining realistic goals, or - if a desired outcome is already known - looking at a variety of different solutions and considering the consequences. This model can also incorporate other types of approaches and questions. For instance, the mentor could ask a 'miracle question' (De Schaza, 1988, p. 5) along the lines of 'if you woke up tomorrow and miraculously the problem of being overloaded had been solved, how would you know this? What would be different?'. As a consequence of considering the 'miracle question', a beginning music teacher might admit that, though she hated being overloaded, the prospect of being under challenged and without stimulation worried her even more.

ABCDE model

The discussion we have just witnessed shows some examples of how unhelpful thoughts can be challenged. This process of thought disputation (sometimes described as the skill of challenging 'cognitive distortions' or thinking errors) is a skill which can assist the beginning music teacher in many contexts. Some types of common thinking errors have been listed in Table 7.1. Albert Ellis, a founding figure of the cognitive behavioural psychology movement, proposed the ABCDE mode as follows (a model which might work within the PRACTICE model or separately from it) in order to 'correct' thinking errors and develop more positive and flexible thinking patterns (Ellis and Dryden, 1997). A brief example is set out next.

A is the activating event
For instance, the beginning music teacher being asked to take on running the production for the whole of the school play.

B is one's belief about the event
The beginning music teacher might say, 'there is no way I can take on this extra responsibility without messing something up, but if I don't take it on, I may fail my probationary period'.

C is the emotional or behavioural response, or cognition
The beginning music teacher feels stressed and conflicted and becomes short-tempered at home and with work colleagues.

D is thought disputation
The beginning music teacher realises it is unlikely she will 'blot her copybook' completely by not taking on this new task and looks at options (see steps 3 and 4 of the PRACTICE model, above) for being involved in the school play which do not involve her taking complete responsibility for it.

E is new the effect or emotion
The beginning music teacher develops her sense of agency, understanding she can say 'no' without it having drastic consequences.

Reflective diary

The value of reflection has been discussed elsewhere in this book (refer also to Chapter 10): reflection can increase self-awareness and depth of understanding in the mentee. What is proposed for this 'intervention', however, is that the beginning music teacher brings a diary (ideally hard copy rather than electronic) to each session. They take notes in the diary during the session, but also record thoughts and feelings in it between sessions. The power of 'journalling' is well researched in counselling and coaching context (see, for instance, Hensley and Munn, 2020). Mentees will sometimes find really attractively bound handbooks to write in, which they become fond of as beautiful objects in themselves. Mentees have confirmed that the seemingly simple activity of keeping a diary has both immediate and long-term benefits:

- The diary provides a place for where the mentee's experiences of their mentoring 'journey' can be recorded, which provides fresh perspectives on problems which had originally seemed intractable and are now solved.
- It allows mentees to keep a record of, and reflect on techniques which have helped them, ranging from the interventions referred to above to basic aspects of self-care, which the mentor might have suggested, such as ensuring they take enough exercise, modify diet, smoking, drinking, and get enough sleep.

- By making notes immediately before and after each session, the mentee can notice how the work in the session contributes to improved mood and sense of self-efficacy.
- The diary can be used to keep track of 'homework' suggested during a mentoring session. The homework might, for instance, involve trying out at home more of the exercises done in the session, or writing down performance inhibiting thoughts and replacing them with performance enhancing ones in order to generate more flexible thinking.
- The diary can be used to enhance mood. At the end of a particularly tough day, the mentee can write down the events which have made the day particularly difficult in one column, and then five positive things (however small) which have happened on that same day. Gratitude has been shown to be very effective at alleviating negative thoughts (Emmons and Stern, 2004, 2013).
- The diary has in some cases been described by a mentee as a 'critical friend', where the mentee can develop a kinder, less hyper-critical relationship with him or herself, which is where self-care begins.

What are your ethical responsibilities when dealing with someone who appears to be suffering from stress?

Please consider the ethical issues which might be raised by the scenario set out as Task 7.2

Task 7.2 Scenario for mentor reflection

Consider the following extract from (fictitious) reflective notes made by a mentor/coach following a mentoring meeting with a beginning teacher.

'My new mentee has had a difficult first half term, where he was offered little supervision and was largely left alone to make his own lesson plans and run after-school music clubs. He was now so exhausted his main issue was 'complete lack of motivation. I cannot find a single redeeming feature to carrying on in this job; I'm completely overwhelmed'. I asked if he had considered that he might need more help than a coach or mentor could give him, for instance psychological help, and he said he really didn't know. He didn't think he felt stressed, he just felt totally demotivated.

I asked how he spent his leisure time. He said largely alone, playing computer games. His girlfriend had left him a while back because he worked all the time. His family lived abroad.

Quite late in the session he told me he'd just been diagnosed as suffering from depression after filling out a questionnaire given to him by his GP; however, the waiting list to see a specialist was several months at least, so he was extremely glad he could talk to me in the interim.

What ethical issues do you think are raised for you as mentor by this scenario?

How you deal with this scenario will vary depend on your prior training and experience, the code of ethics you feel bound by as a mentor and a teacher, including statutory guidance and current policy (see Chapter 1). If you are also independently trained and accredited as a coach and mentor and are a member of a professional mentoring and/or coaching association, such as the Association for Coaching or the European Mentoring and Coaching Council, you will be, in addition, be bound by the ethical code of your membership organisation (for example, see the Code of Ethics on the Association of Coaching website, at www.associationforcoaching.com).

At the very least, it is important to be able to decide when it is acceptable to breach the confidence of a beginning music teacher in order to ensure his or her safety and how to deal with any potential conflicts of interest that might arise between your role (if you have one) as senior manager within a school and what your mentee has told you about their ability to perform their role as a teacher. It is especially important to know the limits of your competence and - in particular - when to advise your mentee to consider seeking the help of a qualified mental-health professional. The initial 'contracting' stages of a mentor/mentee relationship should make these all these points clear as well as noting that the mentor will seek supervisory advice where appropriate.

What steps can you take to look after your own wellbeing

When supporting a mentee who is working in a challenging professional environment, your wellbeing is equally important as that of the mentee's. As discussed above, teaching and coaching/mentoring codes of practice in most jurisdictions will have embedded in them the requirement to know the limit of your own competence. This includes knowing when you are not fit to be undertaking a task entrusted to you, whether due to lack of training or limits on your own physical or mental health (refer also to Chapter 16). Self-care also extends to ensuring you regularly reflect on your work as a mentor both on your own and with others (refer also to Chapters 2, 9, and 16). You might also ask for more formal supervision, offering structured support and feedback from someone more experienced than yourself.

To consolidate your learning from this chapter please consider Task 7.3, below.

Task 7.3 Concluding reflection for mentor

Please consider how the information in this chapter may help you to assist a mentee who is having thoughts such as the ones set out in Task 7.1.

To close, you might find it helpful to consider the following thoughts of an experienced performer, music teacher, and mentor (quoted on an anonymised basis with their consent):

> The relief of being with someone who is not judging but listening and putting total attention on you is far and away the most life-giving aspect of mentoring, I believe. All techniques come after that. Keeping this in mind takes a burden off the mentor in that, even if they do not manage to solve all the problems of the mentee or remember all techniques they could use, at least they are being useful in just being there!
>
> private communication to the author

Summary and key points

Even the most able and organised beginning music teacher is likely to find aspects of their new role extremely challenging from time to time and your role as mentor is to help support them. In this chapter we have:

- Seen how stress can have an impact on our emotions, behaviour, body, and thinking.
- Reviewed a variety of different strategies that you as a mentor could suggest to a beginning music teacher for managing difficult circumstances and situations.
- Considered the importance of knowing the limits of one's competence as a mentor and coach, and where one should look to for guidance (see also Further Resources, below).
- Considered the importance of taking care of one's own wellbeing.

Further resources

The resources listed below will support your thinking when reflecting on the points raised in this chapter.

Bor, R., Eriksen, C. and Chaudry, S. (2014) *Overcoming stress*. London: Sheldon Press.

Written by experienced clinical psychologists for the general reader, this book explains the nature of stress and how it can be managed.

Neenan, M. and Drydan, W. (2014) *Life coaching: A cognitive behavioural approach*. 2nd edn. Hove: Routledge.

An excellent and extremely practical handbook written for mentors and coaches, covering a range of issues you may want to address when mentoring beginning music teachers, including time management, dealing with criticism, developing risks, and overcoming procrastination.

Palmer, S. and Whybrow, A. (2018) *Handbook of coaching psychology: A guide for practitioners*. 2nd edn. Hove: Routledge.

A detailed guide for professional coaches and mentors who are interested in psychology, with a wealth of information and ideas for working with mentees.

Spry, D. (2010) *Cognitive behavioural coaching pocketbook*, Hants: Management Pocketbooks Ltd.

You could recommend this inexpensive, approachable, but extremely condensed book to a beginning music teacher as a quick reference source.

SECTION IV

Supporting specific aspects of beginning music teachers' knowledge, skills, and understanding

8 What are the building blocks? Thinking about musical skills, knowledge, and understanding

Anthony Anderson

Introduction

Skills, knowledge, and understanding (SKU) are frequently referenced in educational literature, academic discussions, policy directives, and practitioner dialogue. Thinking about what these dimensions mean for practices in the music classroom is therefore important for the beginning teacher, where SKU will be a probable focus throughout their teacher training experiences. This chapter will explore what skills, knowledge and understanding might mean, and how with a beginning teacher, you may wish to approach this area. It proposes a model for how SKU interact, followed by discussions about the ways in which SKU are interpreted in policy perspectives, suggesting approaches for reconciling tensions and finding routes into practice, which you can discuss with your mentee. The chapter concludes with a comparison which draws these ideas together and highlights starting points from teacher training and beyond into the first years of teaching experience.

Objectives

At the end of this chapter, following discussions with your mentee, you should be able to:

- Explain differences between skills, knowledge and understanding;
- Understand some of the most significant perspectives which exist of SKU;
- Recognise the importance that interpreting SKU has for your own practices; and
- Identify development ideas for incorporating SKU into music teaching.

What are skills, knowledge, and understanding?

Skills, knowledge and understanding (SKU) often appear in reading you might do about teaching, including statutory documents you are required to follow (such as the National Curriculum or Music Programmes of Study in the school where you are working), non-statutory guidance, such as the Model Music Curriculum (Department for Education (DfE), 2021) and regulatory information (such as OFSTED reports). SKU are frequently employed, but their meanings can go unconsidered, so this chapter is a space to reflect on where to start. We therefore begin by thinking about what these discrete terms mean, how they might be interpreted, and the implications of this for mentoring, before moving on to explore where SKU overlap.

DOI: 10.4324/9781003004196-13

Musical skills

Mentoring for musical skills presents challenges. The notion of skills can be quite varied, so it is important to build in time to address this area for a beginning teacher. Skills can be understood as a set of competencies to be learned, a set of characteristics to be developed, or a way of understanding music. For instance, Evans (2016, p. 131) suggests *keyboard skills* may mean 'learning the layout of the keyboard and individually mastering a performance of a set melody'. *Keyboard skills* may also be interpreted as: chord realisation, melodic reproduction of differentiated repertoire, an approach to composition, or an interface for music technology.

There are other ideas about skills. Skills have been connected with playing instruments (Fautley, 2010), musical performance arising from a 'knowing body' (Savage, 2013, p. 110) and subdivided into learning types in the development of instrumental playing (Hallam, 2006). In such domains, skills are regarded as cognitive rather than physical, even though physical movement is required to interact with a musical instrument to create sound (Lehmann et al., 2007). Skills have also been described as fulfilling other functions. Barrett (1992) has suggested skills form part of necessary learning to control materials of music in their various forms, and Priest (2002) considers skills in terms of aural responses. Swanwick (2012) has proposed that uses of notation can also constitute *skills*, but cautions against concentrating on developing skills for their own sake.

Policy perspectives present a further dimension for how musical skills may be understood. The *Secondary National Strategy for school improvement* (Department for Education and Skills (DfES), 2006, p. 21) suggested that 'intellectual grasp of how' should be followed and informed by 'practical skills', which are the outworking of conceptual understandings. Such a conceptualisation of music is more than a grappling with musical materials and is instead about identifying essential terminologies and applying these to musical contexts. According to this perspective, musical skills cannot be developed before concepts are established. In later developments in policy, the Office for Standards in Education (OFSTED, 2012, p. 52) described musical skills as developing in 'musical sounds, inside the head'. However, in discussing music technology, OFSTED (2012, p. 8) recommended that 'technical skills and knowledge' should be 'supporting, rather than driving, musical learning'. This view also suggests that musical skills come later, after the essence of musical learning has been identified and planned.

Despite these differing perspectives on the nature of musical skills and their place in learning, many regard them as essential to music education. Skills have been acknowledged in music policy guidance (Qualifications and Curriculum Authority (QCA), 2004) as particularly evident in secondary schools, and researchers have emphasised their importance as a peer-to-peer as well as teacher-to-pupil interaction (Adams, 2001). Fautley (2018, p. 1) distinguishes between musical skills and contextual skills (such as the skill of long division in mathematics) by arguing that musical skills have a physical embodiment, which involves a physical response and moves beyond recall and into 'feeling the music'; an aspect that Swanwick (1979, p. 24) previously described as 'the feelingfulness of music'. This dimension of musical feeling leads Fautley (2018, p. 2) to his observation, that 'we music educators really understand skills'.

Thinking about what it means to be musically skilled and how classroom music can enable skills development can take some time to disentangle. It is probably not the same as skills in some other school subjects, and for a beginning music teacher, they may have different perspectives from you on how skills form aspects of musical development. It may be helpful to consider the boundaries between the development of musical skills and musical activity. Whilst an analysis of activity can result in a richer understanding of the classroom environment (Engeström, 2009), unfocused musical activity can dominate music pedagogies aimed at developing skills. Swanwick (1992, p. 28) cautions against composing in the classroom as a 'rarefied activity', instead considering it as a means of engaging with musical discourse. Webster (1990) posits that creative thinking is more than classroom activity and Spruce (2016) suggests it is worth asking if an activity would be considered musical if it took place outside the music classroom. These provide helpful points of reflection when considering the extent to which musical activity enables skill development and the extent to which activity, without a clearly scoped purpose, can feature solely to fill lesson time. Regular moments of candid reflection and discussion in mentor and beginning music teacher meetings can help to delineate and distinguish unfocused activity from musical activity which is part of a skills development approach to teaching and learning.

Before reading further, complete Task 8.1.

Task 8.1 Musical skills modelling

Beginning with overlapping circles, ask your beginning music teacher to create a model of how musical skills intersect and interact.

Now ask them to think about using the model to create a skills map. If a pupil were to travel through this skills landscape, what path could they be taken on? Add lines of progression and arrows to indicate their journey. Where there are multiple options, indicate this with lines that diverge and branch off from each other.

- What does your model and skills map say about musical skills?
- How could this impact the approach to teaching music in the classroom?

Musical knowledge

Following on from considering the substance of musical skills, thinking about musical knowledge in classroom contexts is an important process for a beginning music teacher. Whilst there are some conceptualisations of knowledge as an artefact to be passed on, this may be to confuse knowledge with information. Oak National Academy (2020, p. 3), for instance, describe musical knowledge as 'knowing about', which tends to emphasise music as an object. Distinguishing between knowledge and information is important in music classrooms. Pupils bring a range of experiences and perceptions with them into a space where music is made. Knowledge as a model of transmission is therefore problematic for the music teacher, where music is as much an individual journey of exploration and creation, as it is about engaging with existing musical traditions. In this sense, musical knowledge is not about unlocking the answers which the teacher knows (Wood, 1991). Musical knowledge is both made and discovered.

Thinking about music in this way can be rather inconvenient in some schools, as music does not always neatly fit with prescribed bodies of knowledge. Because of this, it is important for beginning teachers and their mentors to have reflected on a philosophical basis for such an approach. Swanwick (1994) wrote about musical knowing as arising from personal encounters, which takes time to develop. He argued that young people require repeated opportunities to engage with music to develop not only what we might call musical reception, but also musical perception. Such a position did not mean, for Swanwick (1996, p. 29), that music was a 'no knowledge' subject, but rather that musical knowing exhibited its own range of distinct characteristics. Such characteristics have also been discussed by others in the field of music education. Paynter (1992) regarded the development of musical knowledge as an active, rather than passive pursuit and later (Paynter, 1994) suggested that knowledge types needed to compose music were different from those needed when playing a musical instrument.

Concepts of musical knowledge have been further developed since Paynter and Swanwick suggested these ways of thinking about them. Musical knowledge continues to be represented as moving beyond learning about music and is more akin to learning to be musicians (Cain and Cursley, 2017). In other words, musical knowledge is not a static body of components, but an entity. In encouraging a setting where musical participation can occur, musical knowledge becomes a dialogue between learner and teacher. It is an engagement which requires negotiation (Spruce, 2012) to enable musical development. Capturing musical knowledge as a set of propositions is therefore problematic (Murphy, 2002), as musical knowledge is not abstract in this sense (Bate, 2020), but rather takes the form of an interchange between pupils, and between teacher and pupil, and this can take multiple forms.

This way of thinking about musical knowledge can create difficulties for music teachers in schools where music can be required to be expressed in standardised curricular documentation, where the same template is used for all subjects. Formulating *subject DNA*, *building blocks*, *mastery characteristics*, *core elements* or however else a particular school may require musical knowledge to be presented, often for the purposes of creating shared formats and to enable comparisons that school leaders may wish to make across subjects, can be potentially highly complex for music teachers to negotiate. Musical knowledge does not snugly fit a cross-school template. Music is therefore not subject matter to be absorbed (as typified in proposed content documents, such as the Model Music Curriculum (DfE, 2021)), but a discourse (Swanwick, 1999), or what Spruce (2016, p. 26) has described as 'embodied knowing'.

Mentoring to support beginning music teachers to work through these ideas about knowledge will require time and this needs to be accounted for in scheduling arrangements. The opportunity for such discussions can become lost in tangles of written records, observation arrangements, and processes of planning and marking. Time to think and reflect on personal perspectives of what musical knowledge is, and to give these a voice in beginning teacher and mentor discussions, will support their development and enable reflection on their early experiences as a teacher.

Retaining the focus of musical knowledge in mentoring support can also be helpful. Thinking about assessment approaches and discussing whether their formulation is consistent with ideas about musical knowledge could be one useful focus. This can be a challenge where there are requirements to meet training standards. Your experience and perspective will be invaluable at this point. At all stages, thinking about how the beginning music teacher's lessons are seeking to develop musicality in young people and the value of the musical knowledge which such a process is facilitating, will be important. Therefore, the manner in which beginning music teachers perceive the nature and purpose of music (Spruce, 2002), and how this intersects with musical knowledge will directly impact pedagogical approaches, and teacher evaluation of their impacts (refer also to Chapter 11 on curriculum design for a further discussion of pedagogical content knowledge which develops this theme).

Before reading further, complete Task 8.2.

Task 8.2 Musical knowledge and assessment

Spend some time as discussing perspectives on musical knowledge with your mentee.

- How do we evaluate musical knowledge in young people as music teachers?
- What forms of formative, summative or ipsative assessment are observed or used in the classroom?
- Are these forms of assessment consistent with both your ideas of musical knowledge which you have discussed above?

Musical understanding

Following on from skills and knowledge, musical understanding is the aim of classroom music education. Understanding, however, is not equivalent to knowledge and this can be confusing. Knowing something in music, even via musical experience, is not necessarily the same as understanding music, although the two may be found together. It is the role of the teacher and mentor to disentangle authentic musical understanding, from response in musical activity, and this is a highly complex interaction. It requires a dialoguing in music, where the beginning teacher is making music with pupils listening to their response and making further music with them in a manner which consistently urges them on to achieve further musical development. This aspiration needs incorporating *into* episodes of musical learning as they are planned and experienced. This is unlikely to occur where lesson time is filled with music-making activity but is not framed by reflective practices on the part of both teacher and pupil.

Musical understanding has been described as emanating from musical knowledge, where one leads to the other. Philpott *et al.* (2007, p. 78) frame this as 'knowing *of* music' arguing that this needs to be central to musical learning in order to develop musical understanding. Spruce's (2016, p. 26) previously mentioned concept of 'embodied knowing' is again pertinent here where musical understanding is realised through processes of music-making and creating. It therefore makes sense that musical understanding cannot be developed without musical knowledge and musical knowledge is itself facilitated through musical engagement. In other words, it is essentially problematic to think that musical understanding can be developed by activities which do not prioritise musicality and musicianship in pupils. This is important as it will fundamentally frame how teachers facilitate the musical environment of the classroom. Theoretical exercises will not, in themselves, develop musical understanding, but need to be linked to *doing* music in some form. These are the areas which Swanwick (1999, p. 48) described as 'artistic judgement', where making music 'without musical understanding – not really *knowing music* – is an offence against human kind' (Swanwick, 1994, p. 233). Strong words indeed!

What, therefore, might musical understanding look (or sound) like in the classroom and how can teachers recognise and enable it? Fautley (2010) suggests that composing, performing, listening, reviewing and evaluating, musical knowledge, personal learning, and thinking skills, alongside social and environment aspects of learning, all feed into musical understanding, and that these are themselves evidenced through music-making, writing (both text and music), and discussion. Hallam (2006) proposes that repeated listening to music develops musical understanding. Where musical understanding is not part of lesson rationales, these aims can be difficult to realise. Musical understanding therefore stands behind every musical activity, plenary, and the lesson structure as a whole. An evaluation of how planned activities for lessons enable musical understanding is therefore a very helpful starting point.

Before reading further, complete Task 8.3.

Task 8.3 Reflecting on musical understanding

Discuss with your beginning music teacher:

- What moments they can identify from their own educational experience that developed their musical understanding?
- What moments hindered the development of their own musical understanding?
- In what ways do they plan to develop musical understanding in those they teach?

Spending time in reflective discussion is not wasted time, as this allows for beginning teachers to evaluate their foundational principles at the beginnings of their careers. This is significant, because there is so much for new teachers to learn. As well as school systems and aspects of professional practice, subject knowledge as defined in terms of content to be selected and shaped for teaching can dominate, inhibiting wider considerations of the development of musical characteristics in pupils. It is therefore helpful for beginning teachers to evaluate how they are seeking to engender musical understanding through classroom experiences in music. Where there is uncertainty about how an activity might function within an overall music philosophy of education, there may be cause to question its validity. Continually evaluating how a music curriculum enables musical development is useful, and this is discussed elsewhere in this book (for example Chapter 11). At this stage, however, it is perhaps useful to evaluate how musical understanding features in planning and how those teaching it will evaluate its impact. Task 8.4 is designed to help with this. It could be incorporated as a pre-planning exercise each time a beginning music teacher plans a new unit of work, with you, the mentor, acting as a critical friend.

Task 8.4 Skills, knowledge, and understanding planning activity

Use the chart below in Figure 8.1, to discuss both your perspectives and responses to the prompt questions on knowledge, skills, and understanding it contains.

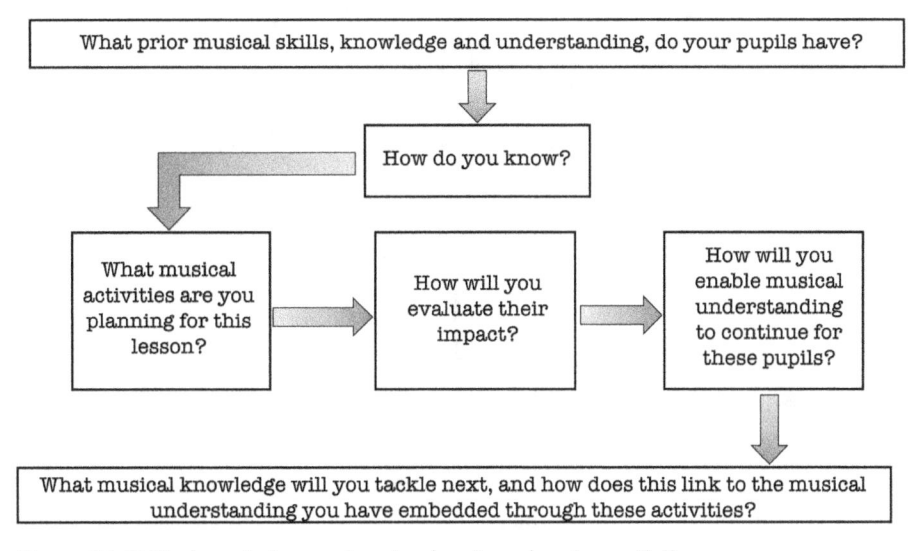

Figure 8.1 Skills, knowledge, and understanding planning activity

How skills, knowledge, and understanding interact

Musical skills, knowledge, and understanding are differing dimensions which unite together to create opportunities for musical learning in the classroom. The interpretation of *musical skills* varies widely – from instrumental proficiency, to a means to control musical materials – and is represented differently in music teacher practices, policy paradigms, and academic literature. *Musical knowledge* requires negotiation and forms a dialogue between learner and teacher, as well as between co-learners. *Musical understanding* is the ultimate goal of music education and embodies processes of music-making and creating in musical expression and an awareness of musicality. It is possible to represent the relationship between skills, knowledge, and understanding as a model of musical practices. In such a model, musical knowledge runs through characteristics of musical learning and is the means by which musical development is enabled. This occurs within an environment of skills, which are constantly practised, with which pupils are continually engaged and which they experience in a back-and-forth interchange. Ultimately, this journey of musical knowledge through skills results in musical understanding, although this is, itself, continually growing and developing and does not exist as an inert bounded entity. This interaction is perhaps the reason that so many have sought to discuss the 'nature' of music in a classroom context (for example Fautley, 2010; Philpott and Evans, 2016; Swanwick, 1992).

In mentoring for SKU, it may be helpful to consider the complexity of the potential interaction between these dimensions and for mentoring and beginning teachers to spend some

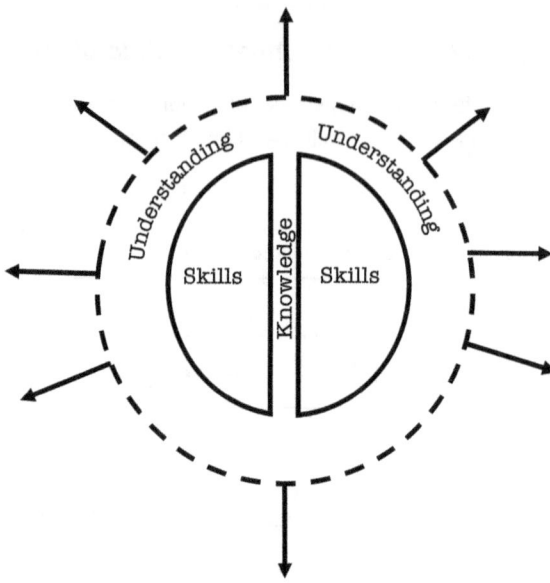

Figure 8.2 The interaction of musical skills, knowledge, and understanding

time discussing how they regard these. There are opportunities for teachers to do this in the earlier activities in this chapter, but if you prefer a pictorial representation, look at Figure 8.2 and use Task 8.5 to discuss together what you think of it.

> **Task 8.5 Reflecting on the interaction of SKU**
>
> - What is helpful about this model of skills, knowledge, and understanding in music and how they interact?
> - What could be added to the model to make it more comprehensive?
> - What does the model mean for to you and the beginning music teacher?

Thinking about skills, knowledge, and understanding in differing contexts

As well as thinking about what skills, knowledge, and understanding might mean in a musical context, it is also helpful to think about how they are used in other educational contexts. Skills, knowledge, and understanding can vary in their use and meaning. This is important to acknowledge in education, where music can be 'schooled' (Spruce, 2002, p. 10), so that it is required to conform to the same approaches adopted by other school subjects. This has implications for assessment, for instance, where assessment processes for science, maths or English are unlikely to be wholly appropriate for music. SKU in a range of contexts bring shades of differing meaning and thinking about these will help beginning teachers to adopt an analytical approach.

OFSTED SKU perspectives

OFSTED, as the inspectorate for schools in England, is highly influential in validating SKU. It is important for the beginning music teacher to understand this perspective, as OFSTED reporting on schools is highly influential. OFSTED (2019c, p. 41) define skills, knowledge and understanding as 'curriculum intent' and expect schools to look for gaps in knowledge and skills, which then need addressing in their school curriculum. OFSTED (2019c, p. 24) consider SKU in relation to 'defined endpoints' and require evidence through work scrutiny to show that they are 'developed incrementally' (OFSTED, 2019c, p. 27). Knowledge and skills are often prefaced with other adjectives such as 'intended' (OFSTED, 2019c, p. 44), 'sufficient' (OFSTED, 2019c, p. 49), or 'detailed' (OFSTED, 2019c, p. 51). OFSTED (2019c, p. 45) also explicitly define learning as an 'alteration in long-term memory' in which pupils 'apply their knowledge as skills'. This is a significant distinction, which may be described as a melding of knowledge and skills.

According to OFSTED (2019c, p. 24), understanding can be 'gauged' and is something that teachers can 'check' (OFSTED, 2019c, p. 44). This is problematic for the discussion of understanding in music already outlined, where it is the ultimate aim of music education, and is continually expanding. Musical understanding is part of ongoing musical development. Connecting 'new knowledge with existing knowledge' (OFSTED, 2019c, p. 45) develops understanding as described by OFSTED. As previously discussed in this chapter, in music, knowledge and understanding are not equivalent, and whilst musical knowledge can lead to musical understanding, this is unlikely where an emphasis on musicality is absent. This makes situating musical knowledge within OFSTED perspectives challenging.

OFSTED has, in previous publications and policies, described its approach to SKU at that time. This distinguished between 'knowledge about' music (OFSTED, 2012, p. 49) from 'musical quality and understanding' (OFSTED, 2012, p. 49). Skills were often attached to domains of musical activity: i.e., 'composing skills' (OFSTED, 2012, p. 18), 'performance skills' (p. 30) and 'listening skills' (2012, p. 30), but were not described in further typological musical detail. OFSTED (2012, p. 7) encouraged teachers to identify 'landmarks of musical understanding', which suggests musical understanding is a fixed point visible from the distance, rising above the surrounding landscape.

OFSTED's approach to skills, knowledge, and understanding, rests on establishing tangible characteristics. However, this has the potential to create tensions for the music teacher between the musical activities of the classroom, and a formulated approach which requires standardised evidence. It is therefore important that the beginning music teacher works through their own rationale for musical learning, supported by you, and articulate this in well-reasoned documentation.

Teachers' standards and SKU

In England, beginning teachers have to meet a set of teaching standards defined by the Department for Education (Department for Education (DfE), 2011) as part of their training. These standards also feature in aspects of professional development throughout teachers' careers in England, where they may serve as objectified measures of teacher competence.

These standards refer to SKU, but their usage differs from characteristics of academic discourse. For instance, 'understanding' is referred to as 'critical' (DfE, 2011, Standard 3.2), 'secure' (DfE, 2011, Standard 5.2), and 'clear' (DfE, 2011, Standard 5.4), but these distinctions in types of understanding are not elsewhere defined. This is also true of supporting documentation for the standards, where teachers are required 'as their careers progress ... to extend the depth and breadth of knowledge skill and understanding that they demonstrate in meeting the standards' (DfE, 2011, p. 7), but the substance of such extension remains undefined. Knowledge is similarly required in the teacher standards to be 'demonstrated' (DfE, 2011, Standard 2.4) and 'secure' (DfE, 2011, Standard 3.1), with teachers able to 'impart knowledge' (DfE, 2011, Standard 4.1), 'extend' knowledge (DfE, 2011, Standard 4.1) and to demonstrate an awareness of pupils' 'prior knowledge' (DfE, 2011, Standard 2.2). There is also an emphasis on professional competencies, where teachers need to demonstrate that they can deploy appropriate strategies for differentiation (DfE, 2011, Standards 5.1 and 5.4) and procedures for accessing 'specialist support' (DfE, 2011, Standard 8.1). Skills are mentioned only once in the *standards* and this is in the 'preamble' where skills are paired with knowledge. The omission of skills in the teaching standards can be problematic for music, where skills and knowledge are so closely connected.

In place of a constructivist approach, where pupils are engaged in making meaning from their learning, the approach in the teaching standards rests on information transfer, or what the standards describe as teaching which is well structured because it 'imparts knowledge' (DfE, 2011, Standard 4.1). This may create challenges for the beginning music teacher, especially as part of lesson feedback from observations from non-music specialists. It is important to recognise this, so that the aspects of musical *knowledge* as musical experiences, *skills* as diverse musical engagements in classroom music-making and creating, and *understanding* as the aim of classroom music-making can be clearly articulated on lesson plans and units of work. These may not be immediately apparent to those supporting the beginning music teacher, who work within alternative pedagogical framings. This means that developments of skills, knowledge, and understanding in music lessons may require explicit annotation on lesson plans and overt explanations embedded into musical learning episodes within lessons. Recognising the differing use of SKU in the teaching standards is a useful first step for expressing pupil-centred musical philosophies existing at the centre of approaches to musical learning. Task 8.6 seeks to facilitate this kind of thinking.

Task 8.6 SKU in lesson planning (for non-music specialist mentors)

Ask the beginning music teacher to create one lesson objective respectively for skills, knowledge, and understanding. Ask them to share with you their thinking. How do they respond? How can they retain the important characteristics of musical learning whilst meeting the planning requirements of your school? Does a colleague from another subject area have any suggestions? Are their ideas valid?

National Curriculum and SKU

The National Curriculum is statutory only in the diminishing number of schools in England which remain under local authority (LA) control. LA schools reduced by over 1 million pupils between 2016 and 2021 (DfE, 2021), to just under 4 million out of a total of around 9 million pupils. However, despite these declining numbers, the National Curriculum remains a significant influence in music teacher curriculum interpretations (Anderson, 2019). Given the centrality of the National Curriculum as the origin for many pupils' musical experiences in school, it is perhaps surprising that skills, knowledge, and understanding receive relatively little attention in these curriculum orders. The subject content for key stage 3 (ages 11–14) requires pupils to 'build on previous knowledge and skills' (DfE, 2013, p. 1), with this realisation occurring through the modes of performing, composing and listening. That pupils are 'expected' to 'know, apply and understand' the 'skills and processes' (DfE, 2013, p. 1) by the end of the key stage further emphasises this developing pathway. There is little distinction between skills, knowledge and understanding as independent elements, which are discussed in an amorphous manner – it is left to the music teacher to unpack and apply their own interpretation of these. This is also evident in non-statutory guidance such as the Model Music Curriculum (DfE, 2021). This document mentions 'skills and techniques' (DfE, 2021, p. 11) without describing their nature, aspires to develop 'mature musical understanding' (DfE, 2021, p. 5) without explanation, and links 'aural knowledge' (DfE, 2021, p. 8) to a chronologically arranged repertoire list. How beginning music teachers think about the nature of 'deepening understanding of the music that they [pupils] perform and to which they listen' (DfE, 2013, p. 2) will therefore be critical to the musical experience with which the pupils in their classroom are able to engage. Thinking about how musical learning is established from the strands of the National Curriculum is therefore a useful starting point, and something with which they will be required to continually re-engage throughout their career.

In considering these differing perspectives of SKU and how to respond to them as a beginning teacher, differing perspectives have come to the surface. In order to give these perspectives further clarity, they are also presented in Table 8.1.

Implications for practice

Implications for mentoring practices and activities to develop these have been included in the discussions during the course of this chapter. Before concluding, however, I here consider three brief observations and recommendations for the development of mentoring practices in SKU:

1. *Be intentional about your approach to SKU.*
   Music teaching can become dominated by musical engagements but lack focus on considered musical learning. After reading this chapter, take some time to consider your own music teaching philosophies. Consider where SKU might be placed and why this is important.
2. *Read and think about SKU.*
   How do the documents and frameworks you work with in your teaching consider SKU? Identify a moment when you can compare them and consider their implications. Include

Table 8.1 SKU comparison table

Approaches	Selections from academic literature	OFSTED	Teacher standards	National curriculum
Skills	Knowing body Learning types Cognitive Controlling materials Aural responses Notation Peer-to-peer interaction Physical embodiment Feeling the music Feelingfulness of music	Defined endpoints Curriculum intent Detailed Developed Intended Sufficient Incremental Apply knowledge as skills	Keep skills up-to-date Extend	Skills and processes Build on previous skills
Knowledge	Not unlocking teacher answers Personally encountered Active Musical knowing with distinct characteristics Learning to be musicians Negotiated Interchange Embodied knowing	Defined endpoints Curriculum intent Identify gaps Detailed Intended Sufficient Apply knowledge as skills Knowledge about music	Demonstrated Secure Impart Extend Prior Strategies for differentiation Specialist support	Build on previous knowledge Know skills and processes
Understanding	Comes from knowing 'of' music Embodied knowing Artistic judgement Music-making Music-creating Listening Musical engagement Musicianship Musicality	Defined endpoints Curriculum intent Gauged Checked Musical quality Landmarks	Critical Secure Clear Extend	Understand skills and processes Deepening understanding

reading on this area as part of your own professional development. You can find some starting points in the 'further resources' section below.

3. *Reflect on your own music lessons.*

How are your own lessons developing musical understanding? If you find it challenging to answer this, think about how your own musical development was enabled and how a beginning music teacher might replicate this in their own practices. Alternatively, consider what barriers to musical understanding you encountered. Work with your mentee to identify appropriate moments in lessons when they can ask the pupils about their SKU and the hindrances they encounter to musical development.

Summary and key points

- Skills, knowledge, and understanding are used frequently in education, but can mean different things.
- Musical skills development is essential in music education.

- Musical knowledge is not the same as information.
- Musical understanding is the ultimate aim of music education.
- Musical skills, knowledge, and understanding are not linear.
- Different educational contexts interpret SKU in different ways.
- Music teacher practices are enhanced through considering how SKU are evident for developing pupil musicality, rather than only meeting organisational requirements.
- It is important to reflect on your own position on SKU and to seek to develop this.

Further resources

Fautley, M. (2010) *Assessment in music education*. Oxford: Oxford University Press.

There is a very helpful introduction and ideas for further thinking about skills, knowledge and understanding as part of the discussions on assessment in this foundational book. Use the index to locate them!

Department for Education and Skills (2006) *Secondary national strategy for school improvement. Foundation subjects: KS3 music*. London: Crown Copyright.

Although published some time ago, this resource also offers some useful starting points in considering the nature of SKU in Music.

9 Mirror, mirror on the wall… supporting beginning music teachers to become reflective practitioners

Martin Fautley and Ian Axtell

Introduction

This chapter will deal with the ways in which beginning music teachers can be helped along their learning journeys from reflection to becoming reflexive. The issue with reflection in the 'mirror, mirror on the wall' situation is that in the fairy tale the mirror answers back. There can be an issue for beginning music teachers that the visible reflection in their mirrors does not do this! To support these beginning music teachers, this chapter describes the ways in which frameworks for thinking have been successfully employed to enable teacher development. An integrated approach involving both practical and theoretical perspectives is employed.

- Context;
- Classroom complexities;
- Reflection in and on action;
- Cognitive load theory;
- Classroom management;
- Observing; and
- From teaching to learning.

Objectives

At the end of this chapter, you should be able:

- To problematise the notion of 'reflection' in the mentoring of beginning music teachers;
- To introduce and discuss some ways in which this can be undertaken;
- To think about the differences between *learning* and *doing* for beginning music teachers; and
- To offer a range of suggestions for developing reflective practice in beginning music teachers.

DOI: 10.4324/9781003004196-14

Context

For many years, the notion of the teacher as a reflective practitioner has been invoked. Much of this work can be traced back to Schön (1983), whose work we return to later in this chapter. In music education Westerlund (2012) has also written of the importance of reflection. Reflection is indeed a good thing, but it warrants unpicking somewhat to be of significant utility in the educational development of beginning music teachers. In the classic fairy tale of Snow White, the evil queen asks the question of her mirror 'mirror, mirror, on the wall, who is the fairest one of all?', and mirror answers that the queen is, until, of course, Snow White usurps this. This version of reflection places the mirror as an active participant in a dialogue, ultimately saying something the wicked queen did not want to hear! But even so, the mirror was agentive in this transaction. In normal everyday usage (outside of fairy tales!), mirrors do not talk back. Let us give a more prosaic example. Every day, before getting ready for work, we look in the mirror. As the authors of this chapter are both men, a singularly male example follows, but doubtless gendered versions of this exist, too. Having a morning shave each day involves looking in the bathroom mirror, and reacting to what is seen. However, this does not guarantee a perfect shave each day, a common experience is that the shaver's partner points out some minutes later 'you've missed a bit!'. This is the partner being agentive, and doing something that the mirror alone cannot do, which is to interact with the looker, in this case, the shaver.

This example may seem trite, but it introduces a key component of reflection, which is that as the reflecting apparatus possesses no agency of its own, a further dimension is required, which is human intervention. The problem for mentoring beginning music teachers is that human intervention is not available 24/7 between the mentor and mentees, and so some way of establishing reflection is needed.

Before reading further, undertake Task 9.1.

Task 9.1 What form does reflection take?

Think about when beginning music teachers have been asked to reflect on their professional practice.

- What form has this taken?
- Have beginning music teachers been required to reflect on teaching and learning using a blank piece of paper?

If active reflection is a good thing, it becomes important to find ways that this can be done remotely, and in a way that empowers the beginning music teacher. In the early days of a beginning music teacher working, it is likely that you, the mentor, will be available to ask questions regarding teaching and learning directly. However, as the beginning music teacher moves towards developing competence, we will want them to be asking themselves the questions which the mentor would do initially. But what does this entail, and what are the sorts of questions that should be being asked?

Classroom complexities

We know that for new teachers of all subjects, school classrooms are sites with a range of complex factors, including immediacy, multidimensionality, unpredictability, and simultaneity (Doyle, 1980, 1986). Indeed, music classrooms, having the added dimensions of sounds (which is not the case in many other school subjects), and which equate to 'noise' in the minds of neighbouring non-music classrooms! Similarly active learning involving musical instruments and singing, mean that active musicing in lessons can be complex and potentially problematic learning situations, in terms of both structure, and, importantly, pedagogy.

Before reading further, undertake Task 9.2.

Task 9.2 Range of music activities in recent lesson

Reflect on a recent lesson you have taught or observed recently.

- Are you able to count how many different activities, tasks, and actions were included?
- What sort of range of things were there?
- Were they practical, did they involve instruments, for example?
- How many of these were happening at the same time?

The shaving example that we gave above may seem overly simplistic, but, even so, let us pursue this metaphor for a little longer. The point of the comment about 'you've missed a bit' is that this is something that the shaver had either overlooked themselves, or was not yet able to see. But in helping beginning music teachers to reflect it is also important to consider what happens if the beginning music teacher had not seen or noticed the matter in question in the first place? This is an important point as Georgii-Hemming (2016, pp. 24-25) observes:

> Reflection is an important tool for teachers to be able to make well-founded pedagogical decisions. But it is a complex concept that can equally refer to pedagogical, philosophical, or cognitive ruminations.

As a mentor, this is an important point; if a beginning music teacher is reflecting as they teach, actively and in the moment, then you need to be able to provide some structure, some scaffolding, for them to be able to achieve effective reflection.

Reflection in and on action

To investigate this structural provision further, it is helpful to revisit Schön's (1983, p. 61) notion of reflection-in-action:

> Practitioners do reflect on their knowing-in-practice. Sometimes, in the relative tranquillity of the post-mortem, they think back on a project they have undertaken, a situation they have lived through, and they explore the understandings they have brought to their

handling of the case. They may do this in a mood of idle speculation, or in a deliberate effort to prepare themselves for future cases. But they may also reflect on practice while they are in the midst of it. Here they reflect-in-action.

This is important for the ways in which mentors work with beginning music teachers. The multiple simultaneity of the classroom situation means that reflection-in-action, which Schön also refers to using the everyday language of 'thinking on your feet' (Schön, 1983, p. 54), is something that is quite hard to do in practice in the classroom situation. The 'tranquillity' of what Schön refers to as the lesson 'post-mortem' provides a good opportunity for a beginning music teacher and mentor to really think together about what went on. There are many ways this can be approached, but it is possibly the case that putting everything into the mix, as it were, may prove too taxing for beginning music teachers, certainly in the early stages of their pedagogic journeys. Ghaye (2010) builds upon the perspective of reflection offered by Schön, indicating the importance of including positive aspects of practice to avoid a focus on negative 'spirals of deficit-based action' (Ghaye, 2011, p.9). This shift in focus, to move from 'fixing' to 'flourishing' (Ghaye, 2011, p. 11), is enhanced by 'reflection-with-action' which is seen as a collective process where professional practice is enhanced by drawing on the expertise of others (Ghaye, 2011, p. 6).

Cognitive load theory

For teaching and learning with pupils, cognitive load theory (Sweller, 1988), or CLT, currently features significantly in the ways in which teachers are asked to think about their pedagogic structuring. As Reif (2008, p. 361) observes:

> The cognitive load involved in a task is the cognitive effort (or amount of information processing) required by a person to perform this task. If the cognitive load needed for learning becomes excessive little or no learning can occur. Hence the cognitive load at any stage of a learning process must be kept within reasonable bounds.

This same theory may also usefully be applied to the ways in which beginning music teachers are placed in the potentially cognitively challenging situation of being both teacher *and* learner in the same educational encounter. What the mentor needs to be aware of is the cognitive load on the beginning music teacher. What this involves is being aware of the multiple simultaneity of the classroom condition, and at the same time, in the very same instant, reflecting-in-action, 'thinking on their feet', about how the lesson is going. This is a task which becomes easier over time but is one of which the mentor needs to be very aware, particularly in the early stages of being a beginning music teacher.

Before reading further, undertake Task 9.3.

Task 9.3 Questions for mentors

- How would you manage an early lesson 'post-mortem'?
- What questions might you ask?

- Can you find 'probing' questions, which involves analysis of action, as well as recall? For instance:
    - Why did you say….after that child played their piece on the xylophone?
    - Why did you answer your own question about the volume change, rather than prompt them further?
    - What makes you think that Jatinder's group did good work? What were your criteria? Had you shared them?

Have you considered the balance between what you think as an experienced practitioner and getting to know what the beginning music teacher thinks as they are likely to be a person who may have very little experience of teaching?

Classroom management

In a music lesson, CLT can often manifest itself in beginning music teachers with a significant concern for actively *managing* a lesson. It certainly is the case, as we have seen, that in a classroom a number of disparate activities are all taking place at once. In the music lesson these include, but are not limited to:

- Furniture arrangement: Does the classroom need re-arranging if desks are in the way?
- Books and writing equipment: Is this a school where, for example, pupils have to write down learning objectives or other didactic features in their workbooks?
- Instruments: Lots of potential for disruption and disturbance here!
- Movement: Do pupils need to move around for practical work?
- Noise levels: If the music room is near other classrooms, how much sound is permissible before complaints will be heard?
- Looking busy: Some practical music lessons seems chaotic rather that purposeful to an outside observer (e.g., Senior Leadership Teams). How to remain in charge of this can be an issue here.
- Time management: coping with all of the above and packing away in time for the end of lesson bell.

These are matters which can be of real concern, not only to beginning music teachers, but newly qualified teachers (NQTs) and recently qualified teachers (RQTs) too. The minutiae of classroom management involves real skills which require developing and honing and can be context specific; in other words what works with *this* class may not work with another class, and systems which are appropriate in one school (because, say the regular class teacher has spent a long time establishing them) may not exist at all in another school, where no such long-term groundwork has been established. It is also the case that beginning music teachers are often 'parachuted in' at little notice for the teaching practice practicum experiences. What the beginning music teacher needs to do in these cases is observe the mentor and other experienced classroom practitioners in action, to see both what they do, and, importantly, how they do it. An important task for you, the mentor, is to help the beginning music teacher with organising such observations, as they are unlikely to have built up the interpersonal relationships with other staff to be able to do this. In many schools with beginning teachers of any subject, there is likely to be a professional mentor who has an overview of such cases and is also likely to be able to offer assistance with organising this. The subject mentor also has an important role to play in proffering helpful support, as the multiple simultaneity of classroom ontology we have already observed above needs careful scaffolding of support, so the beginning music teacher does not feel too overwhelmed.

Observing

However, even this simple act of observation is itself fraught with difficulties. After all, as Sherlock Holmes said to Dr Watson in *A Scandal in Bohemia*, 'You have not observed. And yet you have seen. That is just my point' (Doyle, 1892/2004, p. 11), and we know that this is also the case with new teachers watching classroom lessons. These are often referred to as 'lesson observations', but as is the case with the Sherlock Holmes quotation, there is a real concern that seeing takes place, rather than observation proper. As Loughran (2010, p. 6) notes:

> The way an expert teacher reacts ... may not be immediately noticeable to the casual observer because of the subtle aspects that make a difference and that do not necessarily stand out as being so dramatically different as to draw attention.

And it is here that Loughran gets to the heart of the issue. The aspects that an expert teacher uses 'do not necessarily stand out'. The expert teacher's raised eyebrow of behaviour management, the sharp look, the slight movement of a finger, all of these are within the quotidian repertoire of classroom management techniques, yet are not so apparent as to draw attention to themselves, and are missed by those who are seeing, but not observing. What this means is that these tiny classroom management factors, which may appropriately be termed micro-behaviours on the part of the teacher, need to be made visible to the onlooker. It is possible, however, that the mentors and expert teachers themselves may not be fully aware of what they are doing (Atkinson and Claxton, 2000) in this regard themselves, but that this has become part of their teaching habitus. For the beginning music teacher, first of all learning these micro-behaviours, then using them, will require practising them, and so this can become another aspect of CLT which needs to be taken into account.

What this means is that juggling all of these classroom management issues, and at the same time ensuring that learning is taking place can seem like a major obstacle to some beginning music teachers. As Merrion (1996, p. 188) observed:

> Fortunately or unfortunately, the issue of classroom management within music instruction poses unique problems due to the aesthetic nature of the arts. To maintain a

learning environment free enough to permit personal and individual responses, improvisation, and creativity while providing a structure in which all students can collectively remain on-task and actively involved seems impossible. Just how *does* one manage classroom behaviour?

Addressing this question means that it is likely to be classroom management which occupies the bulk of a beginning music teacher's reflections, certainly in the early stages, and probably well into training, and then out into the profession, too. We alluded earlier to the issue of beginning music teachers being potentially overloaded by being asked to reflect too broadly, at least in the early stages. What might be tried instead is to focus in on a small number of specific pedagogic objectives for both beginning music teacher and mentor to think about in these reflection sessions.

Before reading further, undertake Task 9.4.

Task 9.4 Classroom management

- In your role as a mentor, what would you prioritise as essential aspects of classroom management in the music classroom?
- How can these be communicated to a beginning music teacher quickly and efficiently?
- Are you assuming 'they know'?

From teaching to learning

As time progresses, and in the space of a single year of training (as is the case with many postgraduate training routes), it is important that the beginning music teacher and their mentor move their focus of attention towards the learning of the pupils, whilst balancing the learning wants and needs of the beginning music teacher. There is a fine balance to be had here. In the early stages of a beginning music teacher's professional life it is entirely natural that they will have a focus almost entirely on teaching; however, as their training proceeds, there needs to be a concomitant shift to include a tighter focus on *learning*, as well as on the teaching that results in the learning taking place. This may seem an obvious statement, but we know from experience that when beginning music teachers are asked to judge the efficacy of a lesson they delivered in the early stages of their training, then their responses will almost invariably focus on themselves. Lessons went well from a beginning music teacher's perspective if they 'didn't fall over' pedagogically speaking. In other words, the primary focus of reflection in the early stages for a beginning music teacher is most likely to be on the self, an introspective reflection in which the class can often be relegated to the position of an audience, present in the room, but possibly not intrinsically involved. At some point, which can only be adjudged by mentors working with beginning music teachers, the focus needs to shift away from teaching, and onto learning.

Before reading further, undertake Task 9.5.

Task 9.5 Moving the focus from teaching to learning

- What questions might you ask a beginning music teacher to shift the focus away from themselves and their teaching towards the pupils and their learning? For example:

    - You were quick to praise the pupils for listening quietly to each other, but what were they listening *for*?
    - You were pleased that the instruments had been distributed in an orderly fashion, but how do you know that *all* of the pupils had understood the task?
    - The class were on-task for all of the lesson, which was good. How do you know that they were learning things, and not simply repeating things they had done before?

It may well be the case that in some school subjects learning is relatively straightforward, it is safe to say that music is not one of these! Issues of both what there is to learn, and what learning in music looks and sounds like are the subject of extensive debate within the profession (inter alia Spruce with Matthews, 2012). Indeed, the very nature of what should be taught and learned in music education is itself not straightforward. As Westerlund (2012, p. 9) asks:

> ...should we educate devoted listeners through selected classics or transmit musical hands-on knowledge for amateurs to enjoy in their future lives, or should we simply feed the existing musical institutions, symphony orchestras and the ilk, with new practitioners?

This is a point that all those who are involved in the training of beginning music teachers will need to address at some point, but for the purposes of this chapter, we need to move swiftly on to the issue of what *specifically* is being learned in the beginning music teacher's music lessons. This takes the beginning music teacher fairly rapidly to a realisation that, as Fautley and Savage (2014, p. 25) observe, 'Teaching≠Learning'; in other words, teaching *does not equal* learning. This will be readily apparent and will occur many times in staffroom discussions along the 'I don't know why they haven't learned it yet; I've taught it to them hundreds of times' nature. For the beginning music teacher this dawning realisation needs careful nurturing and reflection, and will involve the carefully adjudged use of classroom formative assessment. For this chapter on reflection, it takes the mentor and beginning music teacher well beyond the 'mirror, mirror' notion we began with. Mentors and beginning music teachers need to really think about what is going on the lesson, what is actually being learned - the beginning music teacher will know what is being taught - and, importantly, how do you actually know? Learning in today's complex examined educational world involves both attainment and progress, with both needing to be apparent, if not clearly visible, in any given lesson.

It might seem an obvious statement that in your lessons pupils should make progress; however, achieving this requires a high level of skilful planning and delivery. Pupil progress is evidenced through the outcomes of a lesson. Put simply, outcomes are what pupils achieve in the lesson ... Sometimes there are unanticipated outcomes. When this happens, you need to understand why and adapt future lessons to accommodate this ... However, outcomes are often seen as the end product. This is not the case. We would want you to focus more on intended learning outcomes. If a pupil has learned in your lesson, if they have met the intended learning outcomes, they will be able to recall this at a later stage and use it in a variety of other contexts.

Shaw and Redfern (2019, p. 115)

This presents one of the well-established dichotomies in music education, that being the difference between planning for *doing*, and planning for *learning*. We know that planning for doing is so much easier that planning for learning. Indeed, books of published materials can be purchased which are essentially things for children and young people to do in their music lessons: sing these songs, listen to these recordings, and the like. But what the pupils are actually *learning* is not clear. 'Keeping them occupied' is well-known and trusted behaviour management strategy in music lessons, but as Custodero (2010, p. 78) asks,

...questions remain unaddressed concerning the locus of meaning making in music educational settings. If what we teach is not what is learned, then what IS learned?

It is in this regard that reflection needs to be developmental between mentors and beginning music teachers. As we have seen, the shift towards a learning paradigm rather than a teaching paradigm entails a shift from the performance of the teacher to the learning of the pupils. This needs to be thought through, and reflected on, with carefully focussed discussions. Again, music is problematic in this regard. Although we have separated learning from doing in our discussions, they are also closely linked, as Fautley and Savage (2011, p. 64) show in this diagram (Figure 9.1):

What this means is that in music, especially in practical music, pupils learn to do something by actually doing it, and then show they can do it by performing. This can be different for those subjects where evidencing learning through writing is the norm (indeed, this can be an issue for SLTs, but hopefully the mentor can deal with that!). But it also means that endless doing might not involve learning. Yes, they can sing more songs, for example, but learning development needs to be not simply quantitative, but also qualitative.

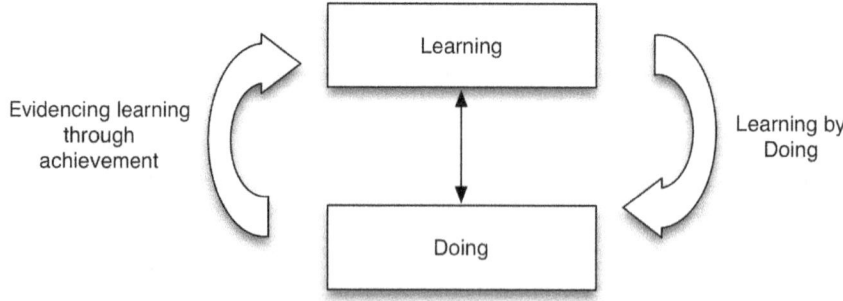

Figure 9.1 Learning and doing (Fautley and Savage, 2011, p. 64)

Before reading further, undertake Task 9.6.

> **Task 9.6 Supporting pupil learning**
>
> - What qualitative processes do you use to identify learning?
> - How do you help beginning music teachers to access the formative or assessment for learning processes that you employ?

Planning for learning is a key activity for beginning music teachers, as for teachers of all subjects. In music, this has the added complication of needing to involve sounds being made as part of the process of learning. Here, some reflective conversations need to be focussed again on what is actually being learned. Musical learning involves being musical, and so to teach it involves, as Swanwick (1999) puts it, 'teaching music musically'. This again is another problematic area. What is it to be musical? What is musicality? What will the doing and learning entail? All of these are key questions for the beginning music teacher to have to get to grips with. The development of musical learning, and the sequencing of how a curriculum is assembled are key areas of interest here.

One of the obvious ways in which a beginning music teacher can get to grips with the pedagogy of their practicum school is to be given access to a copy of the music curriculum and schemes of work. This simple statement belies the fraught complexities that the authors have had to deal with over the years! The curriculum is likely to be a working document, in more or less detail, but it will be important for the mentor to talk through with the beginning music teacher why it exists as it does. After all, that beginning music teacher could end up very soon being a teacher in a one-person department and having to design their curriculum from scratch. So what curricular decisions have been taken by the school? Why the learning, in this order, for these children and young people? These are all good reflective conversations to have with the beginning music teacher. And as we probably want to encourage the beginning music teacher to ask the question 'why?', it is useful for the mentor to have thought about this in advance. After all, we cannot expect our beginning music teachers to engage in deep reflection if they a brushed off with shallow answers from mentors!

Before reading further, undertake Task 9.7.

> **Task 9.7 Digging deeper into learning**
>
> - How would you introduce your Schemes/Units of Work to a beginning music teacher?
> - Can you reveal the hidden assumptions that underpin the text?
> - What are your priorities for teaching and learning in music? Why is this the case? Have your priorities changed over time, perhaps? Again, if so, why is this?

Dealing with reflection in music teacher education is a difficult and complex task. It can also be about the mentor not feeling they have to be in a position of being a 'fount of all knowledge', but rather that they can engage in asking good questions of the beginning music teacher and helping along their journey.

We began this chapter by thinking about the notion of a speaking or silent mirror being held up to activity. We end it by returning to this theme and inviting mentors to reflect on their own interactions with beginning music teachers. Ways in which you, the mentor, take the place of the speaking mirror need to be placed carefully, and enacted with thought. Pedagogic identities can be fragile in beginning music teachers and so words need to be chosen carefully. Along with this, the role of the mentor as talking mirror should be to stimulate reflection on events that have happened, to raise awareness of things that the beginning music teacher may only have been dimly aware of. We have noted, with the help of Sherlock Holmes, how seeing and observing are different. With the benefit of your years of experience as a classroom music teacher, what have you observed in the beginning music teacher's lesson that they may have missed? How can you help this to become a learning experience for the beginning music teacher as much as for the children and young people?

Reflection is not easy, and structured reflection should not just be a simple 'box-ticking' exercise. The place of true stimulated reflection is an important one in the beginning music teacher's learning. Asking good questions to foster this is, as we hope we have shown, far more useful that simply asking for a blank piece of paper reflection exercise, where the beginning music teacher can be adrift. Hopefully the complexities of this personal interaction process will also prove to be of benefit to the mentor, after all, there are very few of us who are beyond learning anything new in music education!

Conclusion

This chapter has outlined the importance of the mentor being involved in active reflection processes with the beginning music teachers. The provision of a blank piece of paper (or its spoken equivalents) to reflect with is not necessarily the best way to proceed. We have suggested a range of activities and focussed questions for the mentor to use when engaged in active reflection with the beginning music teachers, all of which have the functionality of moving intended learning forwards. This applies in equal measure to the learning of the children and young people in the classes, as well as of the beginning music teachers themselves.

Active reflection is not an easy and straightforward process, and it can involve people in making themselves uncomfortable, but it is a key component of developing professionalism in teacher education.

Summary and keypoints

In this chapter, we have:

- Considered the place and role of reflection with beginning music teachers;
- Interrogated what the notion of 'reflection' entails in a range of contexts;
- Thought about Schön's (1983) notions of reflection-in-action and reflection-on-action;
- Considered what cognitive load theory has to offer for mentoring beginning music teachers;

- Problematised the act of observation;
- Offered possible solutions to the ways in which classroom management can be reflected upon and interrogated;
- Considered the shift from a teaching focus to a learning one; and
- Understood why *learning* and *doing* are different processes in classroom music education.

Further resources

Incorporated Society of Musicians. *The national curriculum for music: A revised framework for curriculum, pedagogy and assessment in key stage 3 music.* Martin Fautley and Alison Daubney. Available at: https://www.ismtrust.org/resources/education-resources/the-national-curriculum-for-music [accessed: 2 May 2025].

In this booklet the authors set a series of reflective questions for music teachers to think about their curriculum, and how this impacts upon pedagogy and assessment. This will be of use to both you, the mentor, and the beginning music teacher as conversations about these important issues can be brokered using some of the prompts from this resource. https://teachtalkmusic.wordpress.com/2016/09/03/what-is-ks3-music-education-for/

One of the conversations that you, the mentor, and the beginning music teacher maybe ought to be having is about *why* you teach what you do. This is not as straightforward as it might sound, and this thinkpiece should help provoke some discussions concerning who music education is aimed at. https://www.musicmark.org.uk/resources/10-things-schools-should-know-about-learning-music/

A common task for beginning music teachers is to write an article expounding the benefits of their subject to a sceptical audience. This publication from Music Mark will help with this, and should provide a basis from some fruitful discussions between you, the mentor, and the beginning music teacher, possibly building on the previous resource, and really thinking about music in schools.

Christophersen, C. (2021) 'Educating music teachers for the future: The crafts of change', in Holdhus, K., Murphy, R. and Espeland, M. (eds) *Music education as craft: Reframing theories and practices.* Cham, Switzerland: Springer.

In this book the author describes the situation in Norway with regard to the training of beginning music teachers. This may well be a very different situation and context from other parts of the world. For you, the mentor, this chapter could form a useful adjunct to your discussions about why you teach music the way you do, and how this version may well not be the case internationally.

10 Mentoring for curriculum design

Anthony Anderson

Introduction

Curriculum design forms a central part of music teacher thinking and practice. It follows that this should also be an important area for your development as a beginning music teacher through your mentoring experiences. This chapter will provide an opportunity to explore the domain of curriculum design and to present theoretical understandings alongside practical ideas. It will seek to set out why mentoring for curriculum design is important and its place in your music teacher training. It will also explore ways of thinking about how *curriculum* might be defined and structured in classrooms. There will be a discussion of the place of reflection in curriculum design approaches, and an acknowledgement that, as a mentor music teacher, you *are* a curriculum designer and as a beginning music teacher, you *soon will be*. The chapter will close with some suggestions and ideas for incorporating a curriculum design dimension into mentoring interactions.

Objectives

At the end of this chapter, you should be able to:

- Articulate ideas and meanings of curriculum;
- Identify your rationales for curriculum design;
- Be able to support beginning music teachers in developing their curriculum thinking; and
- Express further ideas for curriculum development in a mentoring context.

Music mentoring and curriculum design

As has been discussed earlier in this book, your understanding of what you think mentoring is, will fundamentally affect how you practice or receive it (see Chapter 1). Definitions in policy documents vary widely and include concepts of personal growth (such as career development) and interactions which can be documented (such as reflective feedback). Mentoring definitions can be relatively fluid, such as 'growing an individual' (National Foundation for Educational Research (NFER), 2008, p. iii) or more prescribed, such as a 'structured and sustained process for supporting professional learners through significant career transitions'

DOI: 10.4324/9781003004196-15

(Centre for the Use of Research and Evidence in Education (CUREE), 2005, p. 3). Mentoring interactions are also subsumed into the UK professional standards for teachers, where Standard 8 highlights 'responding to advice and feedback from colleagues' (Department for Education (DfE), 2013). The framing of this *feedback* may take many and various forms, depending on local contexts and mentoring relationships. Such divergent perspectives also exist in practice literature, where mentoring has been understood as a means to broker access to teacher continuing professional development and learning (CPDL), or as a means to recognise teacher values (Bubb, 2007). Academic discourse has suggested additional complexities inherent in relationships of power between mentor and beginning music teacher, which may lead to 'judgementoring' (Hobson and Malderez, 2015, p. 1) and 'fabrications' (Lejonberg et al., 2015, p. 143), as beginning music teachers seek to conceal what they perceive as their vulnerabilities. Conceptualisations of the substance of *beginning music teacher mentoring* is a further layer in the intricate nature of mentoring processes, and this has only become a domain for more overt study relatively recently (Conway and Christensen, 2006).

Uncovering the nature of musical mentoring in curriculum design also requires careful thought. How you understand *curriculum* impacts on how you choose to interact with young people in your classes, content choices (Plummeridge, 2001), and the sequencing of curriculum content, which is in turn impacted by perceptions of effective musical learning (Philpott, 2007). Curriculum dialogue between you and your music teacher mentor can benefit from acknowledging that there are a range of starting points for designing a musical curriculum. It can be helpful to conceive of musical mentoring for curriculum design as a continual process of enabling musical development for pupils, and to acknowledge that there are multiple ways to realise curricula (Anderson, 2009b). Teaching experiences and musical identities impact not only choices about what to cover and how to cover it, but how to enable colleagues in their interrogation and evaluation of curriculum ethos and culture. In curriculum discussions and interactions, it is helpful for you as a mentor or beginning music teacher to be open to changes in your own musical philosophies so that dialogue enables development and there are opportunities to reflect and evaluate (Anderson, 2009a).

Music curriculum meanings

It is not easy to know where to start in designing a curriculum. Whether you are thinking about your own curriculum or mentoring a beginning music teacher who is involved in curriculum design for the first time, it is helpful to acknowledge that it is a complex task. Although interpretations of what curriculum may mean do exist in policy documentation, such as the *Model Music Curriculum* (MMC) (DfE, 2021), these representations tend to consider music curriculum as an object which can be grasped and passed on. The MMC describes curriculum as 'a benchmark to help teachers' (DfE, 2021, p. 2), for instance, and states that the collaboration of music practitioners and partners, among others, will enable its 'effective delivery' (DfE, 2021, p. 5), as though curriculum is a parcel that can be received. However, outside of these objectified policy narratives, little has been written about curriculum design from the perspective of the music teacher and this is connected to the issue that curriculum design is an under-researched area (Anderson, 2019). Although *curriculum* frequently features in music education discussions, there remain disagreements about its precise nature.

It was proposed some time ago that *the* music curriculum is actually several curricula in simultaneous operation, and this complexity would seem to be likely, as individual teachers interpret curriculum essentials differently (Elliott, 1986). Unless you think about what you understand by curriculum music, pedagogies can become entangled, with Oates (2011, p. 9) warning of such contextual realisations of knowledge descending into 'noise'. There can be differences between what you perceive your curriculum to be and how it is received by your pupils. This *planned* and *received* curriculum in which music teacher perceptions of learning differs from learner experiences (Kelly, 2009), is important to think about in preparation for mentoring work, where an understanding of curriculum may still be emerging. Hidden curricula can also be a concept which is particularly difficult to negotiate, and can cover a multitude of factors, including how and why musical instruments are assigned to learners and the extent to which pupils are granted access to music in extra-curricular activities (Froehlich, 2007; Lamont, 2002). Therefore, understanding what we mean by *music curriculum* is a particularly important beginning in mentoring discussions.

One starting point is to think about music curriculum as more than a documented set of structural approaches. Just as musical knowledge is a combination of knowing *how, about,* and *of* music (Philpott, 2001), so music curriculum is a set of musical interactions. Finney (2017) regards these as dynamic processes and practices, which he sets within historical and cultural discourse. According to these perspectives, curriculum is not static, but fluid and interactive, responding to classroom contexts in all their rich diversity. It has been argued that music curriculum should be conceptualised as lived experiences which enable the emergence of musical knowledge (Cooke and Spruce, 2016). This understanding, just like Finney's, is similarly built on music as an engaging process, not a static document taken from one moment in time. My definition of music curriculum for this chapter, is that it is: intentionally designed and sequenced, evidenced in documentation, but enacted and realised in dynamic musical encounters and experienced in responsive musical dialogue in learning spaces.

Before reading further, undertake Task 10.1.

Task 10.1 Defining music curriculum

Take some time to consider how you would define music curriculum. Write your definition on a postcard and ask the beginning music teacher with whom you are working to do the same. Now compare your definitions. Where do they agree and where do they differ? Discuss these aspects, and try to understand what motivates the areas of agreement and difference.

Thinking about music curriculum structures

Music curriculum sequencing, as it appears in my earlier definition, refers to how you order the topics you have chosen to teach and your rationale for doing so. This is a central activity for practising teachers. There are multiple approaches to sequencing, and whilst the Office for Standards in Education (OFSTED) (2019a, p. 3) connects this to 'a good, well taught curriculum' and suggests it is important to teach the 'right knowledge in the right order'

(2019b, p. 1), this can be problematic to define in music, where musical experiences and pathways are highly individual. However, it is important to consider why you, as a beginning music teacher, have chosen to teach what you have and why you have placed it where you have. If you cannot articulate your rationale for your curriculum design, it may be worth reflecting on this, so that your curriculum is not what Fautley (2012, p. 103) describes as a 'Cook's tour', but represents your philosophy of musical development for pupils.

Structures for music curriculum can overlap and it is important to clarify both your perceptions as a mentor, or your perspectives as a beginning music teacher in your discussions of musical pedagogies. *Lesson plans* are generally the most overt element of curriculum design, as they form the basis for evidence of England's secondary teaching standards (see Standard 4, *Plan and teach well-structured lessons*) and constitute the most regular type of feedback given to beginning music teachers (DfE, 2013). It has been suggested that lesson plans should allow for musical immersion and create flexible frameworks for different types of musical knowledge (Spruce, 2016), but lesson plans have also been conceptualised in more essential terms, as an 'instructor's road map' of what is to be learned and how this is to be done effectively (Singapore Management University (SMU), 2019, p. 34). Such divergences are usually unacknowledged in educational discourse and practice in schools, where it is assumed that the embodiment of the lesson plan as an *object* is known and understood. This creates some difficulties, especially in the light of the complexities of music education as a dynamic process as previously discussed, where such differences can create professional misunderstandings. Further complexities are revealed when beginning music teachers start to develop lesson plans into Schemes of Work, and mentoring is also of central importance at this moment.

Schemes of Work (SoW), also sometimes known as Units of Work, describe collections of lesson plans, often orientated around topics of musical learning. Thus, there may be a scheme of work on *Raggae*, *The Orchestra* or *Chinese Opera*, for example. These are also rarely defined in music education literature. Philpott (2001, p. 46) describes them as a design for 'the overall content which covers a music programme across an age group'. Similarly, The *National Curriculum Council* (NCC) (1992) when discussing the English national curriculum in its first manifestation for music, recommended that advice would be needed on how to develop schemes; however, this support now seems to have largely faded into the background. A lack of clarity on understandings of SoW, can embed further presuppositions of assumed knowledge in educational dialogue, which can create dissonance and unacknowledged complexity.

However, it is in creating *programmes of study* where some of the greatest difficulties for beginning music teachers and their mentors lie. In some instances, opportunities to design these can be absent from beginning music teachers' training experiences, which can later cause difficulties when beginning music teachers qualify and are expected to know how to design one in their first teaching post. Programmes of study are summary documents which outline musical topics as the basis for teaching and learning content in classroom music lessons. These documents are generally categorised into year groups and presented in consecutive layers (see Figure 10.1). They include sequences in which topics are to be taught, their duration and their scheduling in the academic year. It is problematic to determine the origin of this planning practice, although it may stem from the first supporting

	Term 1.1	Term 1.2	Term 2.1	Term 2.2	Term 3.1	Term 3.1
Year 7	African drumming	Musical elements	The orchestra	Gamelan	Programme music	Music of the Caribbean
Year 8	Blues	Indian classical music	Reggae	Ground Bass	Bhangra	Song-writing
Year 9	Music for film and TV		Music Tech project		Pop band performing project	

Figure 10.1 Representative example of a programme of study

documentation for the English national curriculum in Music in 1992, which included planning frameworks and suggestions for conceptualising programmes of study as the basis from which other planning was to emerge (NCC, 1992). The notion of a table of summary topics appears to be a development which has taken hold in the pragmatics of distilling musical learning for 11- to 14-year-olds (Key Stage 3 in England) for the academic year. This is a practice which has rarely been discussed in music education literature, but has become common in schools, in interactions which Bruner (1996, p. 44) described as 'folk pedagogy'. Mentoring interactions whose focus is restricted to lesson plans and schemes of work, but which does not extend into explaining and debating how programmes of study have been designed can create a blind spot. Without the opportunity to explore rationales for programmes of study within whose structures, you may be asked to work as a beginning teacher, an element of curriculum reflection can be absent. Such an absence may be unacknowledged as it has escaped notice: it is an unknown unknown.

Discussing your personal music education philosophies (Cooke et al., 2016) and how these inform your understandings of curriculum design can, therefore, usefully form a part of dialogue in your mentoring interactions. This means that as a beginning teacher you can avoid a tendency to imitate established planning practices, without a rationale which you own for yourself. This will help later, when you have to articulate your curriculum ideas to parents, pupils or your managers in school. It also provides opportunities to discuss and hone music curriculum perceptions and approaches in your mentoring conversations.

Before reading further, undertake Task 10.2.

Task 10.2 Thinking about the purpose of planning

What is the purpose of lesson plans, schemes of work and programmes of study? Take some time to discuss this in your mentoring meetings. Can you create a diagram to explain any interconnectivity and to explore the differences further?

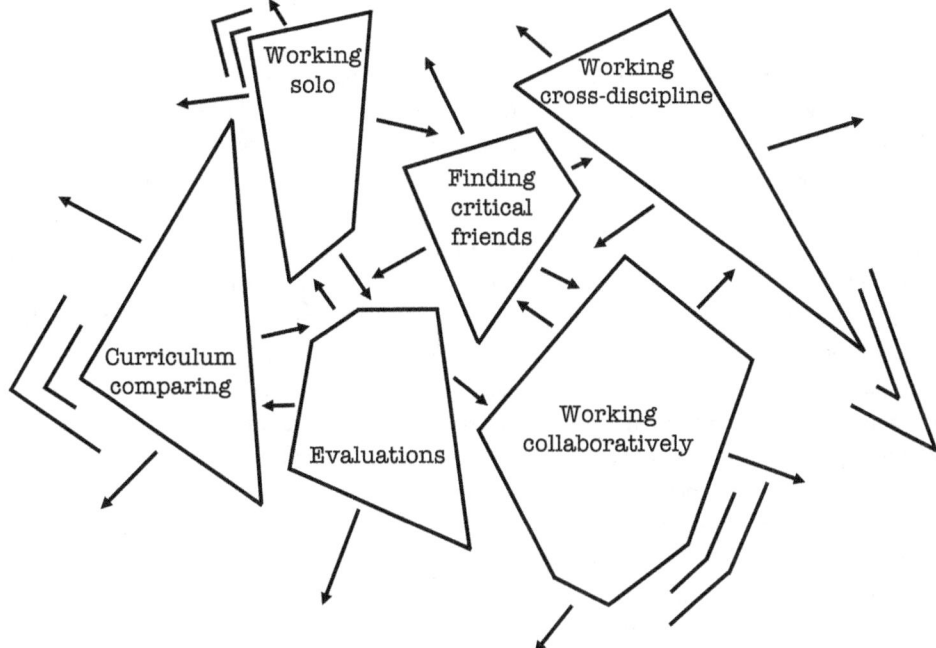

Figure 10.2 Ice floe model of colliding curriculum domains

In considering how you create starting points for programmes of study in music with beginning music teachers, it can be helpful to acknowledge that curriculum design in the music classroom can appear much like an ice floe. Whilst it may seem to be an even and united surface, on closer inspection, it is in fact constituted of multiple smaller fragments of various sizes and shapes, each impacting, rotating and affecting its neighbour. It is this fractured nature of curriculum design which can make distilling a rationale and programme of study such a complex affair. The intricacies of mentoring for curriculum design are represented in Figure 10.2, where these differing domains are represented colliding and interacting with each other:

Unpacking the ice floe: mentoring for curriculum design

For you as a mentor to enable beginning music teachers in curriculum design, it is helpful for time to be spent discussing the different elements which are in conceptual flow and giving these a voice. There are multiple approaches to curriculum design and acknowledging that these exist enables beginning music teachers to make informed choices about their educational outlooks in music, rather than becoming impacted and paralysed by the curriculum ice. This opportunity to develop multi-dimensional pedagogical thinking in place of a series of proposed incremental steps, in turn offers a richer musical experience for pupils to encounter music in a developmental manner.

It is, therefore, useful for you as a beginning music teacher, to reflect on the manner in which music teachers simultaneously interact in a diverse variety of professional domains.

Music teachers collaborate in order to realise musical activity for pupils. Such activities may be formulated as arts projects with an external provider, such as local Music Education Hubs or with other school departments such as drama, dance and design as part of outward facing performing events. The ability to manage dialogue between stakeholders and to work alongside others, are essential skills in the music teacher's toolkit. However, you may be a music teacher who works in a small department, where you may have only one other music classroom colleague, or perhaps not even that. Research conducted by the University of Sussex (Daubney and Mackrill, 2017), which included findings from 705 secondary schools in the UK, found that 30% of music faculties were single-person departments. The ability to work resourcefully and reflectively in such circumstances is challenging, and the tensions that arise between lone and collaborative working is sometimes difficult to negotiate. Mentoring to prepare beginning music teachers for such dynamics is important in creating contextual awareness and equips beginning music teachers with whom you are working to be ready to engage with this undulating educational landscape. Just as music teacher practices embody tensions between lone and collaborative working, so Bruner (1986) describes learning more generally as both a communal activity and one embodying multiple culture-sharing. Identifying the cultures that exist in pedagogical rationales, and understanding where and how they are different, are essential first steps in enabling learning within the school community. Such considerations can be unacknowledged, but mentoring interactions provide ideal spaces in which to explore and evaluate them, before they become immobile and locked in curriculum ice floe.

Before reading further, undertake Task 10.3.

Task 10.3 What is your pedagogy?

Spend some time discussing these questions with your mentor:

How would you describe your musical pedagogy? Can you give your pedagogy a name?
How do your pedagogy and curriculum interact? Is one influenced by the other?

You may as a music mentor find discussions with beginning teachers about how you incorporate differing dynamics of collaboration and lone working into school music provision helpful. For instance, music subject leaders redesign their curriculum on a frequent basis (Fautley, 2015), but it is not always clear why this is the case. Research indicates that there may be a lack of confidence on the part of music teachers about the content of their curriculum (Anderson, 2019), and that they can be influenced by curriculum approaches of other music teachers in local schools, even when the rationales for these alternative music curricula are not explored. Evaluation of curriculum programmes is a well-established feature of educational practices in the USA, where scope and sequence feature in curriculum discussions between music teachers and their leaders (Hale, 2008). However, the approach in England has, in the past, tended to be somewhat less systematic (Adams, 2001). Mentoring relationships provide both a reason and a space for you to evaluate your music curriculum as you have conceived it as a subject-leader, or to explore how you facilitate it as a teacher and consider in more depth how your pupils experience it.

Music curriculum programmes of study can exist in a continual state of flux, in which analysis of what is included and why topics are placed where they are, can be formulated in privileged knowledge (McPhail, 2017), which beginning music teachers are unable to interrogate due to potential inequalities of power dynamics between them and their mentor. The place you give to evaluation is therefore important, as it provides opportunities to explore assumptions, tacit ideologies and concealed perspectives. Even if you are a mentor, you may only rarely have had the opportunity to explain your curriculum choices to colleagues. The mentoring relationship can therefore provide an enriching opportunity for the development of a critical friend (beginning music teacher) who can explore curriculum paradigms with the music teacher designer (mentor). Where you are a mentor but not the curriculum designer, the mentoring dynamic provides an opportunity to explore curriculum choices and approaches to musical development in shared activity.

Reflective mentoring moments can also further facilitate musical cultures for curriculum design. Cultures created by music teachers in their curriculum programmes are diverse, and these are the implicit foundations upon which curriculum is built. These ideological perspectives are communicated in the design of activities and the manner in which they are communicated to pupils, in a process of 'enculturation' (Philpott, 2016, p. 38). Learning is absorbed as much (or more than) it is taught in the music classroom. Enculturation begins with curriculum ethos and if there has been limited time to reflect on what this should be, the musical processes in the classroom with which pupils engage may limit their potential. Your mentoring, therefore, has a key role to play in not only enabling the development of beginning music teachers, but in developing the environment for musical thinking, making their training experiences more fulfilling and the quality of music education more considered.

Before reading further, undertake Task 10.4.

Task 10.4 Thinking about hindrances in curriculum design

What are the aspects of curriculum design which lock ideas into immovable ice floe for you? How could you liberate these areas? Write some of the challenges you have with curriculum design on separate cards and ask the beginning music teacher with whom you are working to do the same. Can you place these issues into an order of priority you would most like to tackle? What emerges as areas for development for you as a teacher and mentor and what will be the areas for development that the beginning music teacher needs to pinpoint as an Early Career Teacher?

Music teachers as curriculum designers

Whether by accident or design, music teachers are curriculum creators. In thinking about what a Key Stage 3 curriculum might look like, music teachers make choices about what to include (and what to leave out) how to sequence musical learning, and how to evaluate its successes. Key Stage 4 (14-16 year-olds) and Key Stage 5 (16-18 year-olds) offer similar opportunities, as even though teachers now have to work within the frameworks of examination board specifications, very few begin by turning to the first page and teaching the first sentence. Deciding where and how you begin in a way that makes sense to pupils in music classes is challenging, and this is often unacknowledged, even amongst music teachers themselves. The act of music curriculum design embodies multiple processes which include bricolage of rationale, content, sequencing of that content, facilitating learning in dynamic musical encounters, and enabling, capturing and evaluating progress in assessment interactions, to name but a few! This is difficult. Acknowledging that this is the case as a music teacher and as a mentor is the first step towards thinking about the intricacies of curriculum design for the music classroom, and making it part of training experiences for the beginning music teachers with whom you are working.

It may be helpful to consider music curriculum mentorship as part of the process of curriculum designer development for beginning music teachers. This approach seeks to make tangible some of the less overt, but essential elements which music curriculum design entails. As an established music mentor working with beginning music teachers, you will work and discuss teaching ideas together, and so move through layers of development in an interactive manner, where one area leads to and impinges on another. Although curriculum design is here suggested as lamination (see Figure 10.3), it may be helpful to acknowledge that its development is rarely this convenient. Curriculum design characteristics may, for instance, occur or recur in different proportions and sequence depending on your own ideas as a mentor and the approaches encouraged by your school. This model seeks to map the potential journey from conceptualised curriculum processes to realised curriculum interactions as facilitated by mentor and beginning music teachers' mutual working patterns:

Turning a curriculum idea into a dynamic classroom lesson, which enables musical experience requires careful thought. Mentoring has an important role to play in this, as potential classroom musical activity is discussed by mentor and beginning teacher. It has been suggested that pedagogical content knowledge (PCK) is required to realise the process of transforming subject knowledge into classroom modality (Shulman, 1986). Shulman (1986, p. 8) argues for a relationship between content knowledge and pedagogical methods, in which teachers are able to present content in a manner that can be understood by learners in a

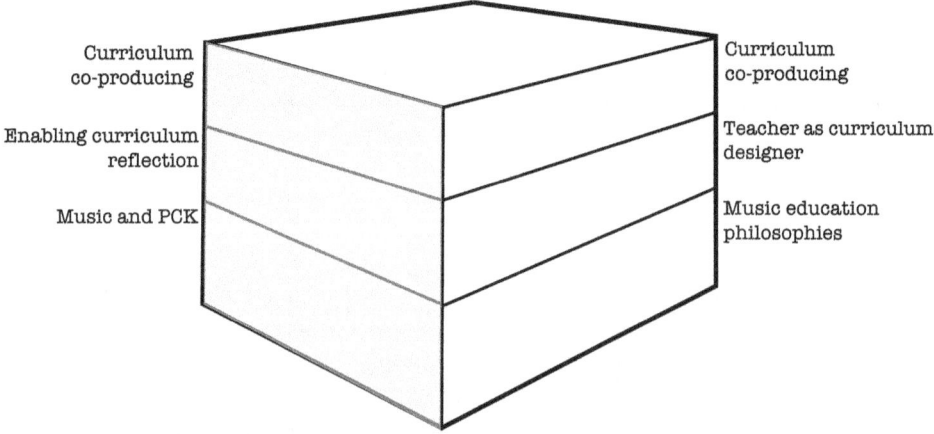

Figure 10.3 Stratified curriculum mentoring

'learning for teaching' process. Thinking about how to transform musical starting points into meaningful musical experience in the classroom is one dimension of PCK. Shulman (1986, p. 10) also defines curriculum knowledge, which he considers as a knowledge of materials in variegated (or 'alternative' as he terms them) form, and a simultaneous knowledge of curriculum which enables the teacher to identify and discuss commonalities of learning in different classes and lessons. A full discussion of musical knowledge is beyond the scope of this chapter, but it is perhaps worth noting that music curriculum design is not solely about content, but also the form that learning will take. This aligns with Shulman's learning for teaching approach, although perhaps not with his concepts of learning materials. However, choosing how musical knowledge is to be explored and developed is a curriculum choice which lies behind the details of perceived subject content. This dimension is difficult and can be an unacknowledged dynamic in music teacher curriculum design. Embedding this into training for beginning music teachers can be challenging as it is an accumulated competency, but this is nevertheless worth highlighting at an early stage of mentoring for music curriculum development.

Alongside PCK, music education philosophies also guide and shape music curriculum design processes. Considering what your personal philosophy is as a mentor, and how it will find expression in your classroom and in your discussions with beginning teachers will be a significant modifier for the shaping of your music curriculum and the way you explain it. Without first considering, for instance, what you would like a Year 9 musician to look or sound like, it is difficult to know where to begin your music curriculum programme for this year group. Your approach may not be the same as a music teacher working in another school, but it is important to know why your differing approach is there in the first place. Cooke et al. (2016, p. 2) express the significance of a personal music education philosophy in their observation that, 'experience suggests that the best music teachers are those who have developed for themselves well-reasoned positions on learning and teaching in music'. While it is not necessary to formulate your understanding of curriculum in the same terms as OFSTED's (2018a) *intent, implementation,* and *impact,* you do need to be ready to engage in professional dialogue with visitors to your classroom, be they inspectors, line-managers, or parents.

Talking to beginning music teachers about what lies behind your music curriculum and how your planning arises from this, can lead to curriculum co-production, where curriculum is modified and developed as the result of discussion. Curriculum co-production can be a powerful learning experience for beginning teachers and for classroom learners. If your work as a mentor permits beginning teachers to work in collaborative partnerships which extend beyond lessons and schemes of work planning, you can build their confidence and allow new ideas to emerge in organic and creative ways. Such a facilitating relationship has links with teacher agency, which when constrained can result in frustration and impoverished achievement for pupils and music teacher professionals. Just as opportunities for deep learning and engagement have been framed as agency (Burnard and Murphy, 2013), within which creative interactions can be inhibited or advanced according to approaches to lesson design, so teacher agency can be a liberating paradigm. Philpott and Kubilius (2015) call for the space for teacher agency in a critical pedagogy of emancipatory discourse, but regard this as a remote possibility. Your work as a mentor with beginning teachers coming together to plan curriculum with distinct but shared values, is one winding pathway towards this destination. It makes agentic collaboration an emancipating possibility in music teacher mentorship, through a distinct and authentic interaction.

Before reading further, undertake Task 10.5.

Task 10.5 Comparing curricula

Compare two programmes of study for music. This may be your own and the example given in Figure 10.1, or you may have access to a colleague's from another school. Analyse the two music curricula. What is included or omitted? What is implied as being of first importance in their structures? How do the programmes connect musical learning with their curriculum structures? How would you like to develop your music programme of study as a result of your discussions? What will be the starting points for the beginning teacher in curriculum design during their first year of practice?

Implications for practice

It is tempting to regard mentoring beginning music teachers as a process in which raw materials are inputted into an organisational melding machine, which churns out classroom-ready practitioners. However, beginning music teachers are not empty vessels any more than pupils in classrooms are (Bunting, 2002) and they bring with them a wealth of musical understanding, experience and skills. Mentoring as a collaborative process embraces these dimensions and is an interchange between mentor and beginning teacher in which you *both* learn, grow, and develop. It is tempting for mentoring to adopt a perspective that focuses solely on classroom practice in terms of models of delivery of musical knowledge as privileged by school contexts and political systems. In this model, mentoring interactions rotate around an axis of the delivery of subject content in its various forms and an evaluation of the effectiveness of such a process. This can then dominate your lesson feedback, mentor meetings, suggestions for reading and planning for lessons.

Developing beginning teachers through mentoring to consider wider issues including curriculum rationales helps to prepare them for teaching practices which can lie outside their primary line of sight. This approach to mentoring centres on the development of musical practices in intersecting domains. Such domains may include (but are not limited to) musicianship, mutual dialogue to debate music education philosophies, tailoring musical interactivity in understanding cultural contexts, and music curriculum design. In this manner, mentoring enables the development of thinking; responding and justifying musical approaches in education which will serve any beginning teacher well in their musical and career development. The most facilitating mentoring is more than feedback on lesson dynamics and is responsive to the needs of the individual beginning teacher, whilst developing thought structures for independent evaluation when the beginning teacher is transplanted into a new school culture or context in their first year of qualified practice and beyond. Encouraging co-thinking, collaborating, co-teaching, and co-evaluating in your mentoring approaches can thus provide a rich training tapestry into which curriculum design philosophies may be stitched.

With these principles in mind, there are implications for practices which merit further thought and consideration and this chapter can only provide a few beginning prompts. These potential starting points must then be worked out by mentor and beginning teacher together. I therefore offer three further ideas for developing curriculum thinking within the mentor and beginning teacher context:

1. *Create time to make tacit curriculum thinking overt*
   As discussed earlier in this chapter, music curriculum processes and discourses can often be tacit interactions, which remain unarticulated. Creating space to draw out overarching philosophies of music education in the classroom and how this is embodied in curriculum realisations, sequences and dialogic learning, enables candid evaluation of classroom music practices, whilst facilitating you as a music teacher to chart courses for future development. Discussions where you as a music mentor present programmes of study from which you are working, with underpinning musical reasoning, which the beginning teacher is permitted to interrogate, can be enriching moments which bring concealed educational motivators to light. Such an interaction goes beyond lesson planning suggestions and schemes of work advice. It may require agreed protocols of engagement, as such a process involves exposing vulnerabilities for both mentor and beginning teacher.

2. *Establish curriculum reflection and evaluation as part of music mentoring*
   Reflection and evaluation are central characteristics of music mentorship and their value has been recognised elsewhere (Savage, 2013). Reflection and evaluation in music teacher mentoring discussions can lack a mutual element, regarding mentoring as something administered to beginning teachers, and can tend to be focused on realised musical encounters in lesson activities. Evaluating curriculum choices and their impact in classroom settings as an ongoing process and a standing item in music mentoring discussions validates curriculum as a significant catalyst in musical learning. Ascribing worth to conceptualisations of musical formulations in education and reflecting on their impacts makes visible hidden motivators and agents. This enables the beginning music teacher to continue to shape music curriculum for their future contexts rather than to be shaped by a curriculum they have experienced and its unacknowledged conceptual boundaries.

3. *Consider curriculum agency*
   The creative agency of pupils can be either inhibited or advanced according to the emphasis placed on lesson design. Regarded as a shopping list of learning, music curriculum design relies on elemental coverage in a standardised form. When opened to democratised development, where pupils are enabled in their chosen musical inspirations, as well as challenged to widen their musical experiences, curriculum can become a powerful agent for musical change. Music teacher agency, in which dimensions of music-making and their application may become more dominant than perceived or prescribed structures, also has the power to radically shape a music curriculum. This breaks away from curriculum as a document in its reified form, as previously discussed in this chapter. Enabling opportunities to allow these dynamics to shape curriculum by challenging assumptions of what a music curriculum is, is therefore an important

interaction which you can facilitate. An outward facing ideology which continually questions decisions about curriculum structures and any underlying assumptions which this reveals, can be helpful in this light. Rather than such questioning betraying a lack of confidence, the courage to continually scrutinise what you consider music curriculum to be and to reframe practices within such a reflection, reveal the importance of mentoring as a facilitating process for beginning teacher and established teacher, even within a high stakes performativity school culture. The very process of mentoring enables music curriculum development, when this is permitted within its frame of reference.

Summary and key points

- A lack of discussion about curriculum design can create a blind spot in the mentoring of beginning teachers, where it has the potential to be assumed knowledge.
- Curriculum is more than documentation and can be understood in multiple ways. Lesson planning, schemes of work, and programmes of study are terms which require discussion to lead to shared understandings in relationships between mentors and beginning teachers.
- Music curriculum can appear united, but closer inspection reveals multiple interacting dynamics. Mentoring relationships can enable dialogue with a 'critical friend' which simultaneously develops mentor and beginning teacher practices.
- Music teachers are curriculum designers. This is a difficult process, and it requires dedicated time and interrogative analysis to enable beginning music teachers to be equipped to design their own curricula.
- Mentoring for curriculum design at its most enriching is not focused solely on lesson feedback, but on making tacit curriculum thinking overt, establishing patterns for curriculum reflection and facilitating teacher agency.

Further resources

Cooke, C. and Spruce, G. (2016) 'What is a music curriculum?', in Cooke, C., Evans, K., Philpott, C. and Spruce, G. (eds.) *Learning to teach music in the secondary school*. 3rd edn. Abingdon: Routledge.

This chapter is an essential introduction to the philosophical underpinnings of music curriculum and includes definitions and discussions of its reified use as an object in a music education context.

Finney, J. (2017) *Music curriculum, pedagogy, assessment and the order of things*. Available at: https://jfin107.wordpress.com [accessed: 30 October 2019].

This blog outlines characteristics of curriculum, considers its nature and substance and how curriculum intersects and interacts with teaching processes and evaluation.

11 Preparing beginning music teachers for delivering lessons focussing on student performance

Terezija Štimec and Motje Wolf

Introduction

Many different types of knowledge are needed to deliver a successful lesson, such as: how to structure lessons, best approaches for each group, underlying educational aim, etc. Teaching music entails many intertwined aspects of teaching, for example: teaching academic aspects of music (such as music history) but also practical parts (such as composing, performing, and appraising of music), which will use different types of knowledge relevant for the preparation and delivery of the lesson.

Teaching academic music will be delivered similarly to other academic subjects and is easily supported through books or chats with other teachers. Though the practical music part, focusing on creating and performing music, requires teachers taking a different delivery approach; not only fostering knowledge but also confidence, creativity and emotional expression. Music experience and expertise are important for this and require reflection.

Shulman (1987) proposed a model of different kinds of teacher knowledge. These are shown in Figure 11.1. Being aware of these, especially the Knowledge of Learners and their Characteristics, empowers beginning music teachers to increase their class's performance level. This can be done through consistent, well-formulated feedback following a performance activity bearing in mind the pupils' background and current abilities. Assessment criteria will help to understand the aspects of educational ends, purposes, and values. This chapter focuses on preparing beginning music teachers for the delivery of music lessons by focusing on enhancing performance levels through appropriate feedback.

> '(Subject) Content Knowledge
> General Pedagogic Knowledge
> Curriculum Knowledge
> Pedagogic Content Knowledge
> Knowledge of learners and their characteristics
> Knowledge of educational contexts
> Knowledge of educational ends, purpose, and values'
> Shulman (1987, p. 8)

Figure 11.1 Shulman's (1987) teacher knowledge

DOI: 10.4324/9781003004196-16

Objectives

At the end of this chapter, you should be able to:

- understand how to empower the beginning music teacher to aim for high levels of performance;
- comprehend how to enable the beginning music teacher to set appropriate standards and learning outcomes for pupils in the music classroom;
- recognise the importance of the effective feedback delivery and how to present it to a beginning music teacher; and
- encourage the beginning music teacher to use the effective questioning in the music classroom.

Offering support for teaching classroom performance

Classroom performance is an essential part of music lessons, allowing pupils to experience music making. However, due to the various knowledge level of the class, with some pupils having peripatetic instrumental lessons and others being new to music, classroom performances that challenge each pupil are a difficult undertaking. Hence, many beginning music teachers might aim for less quality than they could. As music is a time-based art which is different to visual arts where the artefact can be worked on over many sessions, teachers have to capture performances through recording for assessment purposes. There are debates within musicology how accurately a recording captures a performance. Lerch et al. (2019) point out that any professional recording has changes made through audio engineers. Even though this is unlikely to be the case in a school-based recording for assessment purposes, quality of device and room acoustics will influence the quality. More importantly, some aspects cannot be captured in a recording, such as the atmosphere or communication to the audience. It is important that you, as a mentor, point this out to the beginning music teacher to avoid disappointment when listening back to a recording. Furthermore, you should guide beginning music teachers to think beyond the recorded 'physical' outcome and focus on the aesthetic experience that they create within the classroom. Of course, this experience is mitigated due to the many different assessment criteria which we are going to discuss below. Good music education should focus on the aesthetic experience first and foremost (Westerlund, 2012). Assessment, then, has the role to support this process in order to enable pupils to measure their progress and enable them to achieve their full musical potential. This in turn will help to improve the delivery of a lesson.

Offering support in setting the right expectations for classroom performance

Mentoring a beginning music teacher includes introducing them to a beautiful yet challenging world of creating musical minds. There are various factors to consider before lessons are to be delivered, factors that we do almost naturally due to our experience. In this paragraph, we will be describing several issues that beginning music teachers might face whilst learning to 'set high expectations which inspire, motivate and challenge pupils'

(Teachers' Standard 1, DfE, 2013), and offering different actions that beginning music teachers could take.

As mentioned above, the *knowledge of the learners and their characteristics* is crucial for success in delivering lessons. Hence, one of the important, if not the most important, actions that beginning music teachers need to do is get to know their pupils. It is important to guide beginning music teachers to prioritise what information should be gathered and what factors teachers need to take into consideration whilst gathering the information.

As secondary school pupils are coming from various backgrounds (different primary schools, upbringing, cultural differences, financial status of parents/carers), they are likely to have very different prior musical experiences. Many secondary school teachers might feel the urge to 'start teaching students from scratch' (Lamont et al., 2003; Marshall and Hargreaves, 2008), in order to account for a wide range of ability levels of pupils. A benefit of this approach is that it can help smoothen the transition between primary and secondary school and help some pupils adapt faster (Measor and Woods, 1984). While this approach can work well for the weaker or more inexperienced pupils, it can be very frustrating for the more advanced pupils (Symonds, 2015) as they might not feel challenged enough. Therefore, it is important to learn about pupils in order to set the right expectations and teaching styles. Helping beginning music teachers to set the right expectations can improve teachers' confidence, but also pupils' motivation and overall musical performance. Gathering information about pupils' linguistic and special educational needs and disability (SEND) needs could be the first step in helping a beginning music teacher to set the appropriate tasks, organise the appropriate grouping of the pupils, and understand the potential support they might need. The information about whether English is a pupil's first or an additional language (EAL), and whether they have any SEND, such as physical disability, vision impairment, hearing impairment, or a multi-sensory impairment, could influence how tasks are delivered. Also, the information about pupils' economic background (if pupils are eligible for free school meals (FSM) or Pupil Premium (PP) grants) could provide a beginning music teacher with knowledge on how many pupils could have an instrument to practise at home.

The first proposed strategy to address collecting the information is to encourage a beginning music teacher to create a document with pupils' profiles. This could be a spreadsheet or a booklet with data about pupils' needs (EAL, PP, FSM, SEND), previous experience of playing different musical instruments – if possible, to include instrumental grade level (e.g. Piano – ABRSM Grade 2 – Distinction), the experience of public performances (e.g. school concerts), a note about current music theory knowledge, and any other information that is specific to your school. The information could be gathered through the use of a baseline assessment or questionnaire at the beginning of the year. Furthermore, a new teacher could talk to the pupils individually or contact the parents/guardians to find out about pupils' previous musical experiences. Moreover, a mentor could ask the beginning music teacher to talk to other professionals (SENCO, safeguarding, etc.) and, in a meeting, share with the mentor what information has been elicited. This can then help support the planning process. In Tables 11.1 and 11.2, we have listed the different factors that might be useful to find out about the pupils and the different factors that need to be considered. Use the tables as a guide and share them with the beginning music teacher.

Table 11.1 Gathering pupils' data 1

Different factors of pupils to consider	Proposed actions for collecting pupils' data
• Musical experience before Secondary school • Musical and learning abilities • Special learning needs • Cultural capital and upbringing	• Baseline assessment • Questionnaires • Talking to the pupils individually • Communication with parents/guardians • Communication with other school professionals (e.g. SENCO)

Table 11.2 Using pupils' data

Different factors to consider	Proposed actions
• Different pupils' abilities • Sense of self as a teenager (different personalities, different confidence levels)	• Differentiated resources for performances • Wide range of opportunities and styles of performance • Groupings and pairing of the students (e.g. creating seating plan)

From the data gathered, teachers can now adapt their teaching practice: set high expectations, deliver appropriate feedback, and respond to the strengths and needs of all pupils (DfE, 2013). Knowing pupils will help to provide proper 'scaffolding' (Measor and Woods, 1984). An example specific to music learning can include pupils bringing their own instruments and performing them in front of the class, or having tasks specific to their instruments (e.g. learning to play chords on a guitar whilst the rest of the class is playing the keyboard). At the same time, pupils who are only engaging with music performance during the music lesson are likely to take a longer time to learn a piece and play with less confidence than others. These pupils could be asked to learn a short phrase or even the bass notes of the chords in time, whilst the rest are learning the whole melody. This should be done in a way that all students are celebrated for what they can do to create an inclusive environment. It is important to explain to a beginning teacher that inclusivity in the music classroom means encouraging students' participation based on their current abilities and encouraging all students to try their hardest.

Moreover, it is important for a beginning music teacher to understand other aspects that could affect pupils' performance, such as a sense of self and personal identity (Evans, 2015). Some pupils might experience performance anxiety whilst asked to perform in front of others. Helping beginning music teachers to create different opportunities and performance styles could be a solution. For example, if a student is too shy to perform their composition in front of the class, they could record their piece and playback the recording, but still during the lesson. This should be done only as a way to help students build their confidence and reduce performance anxiety. The beginning music teacher should focus on creating a space where pupils feel confident in expressing themselves through music, and the first step in this is to develop in Shulman's terms *knowledge of learners and their characteristics*.

Before reading further, undertake Task 11.1.

> **Task 11.1 Mentor reflection on offering support to set appropriate expectations**
>
> In a meeting, discuss with the beginning music teacher:
>
> - How much do they already know about their classes?
> - How might this knowledge help them in terms of lesson delivery?
> - How might this knowledge help them in terms of enhancing classroom performance?
>
> Use Tables 11.1. and 11.2 as a guide and share them with the beginning music teacher.

Understanding different music assessment criteria

The core guidance for the teaching profession in England is to follow the Teachers' Standards (DfE, 2013), the school policies and the national education laws. It is the duty of all teachers, beginner and experienced, to ensure the high quality of teaching and pupils' learning, to keep the teaching practice up to date and to the highest level (DfE, 2013). Since the 1988 Education Reform Act, assessments in schools have become a vital part of teaching in order to monitor that all schools are following the statutory guidance and ensuring pupils' progress (Hattie and Timperley, 2007; Schartel, 2012). Assessment includes all activities that measure the teaching quality and what pupils have learnt and three main reasons for the use of assessment in music education are: ensuring accountability, certification, and advancement of pupils' learning (Black et al., 2003). In his study on assessment Vinge (2014, p. 299 cited in Ferm Almqvist et al., 2017) explains this even further: 'If there were no grading in the subject of music, the value of the subject would probably disappear, at least with the attitudes that are in society today'. As it is vital that beginning music teachers understand the importance of assessment and ways of delivery, we will be discussing different assessments for music classrooms to ensure that beginning music teacher know how to use assessment in a meaningful way that advances pupils' performance skills.

It can be argued that music is the most assessed discipline, and it has a wide range of assessment opportunities. For example, graded instrumental and vocal examinations, competitions, or testing of musical abilities (Philpott and Evans, 2016). Even before secondary school, pupils are exposed to the various musical assessment criteria through 'pop charts' and various musical shows (e.g. Britain's Got Talent). However, researchers argue that assessment in music education has always been challenging and the construction of different grading systems has been the most challenging part of the assessment practice (Colwell, 2006; Costantino and Bresler, 2010; Eisner, 2002; Murphy, 2007; Olsson, 2001). Due to the nature of the subject, music teachers are the ones assessing the pupils' musical abilities (performing, composing, listening, and appraising) and are responsible for pupils' progress and motivation to learn and improve, which could be overwhelming for beginning music teachers. As there is a wide range of assessment criteria in music, it is good to guide

Table 11.3 Potential issues and proposed actions regarding assessment criteria

Potential issues	Proposed actions
• Understanding Assessment • Knowing what to assess/ Assessment criteria • Knowing how to assess/How to use Assessment criteria	• Ensuring that the beginning teacher understands why we use assessment in the music lessons • Talking to the beginning teachers about the school's assessment and feedback policy • Talking to the beginning teacher about existing Assessment Criteria and different Exam Boards • As a mentor spending time with the beginning teacher showing them how to assess, and making sure they know how to assess independently

a beginning music teacher through different assessments and the school's assessment and feedback policy to avoid them feeling repulsed and confused. Some potential issues that beginning music teachers could face with proposed solutions are outlined in Table 11.3.

Nevertheless, once adopted, assessment criteria can be one of the effective tools for the teacher. They also help with pupils' and parents' attitudes towards Music by showing a clear pathway of expectations and learning outcomes. Therefore, it is important to have classroom assessment criteria in music and to ensure that pupils are aware and familiar with them. It might be a good idea to discuss the different Exam Boards and their Assessment Criteria with a beginning music teacher. There are many: the ISM curriculum assessment criteria for KS3, the different GCSE and A level Exam Boards (e.g. Edexcel, Eduqas, AQA, OCR), the IB diploma, and BTEC in Music to reduce the confusion. It is also important to ensure that a beginning music teacher is familiar with a wide range of criteria and together with a mentor, decides what is the most appropriate criteria to use. It is good to demonstrate how the same criteria can be used across different lessons and units to accumulate summative data about students' progress. Additional important information is to discuss how the assessment is going to be monitored and evidenced. As mentioned above, one way could be to record the pupils' performances and store them safely on the school drive. This way the recordings can later be used to provide more detailed feedback on pupils' progress. Another strategy is creating an Assessment Sheet where the teacher is going to write feedback after the pupils' performances, or where they can write comments to each other. As seen above, understanding various assessment criteria and how to apply them to music teaching is extremely important to ensure pupils' performance excellence. Table 11.4 shows some examples of assessment criteria used in music.

Before reading further, complete Task 11.2.

Task 11.2 Mentor reflection on guiding understanding of the use of different Assessment Criteria for classroom performance

Discuss with the beginning music teacher the use of assessment supporting classroom performance. Focus on the use of the given assessment criteria (school policy or exam boards). Demonstrate how to apply these criteria to concrete situations. For this, the beginning music teacher could prepare some examples of assessment.

Table 11.4 Various examples of different assessment criteria used in music teaching

Group	Framework/exam board	Grading system	Explanation
KS3	ISM-The National Curriculum for Music (Fautley and Daubney, 2019, p. 18)	1-Not yet able to 2-Able to 3-Exceeds	Framework based on assessing pupils' skills and knowledge around six main strands which are adopted to different Units of Work: -Singing -Composing -Improvising -Playing -Critical engagement -Social, moral, spiritual, and cultural (SMSC)
KS3	Music Mark – Radar Diagram Template (Music Mark, 2020)	1-Not yet 2-Can do 3-Can do really well	Framework based on assessing pupils' skills and knowledge around five main strands which are adopted to different Units of Work: -Singing -Playing -Improvising -Composing -Critique and wider skills
KS4	GCSE AQA Music (AQA, 2022)	1-9	Assessment based on three main components: performing, composing, and understanding music
KS5	A-level AQA Music (AQA, 2022)	A*-E	Assessment based on three main components: performing, composing, and appraising music
KS5	IB Diploma Programme: Music (Standard and High Level) (IBO, 2022)	1-7	The course framework is purposefully aligned to assessment components and tasks: -Exploring music in context -Experimenting with music -Presenting music -The contemporary music maker (HL only)
Any	ABRSM (ABRMS, 2022)	Fail Pass Merit Distinction	Focus of grading performance based on qualities and skills of a performer (broadly categorised by pitch, time, tone, shape, and performance) and overall musical outcome.

Encouraging the use of effective feedback for classroom performance

Effective music teaching is determined by several different factors, one of them being the delivery of feedback in lessons. Several scholars (Creech, 2012; Gaunt, 2006; López-Íñiguez, 2017; López-Íñiguez and Pozo, 2016) argue that pupils attain musical knowledge, performance skills, and musical expression through teachers' feedback delivery in the classroom. Hattie and Timperley (2007) explain 'feedback' as the information about pupils' performance and understanding of the task. Therefore, specific types and ways of feedback delivery could have a strong impact, positive or negative, on pupils' motivation and wellbeing (Atlas et al., 2004), nevertheless the confidence to perform in lessons. Pupils' performances are important as they create opportunities for further feedback. It is this 'feedback loop' (Sadler, 1989) between teachers and pupils that can lead to significant progress in obtaining new musical skills. Moreover, the more confident and motivated students are, the more they want to perform, and the more enjoyable and effective music lessons are for students and their teachers. For this reason, it is important to encourage a beginning music teacher to reflect and plan for effective assessment and feedback delivery.

As mentioned previously, there are various ways that pupils can be assessed in music lessons and a beginning music teacher could struggle to understand how to use the criteria. This is not uncommon; a report based on evidence on primary and secondary school music teaching 2008-2011, published by The Office for Standards in Education, Children's Services and Skills (OFSTED, 2012) in the UK, showed that assessment methods used across the country were often inaccurate, over-complex, and unmusical. Hence, guiding beginning music teachers to assess and use effective constructive feedback in their teaching practice is an important factor for effective lesson delivery in secondary education. Besides, due to the nature of the subject, pupils are getting feedback regularly throughout the music lessons; however, some pupils might be struggling to understand and correctly interpret the comments received (Higgins, 2000), which could negatively affect the confidence of both pupils and beginning music teachers. Similarly, OFSTED (2012) suggests that the best assessment practices have taken into account different needs and prior musical experience of pupils. Therefore, it is important to encourage a new beginning teacher to use the students' data, as exemplified in Table 11.5, not only to scaffold the knowledge but for the use of musical assessment.

Whilst a specific formula for delivering feedback effectively has not been discovered yet, there are studies that unpick different feedback characteristics with some being more impactful than others. The characteristics of effective feedback, such as clarity and focus, may seem obvious; however, for beginning music teachers, it might be more difficult to implement it. Moreover, effective feedback can help pupils gain a better understanding of the teacher's expectations, and assessment criteria and develop more autonomy in musical performance. In this way, teachers can have the role of inspiring and motivating pupils, and the pupils can become more aware of their own progress. Duffy (2013) provides a useful framework of the four principles that should be considered to ensure constructive feedback which might form a basis of discussions with beginning music:

1. 'setting realistic goals based on the learning outcomes;
2. gauging students' expectation of feedback;
3. gathering information on students' practice;
4. being immediate and specific' (Duffy, 2013, pp. 22-24).

Table 11.5 Gathering pupils' data 2

Potential issues	Proposed solutions
• Knowing when to deliver feedback • Knowing how to deliver feedback (constructive/destructive)	• Advising the teacher to give feedback after each performance in the classroom • Ensuring the feedback is constructive • Importance of adaptability – knowing the pupils

Moreover, Baron (1988, p. 200) explains constructive feedback as accurate information that links good performance with the pupils' effort rather than the pupil's ability to perform. Some of the practical examples of constructive feedback are: 'I think there is room for improvement', 'You did the best you could under the circumstances', or 'You should give more attention to...' (London, 1995, p. 162). In contrast, Baron (1988) describes destructive feedback as general comments about pupils' performances with an unkind tone of voice that links poor performance as a measure of the pupils' inner abilities and skills, such as 'lack of motivation or ability' (Baron, 1988, p. 199). Additionally, it is important to detach the feedback from the pupils' person, so not 'You are good', but 'your interpretation of the melody worked well because...' This will help pupils to experiment with different versions and not be afraid to make mistakes, without fearing that feedback could be a criticism of them personally. Some of the practical examples of destructive feedback are: 'You didn't even try', 'You can't seem to do anything right', or 'If you don't improve, I'll get someone else to do it' (London, 1995, p. 162). Instead, Hattie and Timperley (2007, p. 120) suggest working with three questions: 'Where am I going? How am I going? and Where to next?'. This facilitates the processes of 'feed up, feedback, and feed forward' (Hattie and Timperley, 2007, p. 86). Use Tables 11.5 and 11.6 for guidance whilst encouraging a beginning music teacher to use only constructive feedback as this positively affects the pupils and their progress.

As stated in OFSTED's report (2012, p. 38), the most effective music assessment teaches pupils to listen more accurately to their own work to identify where improvements are needed. Furthermore, pupils also need to be shown how to improve through exact modelling by their teacher. Through detailed knowledge of the pupils, beginning music teachers will find it easier to use feedback in a way that is guiding pupils to be more self-aware and independent by providing specific instructions on how to improve specific actions by using the examples from Table 11.6. All things considered, effective feedback can be achieved by understanding the pupils' needs, their previous musical experience, musical goals and ambitions, and, of course, their musical abilities and knowledge. The more information gathered about each pupil in the classroom, the higher the chances of constructive feedback delivery.

Table 11.6 Constructive vs destructive feedback

Destructive	Constructive
- You are not talented enough. - You didn't even try. - You can't seem to do anything right. - If you don't improve, I'll get someone else to do it. - You are so bad at playing. - You are bad. - You are good.	- Thank you for trying. For even better results, you could... - You did the best you could under the circumstances. - I think there is room for improvement. - You should give more attention to... perhaps try this instead... - In your performance you have demonstrated... - You have played well because....

Before reading further, undertake Task 11.3.

Task 11.3 Reflection on encouraging the use of effective questioning for classroom performance

In a meeting, discuss with the beginning music teacher:

- What feedback have they given recently?
- How does that fit in with Tables 11.5 and 11.6?
- How might they improve their feedback in future?

Summary and keypoints

- In this chapter, we have discussed how the *knowledge of learners and their characteristics* can help beginning music teachers improve their lesson delivery. This way, the quality of instrumental and vocal performance can be enhanced.
- Knowledge of assessment criteria shared with the pupils and skills of constructive feedback support the goal of improving classroom performance levels.
- Furthermore, examples of assessment criteria and effective feedback have been given in order to support the work with beginning music teachers.
- We hope to have outlined the importance of the right feedback delivery and suggestions on encouraging the right use by beginning music teachers.

Further resources

Hattie, J. and Clarke, S. (2019) *Visible learning feedback*. New York: Routledge.

Combining research excellence, theory and vast teaching expertise, this book covers the principles and practicalities of feedback, including the variability of feedback, the importance of surface, deep and transfer contexts, student-to-teacher feedback, peer-to-peer feedback, the power of within lesson feedback and manageable post-lesson feedback.

Werry, J. (2017) ISM Webinar: Assessment in Key Stage 3 music. https://www.youtube.com/watch?v=pu_2uEXrvHw [accessed: 2 May 2025]

Webinar led by Jane Werry (Head of Music at Hayes School) offers excellent ideas on how to use assessment in KS3 Music lessons.

ISM-The National Curriculum for Music, *A revised framework for curriculum, pedagogy and assessment in key stage 3 music* (2019) Professor M. Fautley and Dr A. Daubney, Page: 18 https://www.ism.org/images/images/ISM_The-National-Curriculum-for-Music-booklet_KS3_2019_digital.pdf

A useful resource for any music teacher to think about the National Curriculum and assessment strategies in a deeper way.

Music Mark (2020) *Assessment in Key Stage 3 Music: Assessment Grid Template* - https://www.musicmark.org.uk/resources/assessment-in-key-stage-3-music/ [accessed: 2 May 2025].

These resources encompass a webinar on assessment in key stage 3 music and some assessment templates.

12 Observing a lesson

Austin Griffiths

Introduction

The aim of this chapter is to make lesson observations constructive and positive experiences for both you and the beginning music teacher you are mentoring. There are various models of observation (Montgomery, 2012; OFSTED, 2018) with a variety of purposes: part of a whole-school inspection; the assessment performance and reward; an opportunity to observe advanced practice; to enable the development of an early career teacher. These distinct purposes dictate the model we might use. As a mentor of a beginning music teacher, you are focusing on the development and understanding of pedagogy in practice. You will act as a critical friend, defined by Ferm Thorgersen as 'a trusted person who asks provocative questions' (2014, p. 61). The purpose of this chapter is to ask you to think about how you can be this critical friend. The key point to keep in mind is that you are observing the person and their potential, and the lesson observation is your vehicle for doing this.

Objectives

At the end of this chapter, you should be able to:

- Understand the features making observation an effective, constructive, and positive experience;
- Understand what qualities and skills you are looking for, and looking to develop, in a beginning music teacher; and
- Consider effective ways to observe and record your findings.

Has this happened to you?

Let's start this discussion with a typical bad observation experience – one that has happened to me and most of my colleagues.

Case study 1: entertaining Mr Sloane

In the regular round of quality assurance, it is pencilled in for Tuesday period 2: your lesson observation by Mr Sloane, the Deputy Headteacher. You have sent in your lesson plan several days in advance, but had no reply. No pre-observation meeting was offered. At 10.15 – five minutes before the lesson begins – everything is laid out. The lesson's objectives are displayed on the board for the pupils. You are confident, but a little nervous. At 10.20, the pupils start to arrive, but there is no sign of Mr Sloane. At 10.22, you begin the lesson. Your warm-up goes really well. The pupils are fired-up and at 10.41, when Mr Sloane arrives, they are animated and engaged in the main activity of the lesson. 'Sorry', says Mr Sloane, 'I was stuck on the phone with a parent – I couldn't get away'.

You ask Mr Sloane if he's got the lesson plan. 'Oh!' he stutters 'er.no…I haven't had time to look at it yet…'. You have made a spare copy which you hand to him. The observation goes well – you get positive feedback and the pressure is off. But you are feeling short-changed. Your lesson was judged 'very good' – but if the start of it had been observed it might have been judged 'excellent'. You had been anxious about it for a few days, but clearly it was not a priority for the school's management. If *you* were late for class, no doubt the 'very good' would disappear.

Furthermore, you are a beginning music teacher. Mr Sloane teaches English. Unfortunately, you are the only music teacher in the school and you have never been observed by a fellow music teacher since you finished your PGCE (teacher training qualification). You have always received positive feedback – but you cannot help wondering if it is actually valid… Verdict on the way the lesson observation was carried out: **Inadequate.**

Points for Mr Sloane:

- Take the observation seriously;
- As a mentor, prepare the date/time and priorities of the lesson observation in advance;
- Meet with the beginning music teacher in advance;
- At this meeting, discuss what you are looking for in the observation and encourage the teacher to suggest any aspects of the lesson/delivery they would particularly like you to give feedback on;
- Remember – the observation might be a small task for you – but it may mean a lot to the person being observed;
- Turn up on time; and
- Give the observation a proper level of priority – don't treat it as something that can be delayed if something else comes up.

Before reading further, undertake Task 12.1.

Task 12.1 Points for Mr Sloane

Rank the points above in order of importance.

What are the possible advantages and disadvantages of a beginning music teacher having a non-music specialist observing their class music lesson?

What are you looking for in your observation?

Rowland et al. (2005) use the term 'Knowledge Quartet' in their study on early career mathematics teaching. And certainly, this can be applied to music (and most other subjects taught at school). The four areas are: foundation, transformation, connection, contingency. However, we can split these into two groups:

- The person (foundation)
- The actions of teaching (transformation, connection, contingency)

The person

Here, we are talking about the knowledge and understanding that the beginning music teacher brings into the classroom. Firstly, this includes their knowledge and understanding of music as a discipline. Secondly, their grasp of the pedagogical principles and practices concerned with music teaching. And thirdly, their beliefs about what ought to be taught, why it should be taught, and why it is important.

The knowledge, skills, and understanding required to be a music teacher have changed dramatically over the last 30 years (refer also to Chapter 9). Before the 1990s, pianistic skills were a pre-requisite. But new technology has brought a new set of requirements. There is a need to be technologically minded. Proficiency in programmes such as *Sibelius*, *Logic*, or *Cubase* is certainly required at GCSE, while a knowledge of more basic programs such as *Garageband* is necessary for lower secondary pupils (11- to 14-year-olds/English Key Stage (KS) 3). And for schools, offering a BTEC or GCSE Music Technology routes the technical demands are high: music production, live performance, live sound, recording techniques, sequencing, knowledge of the music industry, etc. Today's beginning music teachers require a wider range of skills than ever before and, given the huge range of genres now on offer, they need to be adaptable and open-minded. Can anyone cover all of these things? Well, possibly. Certainly, there are many schools with just a single specialist music teacher who has no choice but to cover everything as best they can. The key question is this: has our beginning music teacher got enough in their locker to effectively cover all of the musical and technological requirements of the role? Or - if the answer is no - have they got the capacity to develop the skills they need?

For some subjects - English, maths, history, sciences, RE, to name but a few - most teachers (with a moderate amount of training and effort) could probably cover them up to lower secondary level (11-14 years olds/English KS3) and possibly up to GCSE level. But music in the secondary school does not easily fall into this category. Most professional musicians (and I include music teachers in this category) started learning their skills at a young age. It is difficult to pick up the required skills as an adult. Certainly, as Dascalu *et al.* (2014) point out, the suggestion that 10,000 hours of practice are needed for proficiency (Gladwell, 2009) may be an exaggeration. Nevertheless, the 4000 hours suggested by Dascalu *et al.* (2014) as a more realistic figure remains a sizeable chunk of time.

But why does this matter? Perhaps the answer lies in the fact that, because musical expertise is such a required commodity, teaching and pedagogy can be overlooked. Pedagogy can be both generic and subject specific (see Gudmundsdottir and Shulman, 1987) for an interesting discussion on this topic). The generic aspects tend to fall into what we might call *good practice*. Do the classroom routines align with the school-wide expectations such as seating plans, grouping practices, marking and displaying work, having clearly displayed aims for each lesson, meeting and greeting, enforcing agreed behaviour or uniform expectations, and many more. Good practice emerges from the clearly laid out expectations in Teachers' Standards (DfE, 2011) and their interpretation in the school context. If we observe trainee or early career teachers without regard for these Standards, we will be selling them short because they encompass: 'the minimum level of practice expected of trainees and teachers from the point of being awarded qualified teacher status (QTS)' (DfE, 2011, p. 3).

Part 1 of the Standards give broad headings that we might consider in a classroom observation:

- High expectations;
- Progress;
- Curriculum knowledge;
- Planning and delivery of well-structured lessons;
- Differentiation;
- Formative and summative assessment; and
- The learning (classroom) environment.

Of course, as discussed in Gudmundsdottir and Shulman (1987), classroom craft improves with experience. But what we are looking for is an awareness of these key areas, and the reflective capacity to develop and improve their application.

Reflective practice, too, is essential to the subject-specific elements of music teaching. We may divide this into two areas: what will be taught and how it will be taught. There are various music teaching methods: Suzuki, Kodaly, Orff, and Dalcroize are examples. Class music teachers will not necessarily be familiar with all of these methods. However, what these methods all have is a distinct philosophy. For example, while the Suzuki method emphasises the importance of learning by ear and musical memory, it also stresses the importance of praising the positives and nurturing the social development through music (Hendricks, 2011). I am not suggesting here that class music teachers should adopt the Suzuki method. Rather, I am suggesting that practitioners should have some sort of philosophy or theoretical approaches behind their practice. Sound before Symbol (Kay, 2013) and Informal Learning (Green, 2008) are useful examples of approaches that encourage teacher to ask: why am I doing what I do in the way that I do it? Part of the answer may be to develop skills, for example: listening, singing, playing, composing, creativity. But it may also encompass human aspects: the enjoyment of music, music and cultural identity, cooperation and teamwork, music as a tool for personal expression, to name a few.

It is important to point out here that an observation should not be considered finished at the end of the lesson. For example, evidence of a beginning music teacher's capacity to develop their practice will often become apparent during the pre-briefing and/or debriefing sessions. To what extent do these conversations suggest that the beginning music teacher is a critical and reflective appraiser of their own practice? Do they also bring out the beginning music teacher's pedagogical and philosophical appr approaches?

Before reading further, undertake Task 12.2.

Task 12.2 Reflective practice exercise

As a mentor you are concerned that your beginning music teacher needs to think more deeply about inclusion in their lessons. You observed two lessons with a Year 8 (12-year-olds). The lessons seem to be aimed at pupils who will go on to take music as a GCSE option. But this is less than 20% of the class. What about the rest? The lessons are quite skills-based and focus on theory and note reading. While a small number of pupils seem to do well, you notice that quite a lot of pupils do not seem to be very engaged.

Come up with a list of six questions or discussion points that you can use to support a discussion to help your beginning music teacher to develop more inclusive lessons.

The actions of teaching

While the first part of Rowland et al.'s (2005) quartet looked at the teacher as a person: their theoretical and philosophical approaches to their profession, the next three elements of the quartet looked at what is happening in the classroom. So, as a mentor, by thinking in terms of transformation, connection, and contingency, you can build your framework of what to look for in the classroom. What are the things you need to see to tell you that learning is taking place?

Transformation

The first action discussed by Rowland et al. (2005) is transformation: the ability of the teacher to pass on their knowledge through processes and forms accessible to the learner (refer also to Chapter 4). Often this is intuitive – how we speak to pupils, a natural ability to put things in an understandable way – but much can be planned, practised, and learned. Here is a list of some things you might look for:

- Clear explanations of key concepts and clear instructions at the appropriate level for the pupils (delivery);
- Concepts and tasks broken down into smaller manageable chunks;
- Modelling (by teacher and peers);
- Evidence of differentiation/inclusive teaching (planning/delivery);
- Effective and appropriate use of resources; and
- Formative assessment.

Transformation must go deeper than whole class level – all pupils need to benefit from their teacher's knowledge. For creating an inclusive classroom (by which we mean everyone participating and making progress), differentiation is the key. The observer needs to ask: Is everyone in the class participating and progressing? And as pupils have varying degrees of aptitude and prior achievement, the beginning music teacher must transform knowledge differently for different pupils. In practice, this will often be for groups of pupils and the beginning music teacher's within-class grouping strategies must reflect differences in the transformation of knowledge.

Shulman (1987) discusses how knowledge transformation is tiered. He differentiates between:

- Level 1: simple translation of meaning;
- Level 2: connotations and significance;
- Level 3: interpretation and implications; and
- Level 4: application and evaluation.

Shulman was discussing literature teaching, but the tiers can be effectively applied to music. In your observation, then, you are looking for knowledge transformation that is both differentiated and tiered according to a pupil's need.

Connection

While transformation is about teaching, connection is about progress. How bits of learning connect with each other in a meaningful way. It is useful to think of this at three different levels: micro (within a lesson); meso (between one lesson and another; and macro (between a sequence of lessons and an overall scheme of work).

On a micro level, this covers connections within the lesson. Where does a lesson begin? Where is it aiming to get to? What are the stages in between? As OFSTED (2018) notes, direct observation of 'learning' is difficult. Instead, most observation models observe features that suggest learning is occurring. Certainly, the quality and coherence of connections within a lesson are a very useful indicator that learning has been facilitated. They give the structure for progression by controlling and developing *the* 'discourse within the classroom' (Rowland et al., 2005, p. 7). You might look for:

- An understanding of musical ideas and concepts and how they interlink with each other;
- The ability to break teaching down into small interlinking chunks; and
- The sequencing of these chunks so that they build upon each other to achieve the learning aims of the lesson.

An observer should see some of these chunks in the lesson plan. But you should also see them in action: not all of these micro-steps can be written down. As will be discussed in the next section, they are contingent on the beginning music teacher assessing the pupil's mastery of their current task. You might ask if the beginning music teacher can improvise by breaking down tasks further or differently as required?

At the next level – the meso – you are looking for how a lesson fits into its immediate sequence; the lessons before it and those that follow. Has the beginning music teacher built on prior learning and where will it move on to in the future. Can you see a coherent stepped progression throughout a unit of work?

And finally, there is the macro level. This may be over a term or over a year, or possibly longer. How does what is going on fit in with the overall scheme of things? Why is this lesson, or unit of lessons, being taught at this time?

Contingency

For the beginning music teacher, contingency is associated with the confidence to move away from their lesson plan when required. How the teacher reacts – and possibly changes things – in response to unexpected events. These events fall into two categories:

i. Non-learning-centred events such as:

- Equipment not working;
- Fire alarms going off;
- A pupil being sick or ill in class;
- An unplanned whole-school assembly.

ii. Learning-centred
   - Students finding the tasks too difficult or too easy;
   - Students developing good ideas not on the lesson plan;
   - The teacher seeing a good – but unexpected – learning opportunity emerging.

The second category is linked to the beginning music teacher's informal assessment practice. Can the teacher assess current learning and actions (in individuals, groups, or the class) to harness 'unpredictable opportunities at the time of teaching' (Kula Ünver, 2018, p. 27). An example might be allowing a group to continue a composition or performance beyond the planned time, enabling them to further develop their ideas or understanding. Alternatively, learning-centred contingency could also include curtailing or altering activities that are not working out as expected. We have all been there: delivering the lesson that we thought would work well – but, for whatever reason, the pupils cannot engage with it. The under-confident or non-contingent teacher will plough ahead with their plan. But as an observer, you want to see them change, adapt, and evolve their lesson.

Summary of what you are looking for in:

The person
- Musical and technical knowledge;
- A clear philosophy behind their teaching practice; and
- A reflective and critical capacity for development.

The standards (DfE, 2011)
- High expectations;
- Progress;
- Curriculum knowledge;
- Planning and delivery of well-structured lessons;
- Differentiation;
- Formative and summative assessment; and
- The learning (classroom) environment.

The actions of teaching
- Clear instructions and explanations at the appropriate level;
- Concepts and task broken down into appropriately sized chunks;
- Differentiated and inclusive teaching;
- Effective use of resources;
- Tiered learning becoming increasingly critical;
- Connected learning within the lesson;
- Awareness of previous and future learning; and
- The ability to adapt and react to unforeseen opportunities and circumstances.

The observation process

Your observation should have three stages: pre-brief, observation, and de-brief.

A. The pre-brief

The pre-brief is a meeting between the observer and the beginning music teacher, ideally between three and five working days before your observation takes place. You should ask the beginning music teacher to bring their lesson plan and key resources (e.g. Powerpoints) to the meeting. This means you can:

- be briefed on the intended content of the lesson beforehand;
- assess the quality of the lesson planning and discuss it; and
- ask about any areas you feel might be missing or not covered.

In the pre-brief, you should:

- ask the beginning music teacher to talk you through their lesson plan;
- inform them of any specific points you are looking for (e.g. points from a previous observation; whole-school initiatives) and ask them to highlight any points you would like feedback to focus on; and
- agree the format of your observation (e.g. how long will it last, will you look at books or talk to students, will you stay in one place or walk around, how will you be introduced).

The pre-brief is your chance to put the beginning music teacher at their ease. This is important given the climate of distrust that recently has characterised graded observations (O'Leary and Gewessler, 2014) or observations in OFSTED inspections (Smith and Gallagher, 2019). You should expect the beginning music teacher to be nervous. However, this can be minimised by being clear about the process. Be honest about any short-comings in the plan, but offer solutions to issues. If necessary, give the student the opportunity to revise and improve the plan before the lesson and ask them to email it to you in advance.

B. The observation

At the start
The key here is to set yourself up for success. Arrive in good time so that you are in place before the class enters. Do not undermine the beginning music teacher by introducing yourself or by talking too much when the teacher introduces you – a smile and nod of the head to the pupils is quite enough.

Your role as a researcher
Research methods books such as Denscombe (2017) or Robson et al., (2016) are useful resources to help you develop good practice. As an observer, you are also a researcher. You are collecting data so that you can support the beginning music teacher by celebrating good practice, identifying areas for development, and helping them to become a critically reflective practitioner. You are conducting primary research into the beginning music teacher's practice in the classroom. Many observation proformas are easily accessed with a quick search on Google. These vary from a simple two or three boxes (e.g. what went well/what could have been better) to complicated multi-box A3 giants. However, you might be well advised to devise your own sheet that fits your individual style and needs. However, you may also

find that your school has specific requirements for all observations, and you will need to show these on your form. In some cases, schools have in-house proformas that must be used. In this case, you would be well advised to take a note book in case you wish to record something that does not fit on the proforma.

Often schools take a shortcut by having a single sheet used by the observer during the lesson which then doubles as the feedback sheet handed post-observation to the beginning music teacher. This is a bad idea if for no other reason than it means no post-observation reflection (by the observer) has taken place. It is, therefore, strongly recommended that you use a separate observation notes sheet in the lesson and reflective feedback sheet (filled in after the lesson) to give to the beginning music teacher.

Types of observation

Observations fall into two broad categories: systematic (or non-participant) observation and participant observation. Denscombe (2017) suggests that in systematic observations the observer is aiming not to be noticed, to unobtrusively note actions and attributes of the situation while blending into the background. Of course, in a classroom setting this is not entirely possible. Nevertheless, as a systematic observer you should think about three things: positioning, interaction, and the length of the observation (Denscombe, 2017):

- Position yourself in a place where you are not interrupting the eyeline between pupils and the teacher, but where you can still see the whole class.
- Keep integration with pupils and the teacher to a minimum – you are there to watch not to talk!
- Try to stay for the whole lesson. The longer the observation lasts, the more your presence is disregarded.

There are times, however, when some interaction with pupils will be useful, so a compromise is required. You are becoming what Robson and McCarten (2016) describes as a 'marginal participant'. For example, when the pupils are engaged in their learning activities, you may wish to talk to them to assess their knowledge and understanding of what they are doing. Similarly, you may need to move around the room to see how different individuals or groups are working. Nevertheless, you can minimise the impact of these things by following some simple steps:

- Only discuss the learning activities and understanding with the pupils. Avoid more general conversation;
- Move slowly and quietly; and
- Do not give advice or help with learning – this is not your role.

C. The de-brief

The de-brief is the most important part of the observation process. It is where the dialogue of progress and improvement takes place. As O'Leary and Gewessler suggest, one purpose of this dialogue should be to enable teachers 'to become active agents in their own CPD' (2014, p. 40). It should be a process of empowerment to enable critical self-reflection. Certainly, it should be a discussion - a reflective debate rather than simply a tidied-up version of the notes you took in the lesson. But the nuances of the de-brief may depend on the formative and graded aspects of the observation. In short, is the beginning music teacher being assessed or advised.

In some situations, however, there will be at least an element of grading, although the formality of this will vary. At the very least, the beginning music teacher is likely to want some sort of indication from you on how well the lesson went - even if this is restricted to: excellent, good, good in parts, or requires development. At other times, the extent of the grading element may be dictated by the institution of the teacher or your own institution (if different). However, as a mentor you should keep in mind that that giving an overall grade or judgement is only a minor part of the process. What you actually need to do is initiate a conversation that will lead to critical reflection and critical development for the beginning music teacher.

You should come to the de-brief with three lists to present to the beginning music teacher:

- Good things about the lesson;
- Questions about the lesson; and
- Possible areas for development.

You may consider starting by asking the teacher to reflect on their thoughts about the lesson. While this can be useful in helping you to gauge the teacher's level of reflection, make sure you think about what you will do if their perception if the lesson is radically different to yours. Starting with positives will put the teacher at ease and hopefully boost their confidence in your judgement. Try to find at least four or five positive elements to discuss. You list of questions may include things that you genuinely wish to ask. But it might also include pointers to some of the possible areas for development. You should give the beginning music teacher time to reflect and discuss key points - but have some prompts ready to encourage a deeper conversation if required. Finally, discuss possible areas for further development or focus. Agree a manageable number of key development points (two or three is a good number - but you will need to make an individual judgement here based on your knowledge of your mentee).

It is best not to give the beginning music teacher a formal lesson observation sheet at the de-brief session. A better idea is to fill in a draft by hand during the session. At the end of the session talk it through with your beginning music teacher to secure their agreement on its accuracy and let them know you will send them the final copy via email. But what should you do if you and the beginning music teacher cannot agree on an aspect of your feedback. One suggestion is that you put in both points of view, e.g.:

> The observer felt that the work needed more differentiation to cater for less able pupils. (Note: the teacher disagreed with this point, feeling that it was the pupils' poor behaviour that was preventing them from working).

Of course, this is not ideal - but in the end it should not be a battle about who has the final word. In making this entry on the sheet you have raised the issue while at the same time acknowledging that observations can be subjective. The key point here is that you have encouraged the mentee to critically reflect on differentiation in practice. Critical reflection, as Brookfield notes, is 'the sustained and intentional process of identifying and checking the accuracy and validity of our teaching assumptions' (2017, p. 3). And, in the end, the objective of the observation process is to make your beginning music teacher *think*. Agreeing with your comments is, actually, something of a side issue!

Summary and keypoints

In this chapter, we have discussed:

- Features of an inadequate lesson observation;
- What musical and technical knowledge you might look for;
- The importance of a philosophy or method behind the teaching process;
- The actions of teaching: transformation, connections, contingency;
- Using the Teacher Standards (DfE, 2011);
- The observation process: pre-brief, observation de-brief;
- Techniques for systematic and participant observation; and
- The importance of critical reflection.

Further resources

OFSTED (2018) *Six models of lesson observation: An international perspective*. Manchester: Office for Standards in Education, Children's Services and Skills.

This report neatly sums up six well-respected models of lesson observation from around the world. The report draws out the differences and the common ground in the models.

Brookfield, S. (2017) *Becoming a critically reflective teacher*. San Francisco: John Wiley and Sons.

Brookfield's book is an excellent resource for developing a critical and reflective approach to practice. It helps us to question and reflect on current practices and norms. Challenges brings change and progress – and this book will help both mentors and mentees form and reform their pedagogy.

Denscombe, M. (2017) *The good research guide*. 6th edn. Maidenhead: Open University Press.

Observation is a form of research. Denscombe's introduction to research methods and practice is an excellent starting guide for making your observations robust. It is academically sound – but very practical and user friendly in style.

13 Supporting pupils' learning

Ian Axtell and Martin Fautley

Introduction

There is a common tendency amongst beginning music teachers to privilege *doing* over learning (Regelski, 1986; Chapter 9). This is because it is much easier to plan for doing. Keeping pupils occupied with therapeutic activities, like a calming worksheet or uplifting communal singing, are straightforward assumptions about music teaching, but musical learning is more complex. Building on perceptions of initial teacher education (ITE) with beginning music teachers, developed over a number of years, this chapter will delineate ways in which learning can be identified. This will support mentors to identify how pedagogic encounters can be carefully planned to ensure that learning is to the fore. Musical learning needs to be *musical*, and this chapter illustrates pedagogies for musicality, using case studies as well as descriptions and provocations.

Objectives

After reading this chapter, you will know/be able to:

- Recognise musical learning as an active process;
- Define musical 'knowledge' as musical 'knowing';
- Support the learning of beginning music teachers by highlighting responsive pedagogy: teaching for learning; and
- Prioritise pedagogies for social justice: teaching as learning.

Musical learning as an active process

A focus on supporting learning rather than just teaching music is helpful for beginning music teachers to initiate their perceptions of pedagogy in music education. In this chapter, pedagogy is perceived as: 'The processes and relationships of learning and teaching' (Stierer and Antoniou, 2004, p. 277) where sociocultural and social constructivist perspectives of education underpin process and developmental curriculum priorities (Kelly, 2009). Active verbs are used to identify learning in music education. This approach is adopted by Fautley and Daubney, who suggest: 'singing, composing, improvising, playing' (ISM, 2015, p. 6) as main strands for musical learning during compulsory education. They also emphasise: 'critical engagement' (Fautley and Daubney, 2015, p. 6) where 'The notion of critical engagement … encompasses listening, appraising, evaluating, describing, identifying' (Fautley and Daubney, 2015, p. 6). Identifying the main strands that underpin a teacher's approach towards music education can be a helpful introduction for beginning music teachers and will help to clarify your own curriculum priorities. Now undertake Task 13.1.

Task 13.1 Your priorities for music education

As a mentor for beginning music teachers, what are the main strands that underpin your approach towards music education? Are some strands more important than others? What are your school's curriculum priorities?

Leaving pupils to actively engage in 'doing' without identifying 'learning' is a criticism of constructivist approaches towards education. Social constructivism seeks to retain the focus on meaningful activities for the pupils, whilst at the same time providing access to existing external knowledge through the support of a more knowledgeable other (Vygotsky, 1978). Knowledge is constructed by pupils when they engage in meaningful, knowledge-rich external applications, initially with support through performing existing music, and ultimately independently, where they are composing on their own or with their peers. This creates the potential for pupils to take knowledge in new directions, looking forwards rather than just looking backwards. Vygotsky identified the zone of proximal development (ZPD) as the point at which support is offered. The manner in which support can be offered was identified through the analogy of a scaffold by Wood, Bruner, and Ross in 1976. A scaffold can be built up or taken down, depending on the needs of each pupil. Frameworks for scaffolding learning within the ZPD will be a key focus for this chapter. However, before building or removing any scaffolds, beginning music teachers need to grasp the different types of knowledge that are important in music education. When learning is perceived as a social constructivist process, knowledge becomes conceptualised as *knowing* on the part of the pupil, thus becoming an active process (Beck, 2015). What knowing is important in music education?

Defining knowledge as knowing

Outside music education, Winch (2013) identifies three established types of knowledge: propositional knowledge, know-how, and knowledge by acquaintance. He also describes a further type of knowledge: knowledge who, when, where, when, etc., which he labels as 'knowledge-wh' (Winch, 2017). Propositional knowledge can be identified as *knowing that*. Knowing that relates to key concepts in music education that can be identified through key words or terms. This declarative language associated with music can begin with the basic elements or concepts and gradually move towards more complex structural processes and dimensions that relate to different types, styles, or forms of music. Knowledge-wh or *knowing about* can also be represented through spoken or written language, and identifies cultural, social, historical, and personal contexts in which music was created. *Knowing that* and *knowing about* underpin an academic approach towards music education, essential to gain a deeper understanding of music but often ignored when doing is prioritised over learning. Identifying the *knowing that* and *knowing about* that underpin an education encounter can help beginning music teachers move their focus from doing towards learning:

Before reading further, undertake Tasks 13.2, 13.3 and 13.4.

Task 13.2 Identifying musical vocabulary

Prior to a lesson observation, ask a beginning music teacher to identify the key vocabulary that underpins the lesson. This task can include both explicit and implicit vocabulary. Are both *knowing that* and *knowing about* being identified? Is the vocabulary being 'used' by the pupils and not just 'given' by the teacher?

What is sometimes called an academic approach towards music education is valuable but can objectify music as something that sits outside personal experience. This is not very engaging for the majority of pupils, nor is it inherently musical. An academic approach focuses on the conceptual, scientific, historical, and geographic aspects of music rather than engaging with active music making, what Small identified as musicking (1998). For musicking to take place, *knowing how* is required. An important musical learning activity across the world is as *knowing how* to sing or play an instrument. This involves the transmission of vocal/instrumental skills from particular cultural perspectives which are valued by the teacher and society. Effective music teachers will draw on *knowing how, knowing that* and *knowing about* to link theory with practice. This praxial approach was identified by Elliott as: 'knowledgeable music making' (1995, p. 69) or praxis, where understanding is enhanced when music making is placed within an appropriate context and linked to music theory. Examples of linking music theory (*knowing that* and *knowing about*) with music practice (*knowing how*) can further enhance the move towards learning for beginning music teachers:

Task 13.3 Contextualising *knowing how* and *knowing that*

Ask a beginning music teacher to identify an example where instrumental skills and music theory have been combined to enhance the understanding of a particular type of music.

The opportunity to develop instrumental skills can create a sense of identity and build acquaintances with particular types of music where those instrumental skills are appropriate. However, knowledge by acquaintance or *knowing of* suggests a greater investment by the learner than other forms of musical knowledge. *Knowing of* can be at a surface level, like recognising a familiar melody, or it can be at a much deeper level, understanding why music has value (Swanwick, 1979) and the meta-cognition that lies behind the symbolic and systematic creation of music (Swanwick and Tillman, 1986). This *knowing of* is enhanced when different knowledge types are combined, moving beyond mastery and the manipulation of materials (Swanwick and Tillman, 1986) for particular external, pre-determined purposes towards the realms of value, flow, and metaphor (Swanwick, 1999). Musical learning at this stage begins to access the higher levels of the domains of learning identified by Bloom et al. (1956) where the combination of thinking (the cognitive domain) feeling (the affective domain) and doing (the psychomotor domain) enhance the potential for creativity.

> **Task 13.4 Identifying musical learning**
>
> Help beginning music teachers to identify the musical learning that is taking place in scheme/unit of work. You can use one of your own schemes or the Model Music Curriculum (DfE, 2021). We have provided our own example in Table 13.1.

Regelski (2014) builds on Elliott's (1995) perception of praxis in music education by including the notion of phronesis, practical wisdom, where care for each pupil and their learning are placed at the centre of music education. Table 13.1 recognises that performing together is a key priority for pupils in a classroom context, where different 'voices' are valued and brought together in an inclusive environment. The conceptual process of 'building from the beat' or 'entrainment' (Clayton et al., 2005) recognises the importance of inclusion both in terms of the classroom community and the music being explored. Pupils can focus on performing patterns that are less complex and yet still feel part of the musical community. In Table 13.1, there is a deliberate attempt to introduce pupils to a range of different music where rhythm underpins music for dance. Regelski (2014) recognises that music is varied and open to interpretation. Variety and variation challenge the idea that music education should just be about transmitting fixed norms. Instead, music education should also: 'draw upon children's natural resources of wonder, imagination and inventiveness' (Mills and Paynter, 2008, p. 1). This type of education can then lead to personal discovery and identity building (Lamont, 2002). This identity building

Table 13.1 An example of a lower secondary school scheme/unit of work

Project	Knowing that (concepts)	Knowing how (skill/technique)	Knowing about (context)	Knowing of (understanding)
Patterns and places (Y7: Spring: Project 2)	Key concepts: • Texture • Ostinato/Riffs Extension 1: • Syncopation • Polyphony • Binary forms Extension 2: • Polyrhythms • Ternary/arch forms	Singing and vocal percussion Untuned and tuned percussion techniques How to perform different parts together How to create polyphonic dance music for a particular occasion.	Key contexts: • The Gamelan and Kecak Chorus • Music for the Chinese New Year Extension 1: • Bhangra and Beat Boxing Extension 2: • Dances in Binary and Ternary Forms (Local Folk Music) Extension 3: • STOMP	Prioritising thinking (cognitive) and doing (psychomotor) as logical and structural approaches to creating music. Composing: Can you compose polyphonic dance music that has a purpose? What works? Why?

is a sociocultural process, initiated through making connections with other people who are: 'functioning in a given historical or cultural context' (Antovic, 2009, p. 121), where existing and external musical knowledge can be shared, but then moving towards pupils sharing their own musical thinking through music making (Mills, 2005; Mills and Paynter, 2008). This approach supports the notion that music education is a process of development, rather than content to be transmitted or products to be measured (Kelly, 2009; Wyse et al., 2016).

Before continuing, undertake Task 13.5.

> **Task 13.5 Pupils' music thinking**
>
> Support beginning music teachers to identify where there is time for pupils to engage in musical thinking and to share their own music making in your scheme or unit of work.

Supporting learning through responsive pedagogy: teaching for learning

Where the needs of pupils are prioritised, teachers are able to become more responsive in their pedagogic approach. Base-level teaching for learning needs to be supported by an understanding of functional and procedural aspects of teaching, such as time management during a lesson, organising learning resources, and linking to the school systems for managing behaviour. In music education, teaching for learning can be seen when systems of scaffolding learning create the conditions for pupils to respond musically to a stimulus, sharing their musical thinking. Pupils' musical thinking can be shared through composing: 'part of the "real stuff" in music' (Mills, 2005, p. 45).

Composing opens up spaces for thinking in ways that move beyond the external expectations that frame performing or listening. Nevertheless, performing and listening are fundamental to a pre-generative stage where musical knowledge, aesthetic awareness, and a repertoire of composing techniques can be developed though the sociocultural interactions that underpin performing and listening (Fautley, 2005). During what Fautley (2005, p. 47) calls the pre-generative stage, the teacher has more control and ultimately more input, framing the composing that is to take place (Hallam and Rogers, 2010, p. 107). A scaffolding framework (see Table 13.2), based upon a scaffolding framework for writing identified by

Table 13.2 Pre-generative scaffolding

Intentionality	How can the musical learning be made 'real' and relevant to the pupils involved?
Appropriateness	Is the intention of the musical learning ethical and appropriate for the age group it is aimed at?
Structure	How can this initial musical learning be structured? What musical stimulus/examples can be used to model the intended musical learning? What questions could be asked? What activities are involved? Are they motivating?
Collaboration	How can pupils be involved in this pre-generative stage? Whole class ensemble? Whole class composing? Hot-seating (pupils with instrumental skills act as conduits for ideas from their peers)?
Internalisation	What musical knowing needs to be internalised for composing to begin?

Source: Based on Applebee and Langer (1983).

Applebee and Langer (1983), can help beginning music teachers to structure and support pupils' musical learning:

Underpinning the pre-generative stage for composing should be a focus on the intended learning. This intended learning is framed using conceptual musical vocabulary, moving from basic musical elements towards more complex musical devices, tonalities, and structures that underpin particular musical styles, genres, and traditions (see Table 13.1: *knowing about*). To make learning musical, there is a need to establish the interrelated nature of the concepts that underpin musical learning. Separation can result in unmusical outcomes. However, there is a danger that when too many concepts are covered within a lesson, cognitive overload (see Chapter 10) and confusion for the pupils can be the result. Therefore, a recommendation is that learning should remain focused on a particular conceptual term, particularly when lesson planning. A succession of conceptual terms (see Table 13.1: *knowing that*) can then inform a sequence of lessons that underpin the pre-generative stage. That is not to suggest that each term should be abstracted from a particular musical context but rather that the term is explored through a range of musical 'lenses' that illustrate how the concept can be used to promote 'choice' when pupils are composing. This provides an opportunity to include a range of cultural contexts through which to explore a concept (see Table 13.1: *Knowing about*). During this pre-generative stage, exploring is prioritised through performing and listening. There may even be shorter compositional exercises or whole class composing that feature during this exploration to further establish the intended learning.

The use of: '*An aural-oral transmission process* in which 'musics' are conceptualised and operationalised as sound' (Kwami, 1998, p. 168) during the pre-generative stage can help pupils internalise the intended learning through what Kolb (1984) calls concrete experiences. Pre-generative composing exercises should focus on the process of improvisation, particularly if pupils are going to compose using instruments and their voices as suggested in Table 13.1. Composing in the classroom as perceived here is as a process of moving from improvisation towards internalisation to establish ideas (Burnard, 2012; Burnard and Murphy, 2013). Improvisation can be daunting for those beginning music teachers who have come through an education system that prioritises conventional notation and performance. Their perceptions of improvisation are usually informed by particular types of music that include complex improvisations. However, improvisation can also be perceived as a type of musical 'play' that can be accessed by young children through singing and rhythm games (Marsh, 2013). This opens up the potential for exploring music making through improvisation for everyone, a strategy employed by Carl Orff where rhythm and improvisation underpin a music education using accessible tuned and untuned percussion instruments (https://www.orff.org.uk/). This approached is reflected in Table 13.1 where singing and vocal sounds are combined with tuned and untuned percussion instruments to compose dance music for a cultural festival. The festival can be chosen by the pupils to reflect their cultural background. Where groups are mixed, then the festivals prioritised during the pre-generative stage can provide useful starting points.

It is useful if pupils are provided with some form of booklet that enables them to gather and record ideas from the pre-generative stage. As a mentor, you can also encourage beginning music teachers to do the same. This will be particularly important for those beginning music teachers who lack confidence when composing. The conceptual terms that form the intended learning (*knowing that*) should be prominent within this booklet, but the priority is to create some form of 'composer's notepad' for the pupils so that they are able gather ideas that they have explored during the pre-generative stage through performing and listening. This is where notation systems can be introduced: 'with notation being used as a representational tool or aid' (Kwami, 1998, p. 168) rather than as a main priority. The structure of this booklet will vary according to the learning needs and/or age group of the pupils concerned, but for all pupils, there should be opportunities for them to provide their own input to promote thinking, assimilation, and accommodation. If the booklet is too rigidly framed, and knowledge just given, opportunities for diagnostic assessment on the part of the teacher are reduced. The booklet provides an initial opportunity for teachers to address misconceptions and establish the criteria for assessment that will underpin the composing activities. Throughout composing work of this nature, it is helpful if regular audio recordings are made of the class working. At these novice stages working directly in and with sounds, then recording sound directly is likely to be of use. It is important to emphasise that the booklets being described here are not intended to replace audio recordings from the pre-generative stage. Neither should they replace the teacher/pupil dialogic interactions that accompany reviews of these audio recordings. The booklet is intended to complement these audio recordings which are seen as a foundational aspect of contemporary classroom music education.

Audio recordings of pupils performing and composing are powerful motivational tools in classroom music education. They engender the intrinsic motivation for 'critical engagement' (ISM, 2015, p. 6). Relevant pupil booklets can be addressed while listening to audio recordings made during the pre-generative stage. This listening can be included as homework tasks if recordings are available using some form of virtual learning environment. Beginning music teachers need to be aware of the ethical/legal issues that surround the sharing of data in public spaces, but schools have protected spaces where files can be shared safely. These safe spaces are invaluable to enable pupils to respond to audio recordings of their music making.

Before continuing, complete Task 13.6:

Task 13.6 Composing notepads

Ask beginning music teachers to plan the initial stages of a pupil booklet for the pre-generative stage in a scheme/unit of work. Use Tables 13.1 and 13.2 to support this process.

After the pre-generative stage pupils engage with an initial confirmatory phase (Fautley, 2005, p. 48). This is where they can think about distributing the musical 'parts' that are required. The impact of music education is significantly reduced if pupils are asked to engage in the same activities for assessment purposes. This ignores the distributed nature of musical activity and reduces the potential to replicate 'real-life' music scenarios. Even when technology is involved, pupils need the opportunity to think about music texturally and structurally, recognising the role of different 'parts' within a texture and different 'sections' within a structure in order to create a musical whole. Group composing can bring this thinking to the fore. To support learning, mentors may wish for beginning music teachers to take more control of this distributed process. Music 'conductors' or 'directors' can be identified within pupil groups to challenge those pupils who have more confidence and/or who have had more opportunities to develop their musicality. Cognitive off-loading happens when pupils allow others, or 'tools' like computer software or electronic keyboards that produce ready-made musical riffs, to do the work for them (Pea, 1993). Cognitive off-loading can be avoided by carefully matching parts and/or roles to particular pupils. In the context of Table 13.1, questions during an initial confirmatory stage might include: Who is 'directing' the group? Who is playing what instrument? Are you including voices? Who is providing the 'beat'? Pupils need to 'record' their group organisation. This will help them to remember this organisation for the following lessons, but it will also provide initial evidence for the teacher to monitor how the group dynamics are developing. This record can feature in the relevant pupil booklet.

Before reading further, think about Task 13.7.

Task 13.7 Beginning composing

Ask beginning music teachers to plan an initial confirmatory stage. How will musical resources be distributed across pupil groups?

Pedagogic priorities for social justice: teaching as learning

During group composing in the classroom, pupils respond to the pre-generative stage by generating their own ideas (Fautley, 2005, p. 48). This is where teachers step back and learn from the pupils. Providing choice is an important aspect of this generative stage; by opening up spaces for thinking through choice can be highly informative for the teacher. Pupils' perceptions are revealed. When the pedagogic principles of collective, reciprocal, supportive, cumulative, and purposeful talk through dialogic teaching are prioritised (Alexander, 2008, p. 185), communities of thinking and learning are created. Promoting thinking happens when the teacher asks questions. Referring back to Table 13.1, some questions might include:

- Why are you using these instruments? How are you organising the instruments?
- Is the balance between the different patterns working?
- How can you add variety to your repeated patterns?
- What if you changed the texture?
- What if one pattern changed to become a lead or melody?
- How could the other patterns form a backing or accompaniment?
- What is your structure?
- Why? (see Chapter 10)

Now, complete Task 13.8:

Task 13.8 Teaching composing

Ask beginning music teachers to plan some questions to support pupils during their generative stage of a composing activity (Fautley, 2005, p. 48). Questions should highlight the intended learning.

A phase of 'organisation' (Fautley, 2005, p. 49) occurs in classroom composing after the generation of ideas. This can build upon the initial confirmatory phase and can supported by teacher interventions that centre on organisational questions (see examples above). There needs to be opportunities for pupils to share their initial ideas through a 'work in progress performance' (Fautley, 2005, p. 49). The timing of this performance will depend on the response from the pupils. If too many groups are missing the point, then the class can be brought together again, and a sampling process can take where teachers purposefully select groups that are demonstrating progress to reinforce a focus on the intended learning. The statement of intended learning becomes its own success criteria, in other words it self-produces a notion of formative assessment. Ideally, these criteria are applied in a flexible, evaluative, and dialogic manner wherein pupils offer their own perceptions by using 'supportive, appropriate, fair, and encouraging' (or SAFE) comments. During any initial evaluative stages, the focus on enabling the composers to hear and comment on their own through audio recordings work should be prioritised. Teachers may wish to establish a system where only positive comments or 'strengths' are gained from peer reviews and it is the composers themselves that identify the 'weaknesses and next steps' (a SWANS review) by listening to their own recordings. Pupils can then return to revise, modify, and even transform their initial ideas so that the intended learning or criteria for assessment is made more explicit within the context of their composing.

The final phase within classroom composing is the 'final performance' (Fautley, 2005, p. 50). This is not to be mistaken for the end of a learning journey and so assessment can still include evaluative comments that promote development. However, teachers may be required to provide a grade that summarises a pupil's progress. This might relate to future examination criteria and will depend on the requirements of a particular context. Harpaz emphasises the importance of 'concluding performances' (Harpaz, 2014, p. 114) at the end of any learning episode for pupils. Performances can take place in the context of any subject and act as a 'complex demonstration of understanding' (Harpaz, 2014, p. 114). His perception is framed by three categories of performance (Table 13.3).

Table 13.3 Understanding performances

	Category 1 **To present knowledge**	Category 2 **To think on and with knowledge**	Category 3 **To criticise and create knowledge**
Description 1	To express knowledge in your own words	To analyse and synthesise knowledge	To give reasons why and justify knowledge
Description 2	To explain knowledge	To apply knowledge	To expose contradictions and tensions in knowledge
Description 3	To suggest interpretations of knowledge	To suggest example, metaphor, analogy and comparison	To question knowledge
Description 4	To build a model for knowledge	To generalise form detailed knowledge	To reveal basic assumptions of knowledge
Description 5	To represent knowledge in various ways	To contextualise knowledge	To formulate contradictory knowledge
Description 6	To present perspectives of knowledge	To predict on the basis of knowledge	To create knowledge on the basis of knowledge

Source: Harpaz (2014, p. 115).

In classroom, music pupils are sharing their perceptions of knowledge through both their composing and dialogic interactions with their teacher and their peers. These categories of performance can be applied to live final performances of composing or computer-generated composing. The focus is on how pupils demonstrate their understanding of knowledge and not their technical performing skill. In the context of Table 13.1 and the age group it is aimed at, most pupils will demonstrate aspects of category one but the six descriptions that appear in category one will help Beginning music teachers to frame appropriate questions to enhance the pupils' demonstration of understanding. Pupils should be able to express knowledge through their music, even if they cannot put it into words, and the knowledge being searched for should relate to the criteria for assessment or intended learning. This means that musical knowledge is expressed in the medium of intentionality, in other words, through and in music. In the context of Table 13.1, the focus is on how pupils create patterns and texture in their music. This knowledge can be interpreted in a variety of ways but looking for how pupils manage the balance between repetition and variety is important. How do they make their composing interesting? Do they include syncopation and how is their music structured?

Before reading further, think about Task 13.9.

Task 13.9 Questions to promote thinking

Ask beginning music teachers to plan some questions to support pupils' demonstration of understanding during their final performance stage. Questions should highlight the intended learning.

Concluding comments

Harpaz emphasises the importance of 'fertile questions' (2014, p. 93) to create thinking communities. A fertile question is one that is: 'open, undermining, rich, connected, charged and practical' (Harpaz, 2014, p. 93). The fertile question for Table 13.1 is: Can you compose polyphonic dance music that has a purpose? There is not an expectation that pupils create a pastiche but draw upon a range of ideas to create their own music for a particular purpose. This promotes an inclusive approach to cater for pupils from a mix of cultural backgrounds, moving away from standardisation and social mobility towards a perspective where variety is recognised and valued leading to a focus on social justice (Benedict et al., 2015). This inclusive pedagogy encourages pupils to share their perceptions of the music they have previously explored through their own composing. This can lead to surprising results often reflecting an intercultural perspective that goes beyond what the teacher first envisaged:

> Where students and teachers engage with different types of music in the classroom or the community - play with it, rather than look at it as though through binoculars - the creation of a new type of music through fusion is a normal musical outcome.
>
> Mills (2005, p. 151)

This does not remove the need for a teacher to frame the learning by introducing knowledge to and exploring knowledge with pupils but pupils' learning is at the centre of any teaching activity. As pupils begin their composing, the teacher as a provider of knowledge is gradually replace by the teacher who responds to and even learns from the pupils 'interpretive activity' (Harpaz, 2014, p. 74). The ultimate aim is to provide the conditions where every pupil becomes someone; 'who knows how to relate to and manipulate knowledge' (Harpaz, 2014, p. 81).

What we have shown in this chapter is that *knowledge* is a key and central component of teaching and learning in classroom music. In these days of 'knowledge-rich' curricula, there exists the potential danger that knowledge is perceived simply as being knowledge 'about' music. Throughout this chapter, it is hoped that the notion of music as an activity, involving making music, is an important, if not central component of interest. The place of what there is it to learn, and what there is to do to support this learning, is something that beginning music teachers need to get to grips with in the classroom during the early stages of their professional journeys. The role of the mentor is to help them with this process, and this can involve sometime uncomfortable self-reflective questions about the nature of *what* is being taught and learned and *why* this is the case. This what might be termed philosophical approach to teaching and learning will be ultimately of benefit to the beginning music teachers, but experience has shown that many mentors find it helpful too!

Summary and keypoints

- Musical learning as an active process is emphasised by the use of active verbs, identified by Fautley and Daubney (2015). Musical learning is viewed as a social constructivist process, where pupils are supported to move towards independence.
- Defining knowledge as knowing helps beginning music teachers to become attuned to recognising different forms of knowing through praxial musicking and pupils sharing their own music.
- Supporting learning through responsive pedagogy: teaching for learning focuses on defining perceptions of scaffolding, so that beginning music teachers can engage in systematic ways of enabling access and promoting independence.
- Pedagogic priorities for social justice: teaching as learning informs beginning music teachers about the value of stepping back and allowing pupils to make and share their own musical judgements through the power of choice.
- Concluding comments emphasise to beginning music teachers the importance of inclusive pedagogies that help pupils to think about their music making.

Further resources

1. The third edition of *Learning to teach music in the secondary school: A companion to school experience* (Cooke et al., 2016) provides a comprehensive overview of music education for both mentors and beginning music teachers. The opening four chapters are particularly useful when exploring perceptions of musical learning. Chapter 8, on creativity and music education, also relates to the contents of this chapter.

2. *Debates in music teaching* (Philpott and Spruce, 2012) includes a number of sections that deal with different aspects of music education. Part 3, on the pedagogy of music, would be particularly pertinent for beginning music teachers when they are thinking about supporting pupils learning, but they may also wish to explore Parts 1 and 2 to help them to place their thinking about music education on a secure footing.
3. *The guided reader to teaching and learning music* (Savage, 2013) has a very helpful structure, identifying key reading with summaries; questions to consider; investigations; think deeper; think wider. Chapter 2 through to Chapter 4 relate to supporting pupils learning, but Chapters 5 and 6 provide important perspectives on how support can be extended and enriched.
4. *Music creativities in practice* (Burnard, 2012) provides a comprehensive overview of the rich diversity of music practices that exist, challenging a view that music education should be taught through particular, narrowly defined musical pathways. This resource will support beginning music teachers to question whether they are being sufficiently inclusive in their approach.

14 Facilitating and leading effective discussions with beginning music teachers

Nikki Booth

Introduction

Holding regular and effective pre- and post-lesson discussions with beginning music teachers and engaging and guiding them in the critical reflective process are all key components for developing quality teaching. Teaching, therefore, evolves as an organic process. Not only is having these conversations important but, for the most part, they should be mentee-led rather than mentor-led. With this in mind, this chapter primarily focuses on the notion of facilitating discussions with your mentee; explores various progressive routes into how you can understand, suitably question, support, and challenge the beginning music teachers you work with in the critical reflective process; and, where appropriate, lead discussions effectively in more difficult situations. Although this chapter deals primarily with face-to-face discussions, the information and strategies provided here can also be applied, and adapted where necessary, to online settings.

Objectives

By the end of this chapter, you will be able to:

- facilitate discussions where you understand how different levels of challenge and support can lead to different outcomes for a beginning music teacher;
- facilitate discussions where you know how to identify a phase of development for a beginning music teacher and provide suitable challenge and support to move their practice forward;
- facilitate discussions through video recording lessons and developing early reflection skills;
- facilitate discussions through video recording lessons and using activity theory to develop critical reflection to move a beginning music teacher's practice forward; and
- lead discussions with beginning music teachers in more difficult situations.

Facilitating effective discussions through understanding and supporting the phases of development for the beginning music teacher

Challenge and support are two areas which are key for the successful development of a beginning teacher (Daloz, 2012). Challenge can come through dialogue by means of, for example, questioning the beginning music teacher and enabling and guiding them to critically reflect

Table 14.1 Outcomes of different levels of challenge and support

	Low support	High support
High challenge	**Retreat**	**Growth**
	The beginning teacher is unlikely to cope with the demands of the challenge.	In order for the beginning teacher to develop effectively.
Low challenge	**Stasis**	**Confirmation**
	Development for the beginning teacher is extremely limited.	The beginning teacher is unlikely to move beyond where they are now despite the potential for growth.

Source: Adapted from Daloz (2012).

on their own current views, behaviours, and attitudes towards teaching and learning. Asking a beginning teacher to reflect is very difficult and they will require support; you will need to actively listen and encourage them to find their own solutions in order to grow. According to Daloz (2012), there are different outcomes depending on the level of challenge and support given by a mentor, as Table 14.1 exemplifies:

Based on Daloz's (2012) work, it clear is that, as a mentor, you need to be aware of both the level of challenge and support you give to the beginning music teacher. Once you have established what the appropriate level of challenge and support would be for the beginning music teacher to 'grow', you can then start thinking about their phases of development.

Before reading further, undertake Tasks 14.1a and b.

Task 14.1a Discussing and planning for growth of a beginning music teacher

Beginning teachers will always need different levels of challenge and support in order for them to 'grow' successfully. Discuss with the beginning music teacher their experiences of teaching so far. What would they say their current strengths and areas for development are? What challenge and support do they feel they require at this point of their journey?

Task 14.1b Reflecting and planning for growth as a mentor

If mentoring a beginning music teacher is a relatively new journey for you, consider what challenge and support you might need in order for you to 'grow' successfully. Discuss with another professional who has some experience of mentoring what their experiences are. What challenge and support did they receive in order to fulfil this important role?

A particularly useful model for understanding the phases of growth for a beginning teacher is Katz's (1995) development model which consists of four stages: survival stage, consolidation stage, renewal stage, and maturity stage, as exemplified in Table 14.2: (see also chapter 1).

Table 14.2 Stages of development model

Developmental stage	Examples
Survival	• Very self-focused. • May be reluctant to take responsibility for things and, therefore, blame others (pupils, colleagues, the school, for example). • Confused. • Lack of clear routines and rules in lessons. • May demonstrate little consistency to behaviour management. • Teaching is heavily teacher-orientated with a reluctance to come away from the lesson plan script.
Consolidation	• Beginning to implement clear routines and rules in their lessons. • Starting to question their own teaching practice. • Being more open to alternative ways of doing things. • Lessons are generally well-managed. • More awareness of individual pupil needs which are being catered for. However, there is still a developing need for pupils with specific needs, for example, pupils with Special Educational Needs and/or Disabilities (SEND), English as an Additional Language (EAL), or more able pupils.
Renewal	• More self-aware and self-critical. • Regularly finding ways in which practice can be even better. • frequently seeking and embedding more creative and innovative activities into lessons. • Self-motivated and contribute to departmental (or even whole school) discussions, offer suggestions to others, design resources for themselves and others, become involved as a whole-school member of staff (for example, a lunch-time or after-school club).
Maturity	• Develops and regulates their own teaching style, strategies, and beliefs. • Questions themselves for deeper reflection. • Has an interest in the regular impact of their teaching and pupil progress.

Source: Adapted from Katz (1995).

It is important to note that although Katz's (1995) model uses the term 'stages', this can be somewhat problematic; to some, the term might represent development as a linear structure where progress can only move forward. The problem is that this is hardly ever the case. Instead, the term 'phases' within the notion of a spiral might be more appropriate when discussing development and growth, as Daubney and Fautley (2015) make clear in the context of a pupil's musical progression. The important point when thinking about growth within a spiral is that it can move forwards and backwards as well as up and down. This is likely to occur when, for example, the beginning teacher teaches different aspects of the music curriculum where they have less knowledge or confidence compared to others, as well as starting to teach at a new school. In short, if a beginning music teacher has moved backwards or downwards this does not necessarily mean that there are not developing, but more like they have shifted their position on the spiral.

Before reading further, undertake Task 14.2.

> **Task 14.2 Identifying the current phase of development and planning for support**
>
> Following Katz's (1995) developmental model, there are responsibilities for both you, as a mentor, and the beginning music teacher. Using the list of examples in Table 14.1 as a starting point, identify which phase the beginning music teacher is currently working at and consider what support you need to give to support their ongoing growth. If possible, discuss with them the next unit of work. Is this something they feel confident in teaching? In relation to Katz's (1995) developmental model, where might the beginning music teacher's position on the spiral change to? What support might you be able to offer in advance of this unit taking place?

Although a beginning music teacher might need a lot of support initially, you need not only advise them, but ask questions and give them thinking time in order for them to arrive at and devise their own solutions to move their teaching forward. This is an important aspect for you to consider because research suggests (for example, Mena et al., 2017) that all too often mentors tend to dominate discussions which can limit the development of the beginning teacher. As such, creating and engaging beginning music teachers in effective discussions where they are developing their practice through critical reflection is a learning dialogue which is a fundamental aim for their growth (Caddick, 2017).

Facilitating effective discussions through developing early reflection skills

According to Black and Plowright (2010, p. 246), reflection is:

> the process of engaging with and/or professional practice that provides an opportunity to critically analyse and evaluate that learning or practice. The purpose is to develop professional knowledge, understanding and practice that incorporates a deeper form of learning which is transformational in nature and is empowering, enlightening and ultimately emancipatory.

Similarly, according to Boulton and Hraniak (2012), teachers who explore critically why they do things, for example, making links with learning theories and considering why they might or might not use them in their future practice, move from evaluation to reflection. As such, beginning teachers need to learn to evaluate and question their own beliefs in light of alternative, and even more effective, methods of teaching (Hobbs, 2007). For you, as a mentor, it is also important you are aware of any pre-conceived ideas the beginning music teacher might have as to what high-quality music education might look (or sound) like. As such, you need to make a deliberate effort to understand the beginning music teacher's beliefs and attitudes so that you can begin to relate to their thinking.

Before reading further, think about Task 14.3.

> **Task 14.3 Discussing beliefs about music education**
>
> In a meeting with the beginning music teacher, ask them to write down what they consider are the three most important aspects of a high-quality music education, and why. You do the same. Share this information with one another and discuss each of your answers. Encourage the beginning music teacher to reflect on why they have given these answers.
>
> At the end of the discussion, what did you learn about the beginning music teacher's beliefs? What did you learn about your own beliefs as a result of this discussion taking place?

Posing questions during pre- and post-lesson discussions and asking them to explain and justify the rationale behind the lesson activities and pedagogical approaches is an effective way of developing the beginning music teacher's ability to reflect, particularly in the early phases. It is also an effective way of beginning the discussion. It is important, however, that in developing the beginning music teacher's reflection skills they are given appropriate thinking time. For example, during a pre-lesson meeting it could be particularly beneficial to ask the beginning music teacher to re-read the lesson plan (or PowerPoint) and consider why they made certain decisions about lesson content and teaching strategies. Similarly, following a lesson, if the beginning music teacher had to deviate from the lesson plan (which can be perfectly acceptable) why was this and what did they do that was a suitable alternative? This will provide a good basis for the discussion which then follows. Upon hearing the beginning music teacher's reflection, this will allow you to pose open questions that will establish a learning dialogue. As a result of this dialogue, and you sharing your own ideas and experience, this may lead to appropriate adaptations of the lesson direction and/or choice of pedagogical decisions. The important point, however, is that, as a result of the beginning music teacher's reflection, they largely arrive at the decisions themselves.

For the beginning music teacher, daily reflections are key and allow the opportunity for them to frequently identify strengths and areas for development which can then be used to inform the next lesson. Furthermore, it can be argued that reflecting immediately after a lesson, even for just a few minutes, is crucial in facilitating reflection; it allows the beginning music teacher to consider three main ideas: What went well? What areas for development are there? How can areas for development be strengthened? It is important that these fundamental questions are established with the beginning music teacher from the start, especially because there is usually very little time between lessons, also the beginning teacher's phase of development (see Table 14.1) would need to be taken into account. That said, video recording lessons, for example, is a highly useful tool which allows for powerful and deep reflective discussions to take place.

Before reading further, think about Task 14.4.

Task 14.4 Supporting a beginning music teacher's reflective practice

Before attending a pre-lesson mentor meeting, ask the beginning music teacher to re-read their lesson plan (or PowerPoint) and then discuss with them their decisions behind the lesson content and teaching strategies.

In a post-lesson meeting, ask the beginning music teacher to consider these main ideas: What went well? What areas for development are there? How can areas for development be strengthened? Did they have to deviate from the lesson plan? Why was this? How did they deal with that situation? What did they do instead that was a suitable alternative?

One of the most promising methods to develop self-reflective practice is videoing lessons (Welsch and Devlin, 2012). Using video recording provides a unique opportunity for the beginning teacher to play and re-play the lesson(s) and clearly identify strengths and areas for development which might not have been spotted under the traditional post-lesson reflective discussion. In fact, Harford *et al.* (2010) argued that video 'captures the immediacy of the classroom, offering detailed and rich data on the teaching and learning process' (p. 59). Similarly, for you, as a mentor, you are able to support the beginning music teacher in developing their reflective skills. Reflective collaboration between mentor and mentee, it has been argued, has the greatest impact on reflection (van Es, 2012). An important point, however, is that this not just about you giving feedback; rather the beginning music teacher watching themselves and discussing *their* reflections with you. In other words, for an effective discussion to take place, it should be beginning teacher-led, rather than mentor-led.

There are two key issues that need to be considered when thinking about video recording lessons: first, video recording can be a sensitive issue, particularly for pupils, and permission should be sought for it to take place; and second, recorded lessons are better when they are done over a period of time throughout the year; the beginning music teacher will, perhaps, be an even more willing participant in the process, and you will have become even more comfortable in assisting them in the reflection process. As a result, these can lead to better development. As Harford *et al.* (2010) state above, the use video-recorded lessons will provide detailed and rich information about the teaching and learning process. What is needed, then, is an appropriate framework to ask detailed and focused questions to deepen the reflective discussion in order to allow you, and the beginning music teacher, to share reflections and thoughts effectively.

Before reading further, think about Tasks 14.5a and b.

Task 14.5a Supporting the beginning music teacher with a video reflection

Ask the beginning music teacher to organise the recording of a lesson with a class of their choice. Following the lesson, ask them to do an initial reflection of the lesson based on the post-lesson reflection points listed in Task 14.4 above. In a mentor meeting, watch the lesson (or as much of it as you can/need to) together and ask the beginning teacher to discuss with you their reflections. What similarities and differences are there between your observation thoughts and the beginning music teacher's reflections?

Task 14.5b Mentor reflection for supporting the beginning music teacher with a video reflection

Think back to the mentor meeting you had with the beginning music teacher for Task 14.5a. How effective would you say your questioning was? What challenge and support did you offer the beginning teacher to help them move into the next phase of their development? In addition to challenge and support, what praise did you offer them? How effective was this discussion in helping the beginning music teacher to develop their critical reflection skills? Following this discussion, what would you say your strengths and areas for development are as a mentor?

Using activity theory to lead and facilitate effective, deep, and critically reflective discussions

The origins and development of activity theory

Activity theory is rooted in the work of Vygotsky (1978) whose focus was on a triadic interaction between the *subject, object* and *tool(s)* (artefacts), as shown in Figure 14.1:

Within the triangular model:

- the *subject* represents a person whose perspective is the focus;
- the *object* is the goal of the activity system; and
- the subject and objects are influenced by *tools* (mediating artefacts).

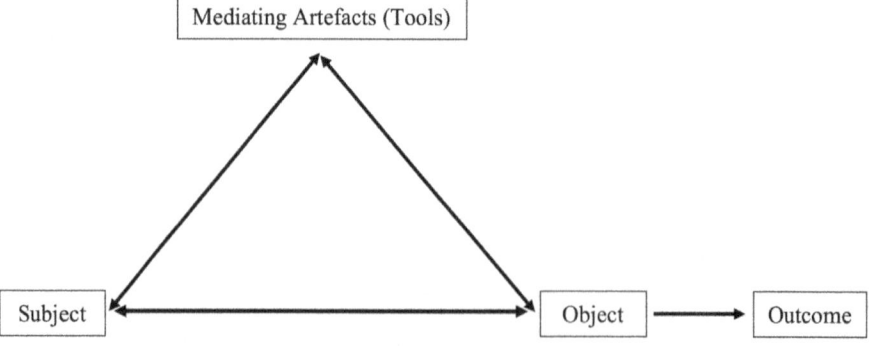

Figure 14.1 Activity Theory model (adapted from Vygotsky [1978])

Vygotsky's original activity theory model provides a framework in which social and cultural practices can be considered with regards to how individuals learn by engaging in these practices as well as how tools (for example, physical tools such as writing, technology, or a musical instrument, or mental tools like gestures, expressions or language via questioning and/or discussion) are mediated to shape human activity.

Some might argue (for example, socio-constructivists) that we are not individuals who 'interact with our environment on a purely biological basis' (Wilson, 2014, p. 21), but that we engage and interact with our environment based on the mediation of other people and the context of which we live (Wilson, 2014). Following Vygotsky, an 'Activity System' (Figure 14.2) was developed by Leont'ev (1978) and subsequently Engeström (1987). This is because 'mediation by other human beings and social relations [were] not theoretically integrated into the [original] triangular model of action' (Engeström and Miettinen, 1999, p. 4) nor did it suitably present the complex interactions of an activity system (Asghar, 2013). This is particularly the case within the classroom setting which has to account for 'different identities, intelligences, modes of learning and pedagogical processes' (Kinsella, 2015, p. 36). Within this updated system, Leont'ev distinguishes between 'action' and 'activity' where 'action' is conducted by an individual, and an 'activity' is undertaken by a community to fulfil a goal (Bakhurst, 2009).

In addition to *subject*, *object*, and *tools* described above:

- the *community* is where the activity system belongs or takes place;
- the *rules* characterise the behaviours and norms (for example, the dos' and the don'ts) within the community; and
- the *division of labour* relates to hierarchical power structures and social relations within the system as well as how labour is divided.

According to Gedera (2016), using activity theory within an educational context requires changes to activity theory terminology. This is because Engeström's framework is limited to work-related contexts and, therefore, in Gedera's (2016) view, the terminology does not

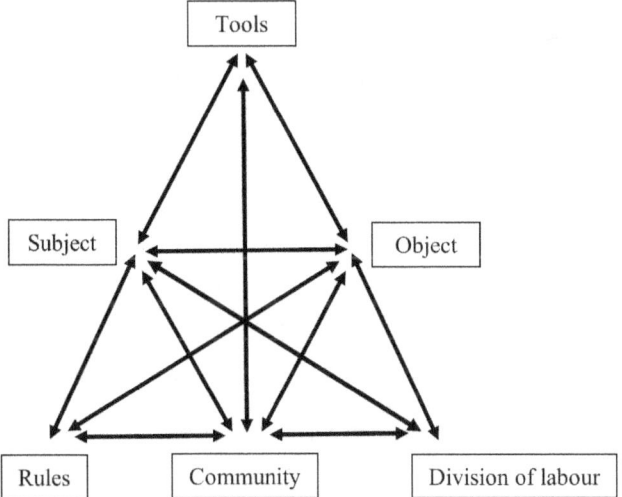

Figure 14.2 Engeström's (1987) activity system model (adapted)

translate into an educational context. For example, the term 'object' is used in place of 'objective' to refer to the purpose of an activity. Furthermore:

> Semantically this use can be considered correct; however, practically, in referring to the purpose of an activity in a classroom, this creates confusion as the term object can mean a real object (i.e. a computer or a book) ... In Activity Theory the term object means a purpose or an objective of an activity.
>
> Gedera (2016, p. 59)

Gedera (2016) also asserts that to avoid any confusion with the use of activity theory terminology within educational contexts the following adaptations (shown in Table 14.3) are considered for clarification:

Within education, Wilson (2014, p. 23, italics in original) gives the following description to clarify the notion of activity theory within the classroom:

> [A] class teacher *(subject)* wishing to improve pupils' achievement *(object)* within a particular school *(community)* might want to introduce a new strategy for learning *(tool)*. Depending on the management structure within the school *(division of labour)*, the teacher may be constrained on the basis that the new idea is seen as deviating from implicit norms *(rules)*, or encouraged if the attitude within the school is to support innovation – also an implicit *rule*.

An activity system does not remain static; in the example provided by Wilson (2014) above, if the new learning strategy proved to be successful, it may become developed by other teachers within the school thus becoming a rule within the school. Furthermore, as Cole and Engeström (1993, p. 8) assert:

> [schools] appear to reproduce similar actions and outcomes over and over again in a seemingly monotonous and repetitive manner that gives cultural constraints on action a seemingly overpowering quality. However, closer analysis of apparently unchanging activity systems reveals that transitions and reorganizations are constantly going on within and between activity systems as a fundamental part of the dynamics of human evolution.

Table 14.3 Clarified activity theory terminology for use in educational contexts

Activity theory element		
Engeström (1987)	Gedera (2016)	Description (Gedera, 2016)
Object	Participant	The main participant(s) of the activity.
Tools	Tools	These can be physical (instruments), mental (a plan), symbolic (language).
Object	Objective	The purpose of the activity
Rules	Rules	These are the norms, practices, and expectations that may control or influence interactions within the activity system.
Community	Community	This represents the co-participants of the activity, for example, peer-pupils.
Division of labour	Roles	The distribution of responsibilities towards the objective. Roles also refer to status and power relations.
Outcome	Outcome	This is the desired results of an activity. Objectives are transformed into an outcome through the mediation of tools.

Consequently, activity systems are best viewed as complex formations in which equilibrium is an exception and tensions, disturbances, and local innovations are the rule and the engine of change. When an activity system is followed through time, qualitative overall transformations may also be found.

What this shows is that by unpicking each component of the activity system, you are making visible the complex and multifaceted nature of the music classroom and are able to critically analyse, reflect and question teaching and learning approaches with the beginning music teacher. What will happen, therefore, is that during the process of examining each component of the activity system you will identify, describe, and problematise *contradictions*.

Contradictions within the activity system

By analysing each node of the activity system, tensions and contradictions between each of the nodes are revealed and are important for the beginning music teacher (as well as teachers in general) to develop and change (Postholm, 2015). Such disruptions can be identified which may affect the process of teaching and learning and, therefore, allow opportunities for the development of practice (Addison et al., 2015). Engeström (2001) refers to these contradictions as 'aggravations' where current existing practices (or norms) are questioned, probed, challenged, and reflected on in order to develop a new viewpoint. He writes:

> [a]s the contradictions of an activity system are aggravated, some individual participants begin to question and deviate from its established norms. In some cases, this escalates into collaborative envisioning and a deliberate collective change effort. An expansive transformation is established when the object and motive of the activity are reconceptualised to embrace a radically wider horizon of possibilities than the previous mode of activity.
>
> Engeström (2001, pp. 136-137)

Pohio (2016) asserts that of all the elements within the activity system *tools* arguably play the most central role in research investigations. This is also the case within some music education research. For example, Burnard and Younker (2008) found that lower-secondary school pupils (aged between 10 and 12 years) tended to focus on 'choice and use of instruments and knowledge to drive compositional ideas' (p. 72). This was not the case, however, in research by Devaney (2018, p. 283) where, in composing music for accreditation towards a national qualification:

> teachers expressed frustration with the examination many felt obliged to TTT [teach to the test] due to high levels of accountability, even to the detriment of their students' learning.

Whilst Cole and Engeström (1993) posit that the inclusion of *rules* is important within an activity, Fautley and Kinsella (2016) warn that rules of an activity can potentially 'dominate practice' (p. 30), with Burnard and Younker (2008) additionally cautioning that *rules* could limit and constrain actions. In light of formative assessment to move musical learning forward, Kinsella and Fautley (2016) observed that, in a multi-session project, where pupils were engaged in composing for examination purposes, teacher comments were far more focused on matters which were directly related to task completion, whereas comments from professional composers brought into the lessons were more grounded on the quality of the outcome of the task. In their findings, what this meant was that composers dealt more with the composing process, and the teacher on the completion of the composition. Furthermore, they found that teacher-based dialogue was more focused on keeping pupils on task by ensuring that they knew how much time they had left and what they still needed to do. Composers, on the other hand, were observed using higher-order questions relating to composing techniques and musicality, that is '... what they did and why they did it, and of how the resultant composition emerges from such procedural choices' (Fautley, 2014, p. 201). As has been previously mentioned, by analysing the separate components of the activity system we are able to make clear and visible the complexities of the music classroom. The information you and the beginning music teacher elicit from the analysis, then, can be reflected upon, discussed, and used as an effective means for moving the beginning teacher's pedagogical practice forward.

Using activity theory as a framework to move teaching and learning forward

Using the information presented above and adapting Kinsella's (2015) work for the art and design classroom, Table 14.4 uses the activity theory framework and shows a list of starting-point questions, on each of its components, to allow for an effectively deep and critical reflection by the beginning music teacher. Depending on when the reflective discussion is due to take place, the questions are in pre- and post-lesson format.

Table 14.4 Starting-point reflective questions using the activity theory framework

Activity theory component	Pre-lesson critically reflective questions for the beginning music teacher	Post-lesson critically reflective questions for the beginning music teacher
Activity	• What musical learning activity would you like to plan? • How does it fit into the overall unit of work?	• What musical learning activity was planned? • Where did this activity fall in terms of the overall scheme of work?
Objective	• What is the purpose of getting pupils to do this activity? • How will pupils' musical progression develop as a result of doing this activity? • What musical knowledge, understanding, and skills will be needed as a prerequisite for this activity to be a successful learning opportunity?	• Why was it important for pupils to do this musical activity? • Did pupils' musical progression develop as a result of doing this activity? If so, how? • Did pupils possess the relevant musical knowledge, understanding, and skills for the activity to be successful?
Participant(s)	• Who will be involved in carrying out this activity? Is it a whole-class, group, paired or individual activity? Why is this the best choice for this activity? • Is everyone going to do the same activity? How might differentiation be used effectively here for differing learning needs?	• How was the activity organised? Was it whole-class, group, paired, or individual? Was this the most effective way of organising this activity? Why? • Did everyone do the same activity? How was differentiation planned for and used to help support differing learning needs during the activity?

(Continued)

Table 14.4 (Continued)

Activity theory component	Pre-lesson critically reflective questions for the beginning music teacher	Post-lesson critically reflective questions for the beginning music teacher
Tools	• What learning resources (for example, success criteria, instruments) will be needed for pupils to carry out this activity successfully? • Are these tools predetermined? By whom? • Will pupils need support in being able to use these tools successfully? • What pre-planned questions might be asked of pupils to help develop their musical progression?	• What learning resources were available to pupils for the successful completion of the activity? • How were these tools used during the activity? • Did some pupils need any additional support with using the tools of the activity that was, perhaps, not foreseen? How was this dealt with during the activity? • What sort of questions were asked to pupils during the activity?
Rules	• What cultural/social/political rules will govern the music activity? Who will determine these? (For example, will pupils follow teacher guidelines when engaged in the activity, or will some rules also be pupil-orientated?) • How might difficulties with these rules be overcome for an effective teaching and learning experience?	• What rules were evident during the activity? (For example, did pupils follow the teacher guidelines? Were there any points where rules needed to be adapted to enhance learning for some pupils? Did pupils have the opportunity to create their own rules? What was the impact of this on their learning?) • Were there any points during the activity where the rules may have hindered learning?
Roles	• How will roles be organised in this activity? (For example, is everybody going to have the same role or might some pupils take a leading role in group work? If this is the case, why these pupils?) • What will your role be as the (beginning) music teacher?	• How were roles organised during the activity? If roles were different for some pupils, how effective was this? • What was your role as the (beginning) music teacher? How effective would you say your role was during the activity?
Community	• How will the roles discussed in the row above be supported? • Where will this activity take place? (For example, will everybody be in the music classroom, or will pupils go to practice rooms?) • How will the learning environment act as a supportive learning mechanism?	• What support was needed to support the rules discussed in the row above? • Where did the activity take place? Was this the most effective way of enhancing musical learning for this activity? • How was the learning environment used as a supportive learning mechanism?
Outcome	• What will the desired learning outcome be for this activity? • How will you (the beginning music teacher) and the pupils know this outcome has been reached? • How will feedback to pupils be elicited and used effectively throughout this activity?	• What was the desired learning outcome for this activity and did it differ in any way from the actual learning outcome? • How did you (the beginning music teacher) and the pupils know that the learning outcome had been met? • What feedback was elicited and given to pupils during the activity which helped move their musical learning forward?

Source: Adapted from Kinsella (2015).

Before you continue, consider completing the following two tasks, 14.6a and 14.6b.

Task 14.6a Using the activity theory framework for a deep and critical pre-lesson discussion with the beginning music teacher

In advance of a mentor meeting with you, give the pre-lesson questions (shown in Table 14.4) to the beginning teacher and ask them to use them to reflect on a lesson they are yet to teach. If not completely relevant, the list of questions should be adapted to suit the needs of the school context, and pupils, as well as the developmental phase of the beginning music teacher.

In the meeting, discuss with them their responses to the questions. What contradictions have become evident within the activity system as a result of the discussion that need to be considered before the (next) lesson takes place?

Task 14.6b Using the activity theory framework for a deep and critical post-lesson discussion with the beginning music teacher

Ask the beginning teacher to video record a lesson of their choice. In advance of a follow-up mentor meeting, give the post-lesson questions (shown in Table 14.4) to the beginning music teacher and ask them to use them to reflect on the lesson. If not completely relevant, the list of questions should be adapted to suit the needs of the school context, and pupils, as well as the developmental phase of the beginning music teacher.

In the meeting, discuss with them their responses to the questions. If the beginning music teacher has struggled with this particular level of reflection, arrange to watch some of the videoed lesson with them. What contradictions would the beginning teacher say became evident during the activity? Discuss with them how these contradictions might be overcome the next time a similar activity takes place.

Leading effective discussions with beginning music teachers in more difficult circumstances

It is unfortunate that relationships between mentor and mentee sometimes break down. Although there can be many reasons for this, the main reasons can be said to relate to differences in expectations (for example, professionalism), breakdown in trust, and occasionally clashes of personality. In cases such as these, how discussions are led and managed are important for continued professional working. What follows is two examples of difficult circumstances with possible solutions.

The non-reflective beginning music teacher

Whilst you may mentor many beginning music teachers who develop consistent reflective practice you may work with one who can be described as non-reflective. Furthermore, as

Hobbs (2007) makes us aware, there may be beginning teachers who value the notion of reflective practice but simply do not know where to start, whereas others may be capable of self-reflective practice but choose not to do so and see it as a pointless exercise.

The differing levels of strategies discussed within this chapter will help you support a beginning music teacher who values self-reflection but is not capable of doing it. A fundamental point may have arisen here in that the beginning teacher may not be where you (and even they) have thought they are in terms of the phases of development. Similarly, the notion of challenge may be too great for the beginning music teacher in which they may require additional support. For example, arranging reflective practice workshops or allowing the beginning teacher to observe you and co-reflect in a follow-up meeting can offer valuable insights into developing practice. Furthermore, you could provide your mentee with a sample of reflective journals of varying quality and the beginning teacher has to rank the accounts in terms of reflective quality. By doing this, you are exposing the beginning music teacher to the underlying thinking behind good reflective practice.

Supporting beginning music teachers who are capable of reflecting but do not see the value in it is challenging. A key role for you, as a mentor, is to convince your mentee the important role reflective practice has on a teacher's professional development. In short, as Wiliam (2015) asserts: '[all] teachers need to improve, not because they're not good enough, but because they can be even better'. This is an important stance to take as it makes it clear that good reflective practice is something that *all teachers* do and not just those at the beginning of their teaching career. Getting the beginning music teacher to observe you, making a note of strengths and areas for development, and co-reflecting in a post-lesson meeting might be an effective way of breaking down this barrier. It would be important for the beginning music teacher to witness first hand that lessons might not go as well as we have anticipated. The discussion which follows would be important for the beginning music teacher to understand how you reflect and how you will be addressing the issues (or contradictions) in the next lesson as well as the valuable opportunity for you to explain your pedagogical decisions. Leading by example in this way would be a valuable way of showing clearly that all teachers need to reflect.

Planning

A beginning music teacher who continuously relies on you to provide lesson resources, asks for an excessive amount of feedback on planning, or does not submit lessons plans (when appropriate to do so) might not be showing the professionalism that you would expect. This may affect the progress of a class and you may find that you are needing to sort things out. Naturally, this will cause you frustration and additional pressure which may affect the working relationship with the beginning teacher. In scenarios such as this, you need to understand why this is causing the beginning music teacher a problem and this may require a sensitive discussion. The important point is how you move forwards and it may be that you need to provide modelling as scaffolded support of the planning process which can then be gradually removed overtime. You would also need to review the expectations of the beginning music teacher and, where necessary, closely monitor them, so they are aware of their professional responsibilities and maintaining a positive working relationship with you.

Disagreements

We cannot agree all of the time. However, you might find that a beginning teacher disagrees with your thoughts and/or comments, challenges your teaching decisions, or even discusses this with other colleagues. Whilst you should always be open to feedback to improve your practice (even from beginning teachers), it could be how the feedback is articulated which might be the problem for you. As such, you should avoid taking the feedback personally. In such cases, it would be important for you to gain a clearer understanding as to why the beginning music teacher is thinking that way. Depending on what has been said, you may feel uncomfortable with the beginning music teacher discussing lessons in such a way with other colleagues. Again, it would be important to discuss with them why they are making the comments and, where necessary, establish clear boundaries.

However, if you are particularly concerned about this, a conversation with a more senior member of staff (or line manager) might be useful. In any case, you need to be aware of the guidance your school has on having difficult conversations and how you, as a mentor, can be best supported when the need arises. As mentioned above, setting clear boundaries and re-establishing expectations might be all that is required, however, in the rarest circumstances, you may need to consider how you can extract yourself from the relationship completely.

Task 14.7 Reflecting on leading discussions in challenging circumstances

Think about the challenging scenarios discussed above or an additional one of your own. How might you, as a mentor, deal with leading a difficult conversation? Write down a description of what you would do and discuss your thoughts with another colleague (for example, your line manager or another colleague who is experienced in mentoring beginning teachers).

Summary and key points

- Challenge and support are two key areas for the successful development of a beginning music teacher:
  - Challenge can come through, for example, questioning and enabling and guiding them to think critically;
  - You need to actively listen to support, however you must also be mindful that beginning teachers should, as often as possible, find their own solutions in order to grow. This is important because some mentors have been found to dominate discussions with mentees.
- According to Katz (1995), there are four phases of development: survival, consolidation, renewal, and maturity. With each phase comes a deeper level of critical discussion between mentor and mentee.

- Beginning music teachers who explore critically why they do things move from evaluation to reflection.
- For an effective reflective discussion to take place, thinking time is important to allow the beginning music teacher to think deeper and more critical about their practice.
- In the early stages of reflective discussions, there are three useful starting-point questions that can lead to a meaningful discussion:
    - What went well?
    - What areas for development are there?
    - How can these areas for development be strengthened?
- Videoing lessons can be a highly effective way of capturing and discussing in detail strengths and areas for development.
- Using activity theory as a framework offers a focused, detailed, and critical way of moving teaching and learning practice forward.
- Identifying contradictions in the activity system allows opportunities for the development of practice to be discussed.
- Sometimes, relationships between mentor and mentee breakdown. It is important that any difficult discussions are led effectively and, as often as possible, problematised to find a working solution, in order to secure a continued positive working relationship.

Further reading

Lawrence, J. (2017) 'Reflecting on your teaching', in Jolliffe, W. and Waugh, D. (eds.) *NQT: The beginning teacher's guide to outstanding practice*. London: Learning Matters.

This is a short chapter on engaging beginning teachers in the reflective process.

O'Leary, M. (2014) *Classroom observation: A guide to the effective observation of teaching and learning*. Abingdon: Routledge.

This book provides clear guidance on observations, discussions and critical reflections.

Kinsella, V. and Fautley, M. (2016) 'The use of activity theory as an analytical tool for the music learning processes', in Bugos, J. (ed.) *Contemporary research in music learning across the lifespan: music education and human development*. Abingdon: Routledge, pp. 26-38.

This is a chapter exploring the use of activity theory in the music with a particular focus on classroom composing.

Spendlove, D., Howes, A., and Wake, G. (2010) 'Partnerships in pedagogy: Refocusing of classroom lenses', *European Journal of Teacher Education*, 33(1), pp. 65-77.

This is an academic article exploring how activity theory can act as a meaningful tool for a beginning teachers' professional preparation.

SECTION V
About moving beginning music teachers on

15 Using formative assessment effectively to see the wider picture

Nikki Booth

Introduction

Engaging beginning music teachers in the critical reflective process and regularly acting upon areas for improvement is an important part of their development as a professional; therefore, it is part of the formative assessment process. What can happen, though, is that lessons (and learning) might be seen as separate, isolated learning events rather than a series of phases which occur overtime. Given that there is substantial research evidence to suggest that formative assessment can have a significant impact on pupil outcomes, this chapter looks at how you, the mentor, can scaffold the beginning music teacher in helping them see the wider picture, and how you can support them in developing the ability to make meaningful inferences about learning, not only between lessons, but during them, also. Although this chapter deals primarily with in-school lessons, the information and strategies provided here can also be applied, and adapted where necessary, to remote learning settings.

Objectives

By the end of this chapter, you will be able to:

- explain and give examples to a beginning music teacher so that they can see assessment as both a process and product of teaching and learning;
- explain and give examples to a beginning music teacher so that they can see a variety of starting points for pupils not just one;
- explain and give examples to a beginning music teacher so that they see lesson planning as a means for what pupils are doing to learn not just do;
- explain and give example to a beginning music teacher so that they see pupils' musical progress as something which happens overtime not just in a lesson; and
- explain and give examples to a beginning music teacher so that they see learning through the eyes of their pupils not just themselves.

Seeing assessment as a process not just a product

Before reading this section, discuss the following questions in Task 15.1 with the beginning music teacher during a mentor meeting.

186 Mentoring Music Teachers in the Secondary School

> **Task 15.1 Understanding assessment in music**
>
> 1. What are their own memories of assessment at school? What did this look (or sound) like in music compared to other subjects?
> 2. What do they understand by the term "assessment" and has this understanding changed during their teacher training? If so, how?
> 3. How often can assessment occur?
> 4. What is the difference between summative and formative assessment and what might this look (or sound) like in music?
> 5. How can assessment information be used to improve teaching?
> 6. How can assessment information be used to improve pupils' learning?

In general terms, "assessment" can be seen as the collection of evidence(s) in order to make some sort of judgement. Typically, as Figure 15.1 shows, a beginning music teacher (or even yourself, perhaps) may hold the view that assessment only occurs at the end of the teaching and learning cycle, that is, at the end of a unit of work which might be referred to as "assessment week" or the "assessment lesson". This is when, for example, pupils produce a "product" by doing a listening test or end-of-topic performance or a composition and from this collection of evidence it is ascertained exactly what and how well pupils have learned and move on to the next topic.

Fautley labels this separation of assessment from the teaching and learning cycle as the "folk view of assessment" (2010, p. 3) where assessment takes place at a series of fixed-points during the school year in order to determine pupil progression. The issue with this "folk view" is that it "downgrade[s] teachers' judgements" (Fautley, 2010, p. 4) by placing the complexities of learning into such a narrow-focused, single event (the half-termly "assessment lesson", for example). Whilst these "products" (also commonly referred to in schools as *summative assessments*) are indeed important, valuable evidence, as shown in Figure 15.2, can also be collected before this point by means of, for example, teacher observations of and frequent conversations with pupils. In other words, assessment can also take place *within* the process of teaching and learning and not just after it. As such, this can be said to be *formative assessment*.

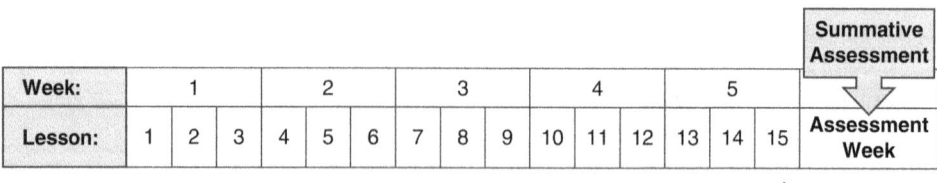

Figure 15.1 Assessment *after* the teaching and learning cycle (taken from Booth, 2019, p. 412, and used with permission)

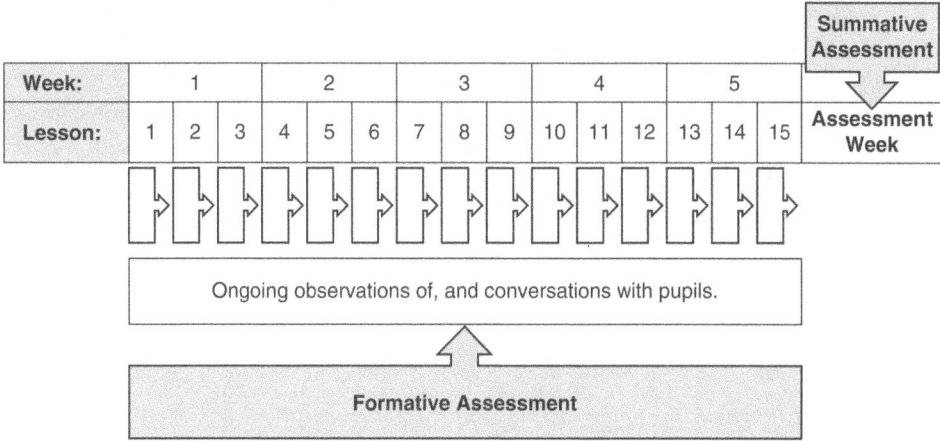

Figure 15.2 Assessment *within* the teaching and learning cycle (taken from Booth, 2019, p. 413, and used with permission)

For many years, research literature has pronounced summative and formative notions as descriptions of assessment. For example, in performing a piece of Bach on the piano, a summative assessment would typically refer to what score or grade the performance is, and a formative assessment would normally refer to the comments given to the pupil to improve. However, more recent thinking (for example, Black and Wiliam, 2018) suggests that these two notions are better when referred to as *inferences* of assessment. Taking the performing example above, it could be inferred that the pupil's right-hand technique is secure, however they seem to have particular difficulties with the left-hand. If this is the only inference made then this is a summative assessment; it relates to the status of the pupil since it has been "summed-up" that they are good at one thing and not another. What could also happen as a result of eliciting this information is that the pupil could be provided appropriate technical exercises to develop further the left-hand technique. Where formative assessment takes place, in this example, is not only that a developmental point has been identified, but, more importantly, that opportunities have been provided to practise and get better. In other words, for formative assessment to be truly *formative*, the information elicited has to be acted upon. The difference between summative and formative as "inferences" rather than "descriptions" of assessment is important because a mode of assessment (whether an observation of group composing or listening test, for example), according to Black and Wiliam (2018), cannot really be said to be summative or formative until inferences are drawn from the information collected.

Despite the change of definition, there is over 50 years' worth of research evidence to suggest that formative assessment, when used effectively, can have a significant impact on pupil outcomes (Wiliam, 2016). An important aspect of formative assessment is that it is not just for beginning music teachers to see whether learning is heading in the right direction and to use information to inform and change the direction of teaching, but requires pupils, and their peers, to take greater responsibility for their own learning, also. From this, it becomes clear that assessment can also be a process and involves working *with* pupils, so they understand where they are at in their current learning, where they need to be, and how they are going to get there. Through frequent and responsive formative assessment, you can support the beginning music teacher to see a much wider picture of ongoing and developing pupil learning on a lesson-by-lesson, even minute-by-minute, basis, something which cannot be done with single "assessment lesson" events. An appropriate starting point for making valuable inferences, therefore, would be at the beginning of the lesson. Consider undertaking Task 15.2 as a reflective activity in a mentoring session.

Task 15.2 Reflecting on the effective use of assessment in music

During a follow-up mentor meeting, ask the beginning music teacher to identify some summative and formative inferences they had made during the last week with a range of classes. What did these inferences tell them about moving teaching and learning forward? On further reflection, is there anything they would have done differently that might have had an even greater impact on pupils' learning? Why?

Seeing a variety of starting points for pupils not just one

With your support, it is important for the beginning music teacher to recognise that pupils will bring with them a lot of different prior experiences with them into the classroom. For example, outside of normal curriculum music lessons, some pupils may have instrumental or vocal lessons, some may engage in group-based social jamming even though they do not have additional peripatetic lessons, some may compose their own music, some might enjoy listening to certain genres of music either by themselves or in friendship groups, and some may have musical relatives who support and encourage music outside of school. Other pupils, of course, may not do or have any of these things. Furthermore, some pupils learn things quicker than others. The important point is that, as a class, pupils will not have the same starting point whether it is at the beginning of the lesson or even a new unit of work.

Your role in supporting the beginning music teacher to establish the range of pupils' starting points is an important one for effective formative assessment to take place. As Ausubel (1968, p. vi) comments:

> ...if I had to reduce all the educational psychology to just one simple principle, I would say this, The most important single factor influencing learning is what the learner already knows. Ascertain this and teach him [or her] accordingly.

Pupils build new knowledge from what they already know (Fautley, 2010) and by establishing the level of knowledge they have prior to beginning a lesson or new unit of work can carry with it certain benefits to enhance learning. For example:

1. What pupils already know can be taken to a deeper level of understanding;
2. Any misconceptions, from previous learning experiences, can be identified and corrected before the new, or correct, learning takes place; and
3. Current gaps in knowledge can be established before new learning takes place.

What follows is a useful strategy for you to consider, discuss, trial, problematise, and then embed within the beginning music teacher's practice as they continue to develop.

Entrance tickets

The best way to find out what pupils have learned is to ask them. Entrance tickets (or entrance passes), for example, can be a very useful formative strategy to quickly identify where all pupils in the class are currently in their learning based on previous learning experiences. Although oral questioning is a particularly powerful teaching strategy, it, perhaps, will not be as effective at this particular point; the idea here is to have an idea as to where *all pupils* are as a starting point, something which cannot be done effectively with large classes of pupils without slowing the pace of the lesson right down. Whilst pupils are responding to a given task on, say, scrap paper, post-it note or mini whiteboard, you can encourage the beginning music teacher to walk around the room, look at pupils' responses, and build up as knowledgebase as to who already knows and understands what, and establish what misconceptions or gaps (if any) there are which need to be addressed.

In music, entrance tickets can be used effectively for supporting teaching and learning in listening and appraising, composing, and performing activities as the following figures (Figures 15.3–15.5), taken from Wolgarston High School, Staffordshire, show. For example, at the

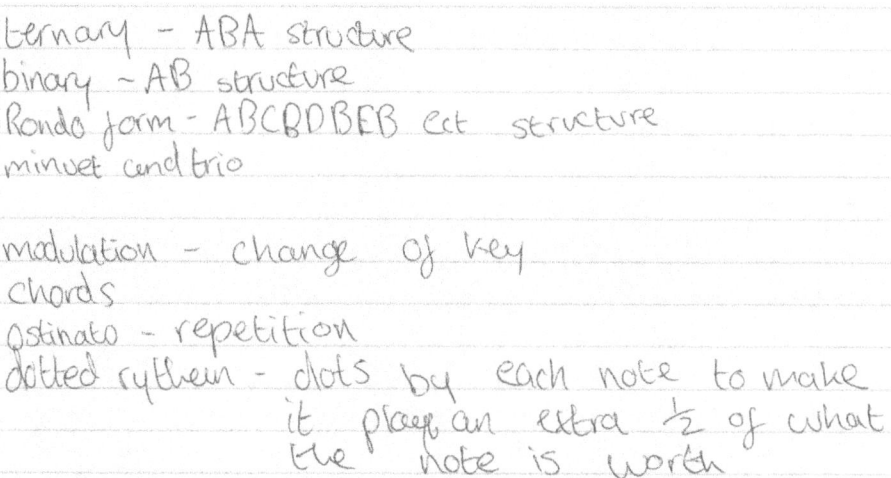

Figure 15.3 Pupil 1 example Year 10 entrance ticket, used with permission

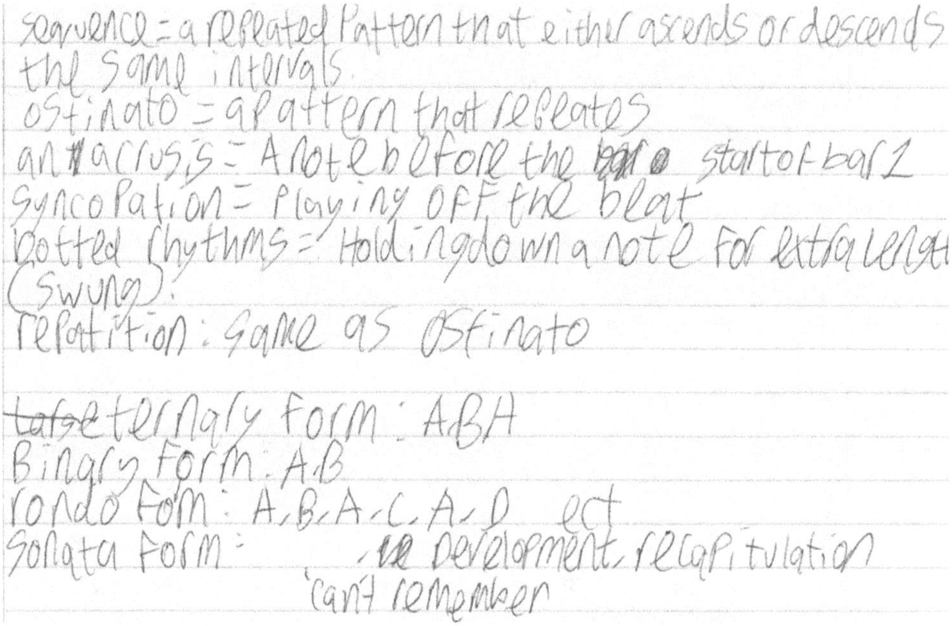

190 Mentoring Music Teachers in the Secondary School

> sequence = a repeated pattern that either ascends or descends the same intervals.
> ostinato = a pattern that repeats
> anacruss = A note before the start of bar 1
> syncopation = Playing off the beat
> dotted rhythms = Holding down a note for extra length (swung).
> repatition: same as ostinato
>
> ~~tage~~ ternaly form: ABA
> Binary form: AB
> rondo form: A,B,A,C,A,D ect
> Sonata form: , te Development, recapitulation
>   'can't remember

Figure 15.4 Pupil 2 example Year 10 entrance ticket, used with permission

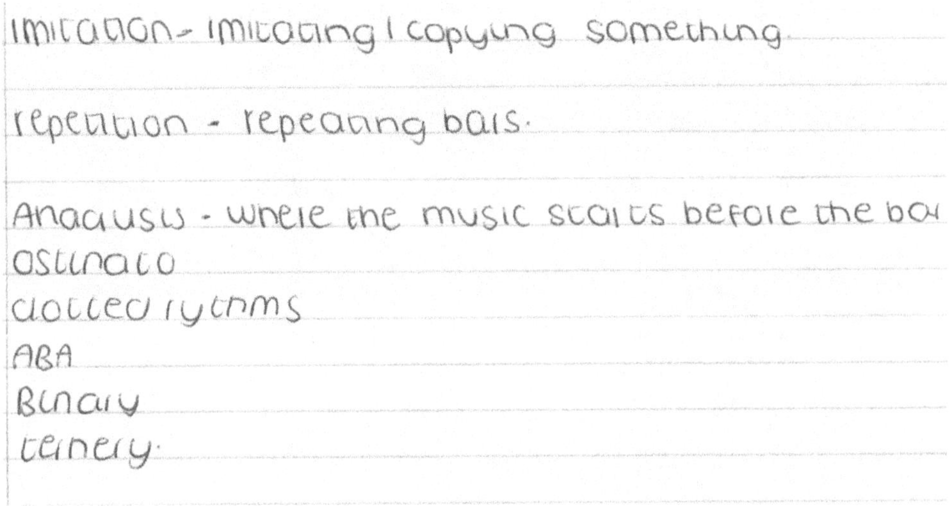

> Imitation - imitating / copying something.
>
> repetition - repeating bars.
>
> Anacusis - where the music starts before the bar
> ostinato
> dotted rythms
> ABA
> Binary
> ternery.

Figure 15.5 Pupil 3 example Year 10 entrance ticket, used with permission

beginning of a new unit of work on musical structures and devices, this teacher asked his Year 10 musicians to list as many musical structures and devices as they could, with examples to demonstrate their understanding of each one. Samples of what pupils wrote are shown below.

From looking at pupils' responses, it is clear that Pupil 1 could correctly identify and describe three musical devices, however was unable to define what chords were. Similarly, with musical structures, the pupil had a clear understanding of Ternary and Binary forms, however was not sure how to define Minuet and Trio and they also had a misconception as to how the Rondo structure is organised. Pupil 2 knew and understood a larger number of musical devices and structures by comparison to Pupil 1. In this particular case, however, they forgot "exposition" as part of the sonata form structure. Pupil 3, on the other hand, could identify some musical devices and structures, however, appeared to struggle with showing an understanding as to what these key terms were. From eliciting this evidence, it is clear that, based on previous learning experiences, these pupils are beginning the new unit or work from very different starting points and because this particular teacher had an idea as to who knew and understood what, they could respond accordingly.

A beginning music teacher who is not supported in how to effectively use this information formatively will just carry on with what they have planned with little regard for pupils' needs. The likely consequence of this, for some pupils, will be boredom and disengagement. Effective pre-planned questioning (Fautley, 2009), though, can be a highly useful tool for meeting a variety of learning needs without creating additional, last-minute workload. For example, if the beginning music teacher had already planned the first lesson of the new unit of work on binary and ternary forms and it was revealed, from looking at the entrance ticket responses, that approximately 50% of the pupils already appeared to know and understand these terms, it needs to be considered, then, as to what these pupils are going to learn from this lesson that they, perhaps, *do not* already know, and how their current understanding can be deepened further. As such, supporting the beginning music teacher to develop a range of pre-planned, progressive questions, which can be shared visually with pupils on a PowerPoint slide, for example, can help cater for the variety of different starting points, as Figure 15.6 shows.

Listening Activity

Listen to the following piece of music. Choose the question you are going to answer from the appropriate column.

I'm just getting started	I already know a little bit	I think I'm ready for a challenge!
1. Identify the structure of the piece. Is it: a) Binary (A-B), or b) Ternary (A-B-A)	1. Identify the structure of the piece and give musical reasons for your choice.	1. Identify the structure of the piece and describe the similarities and differences for each section you hear.

Figure 15.6 Example of progressive questions for different starting points, used with permission

192　*Mentoring Music Teachers in the Secondary School*

The aim of responding to entrance ticket replies like those shown above is to make teaching more effective by developing a wider picture as to where learning currently is and where it needs to go for pupils with different starting points. As can be seen from Figure 15.6, this does not mean completely different activities, for some pupils, so that they know more; it focuses on knowing things at a deeper and analytical level. Although the beginning music teacher could simply pre-plan a range of progressive questions without the use of entrance tickets, you could suggest to them that they would, in fact, be unsure whether some pupils were just taking the easy route and that the beginning music teacher would not have the information to challenge any pupil who does this. Furthermore, having read the entrance ticket response examples above, you could suggest to the beginning music teacher that they would also become more aware that there are learning gaps and misconceptions with the Rondo, Minuet and Trio, and Sonata Form structures, something, you might suggest, which can be effectively planned for in future musical lessons.

Exit tickets

Just like entrance tickets can give useful information at the start of the lesson, exit tickets (or exit passes), which take place at the end of the lesson, can be equally meaningful for developing a wider picture of learning. For example, following Year 9 group composing (Figures 15.7 and 15.8) and Year 10 Solo Performing (Figures 15.9 and 15.10) lessons at Wolgarston High School, Staffordshire, pupils reflect on their work at the end of the lesson.

In the Year 9 group composing exit tickets, where one pupil would be nominated as the "scribe" to represent the views of all members of the group, we can see that one group (Figure 15.7) spent quality time listening to their work-in-progress composition and identified areas for development which they could respond to next lesson. They also said that they included

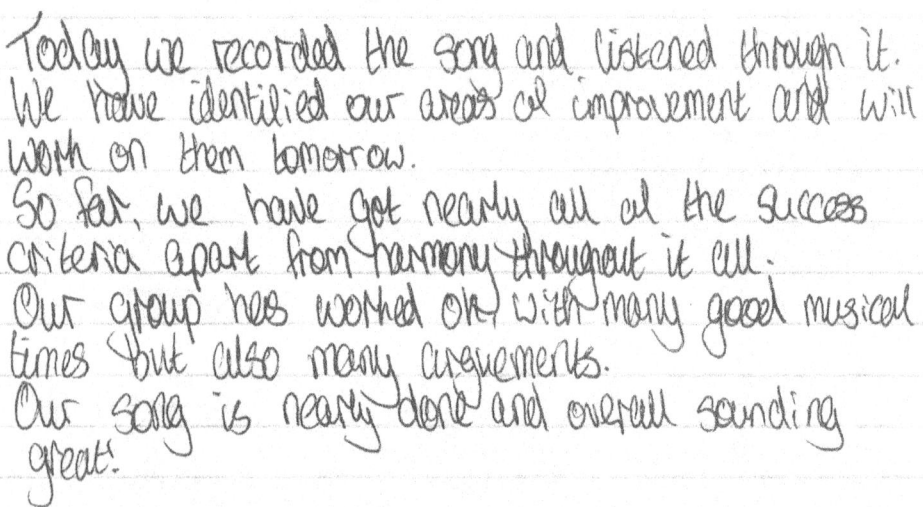

Figure 15.7 Pupil 4 example exit ticket after a Year 9 group composing lesson, used with permission

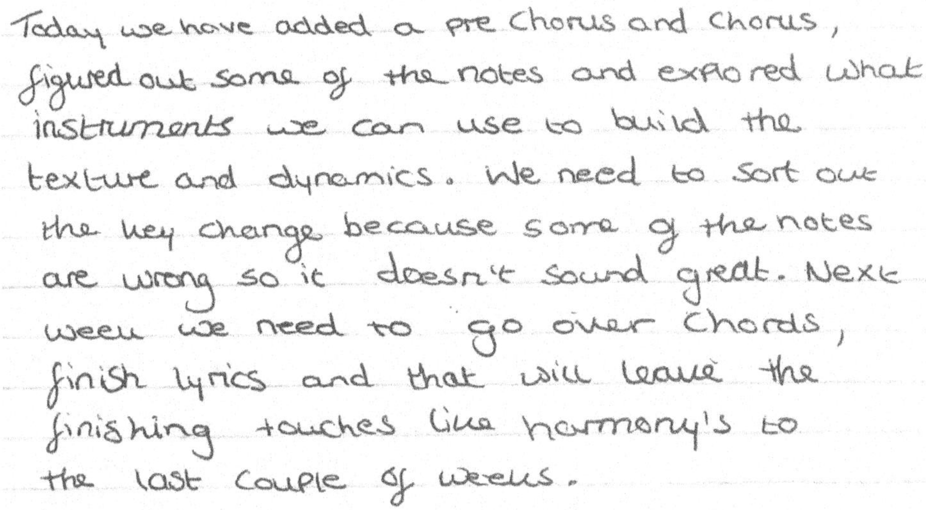

Using Formative Assessment Effectively to See the Wider Picture 193

> Today we have added a pre chorus and chorus, figured out some of the notes and explored what instruments we can use to build the texture and dynamics. We need to sort out the key change because some of the notes are wrong so it doesn't sound great. Next week we need to go over chords, finish lyrics and that will leave the finishing touches like harmony's to the last couple of weeks.

Figure 15.8 Pupil 5 example exit ticket after a Year 9 group composing lesson, used with permission

a lot of the success criteria, although they recognised that harmony still needed some work. If this were the beginning music teacher's lesson, you could suggest that this is a meaningful agenda to discuss with the pupils during the next lesson. For example, they could check whether the success criteria have been addressed in the composition, they could find out exactly what the areas for development were, and also provide support as to how these, as well as their group's comment about using more harmony in the piece, could be turned into strengths. Similarly, with the second group's reflection (Figure 15.8), it seems that they spent time working on the structure of their song as well as considering how their instruments could be used effectively to build texture and dynamics. If this were the beginning music teacher's lesson, you could suggest that they listen to how this is developing as well as provide support for the group in helping with how their choice of notes fit into the key change. Following this same idea, in the Year 10 Solo Performing exit tickets (Figure 15.9) you could suggest to the beginning music teacher that the pupil could be supported with how to maintain a

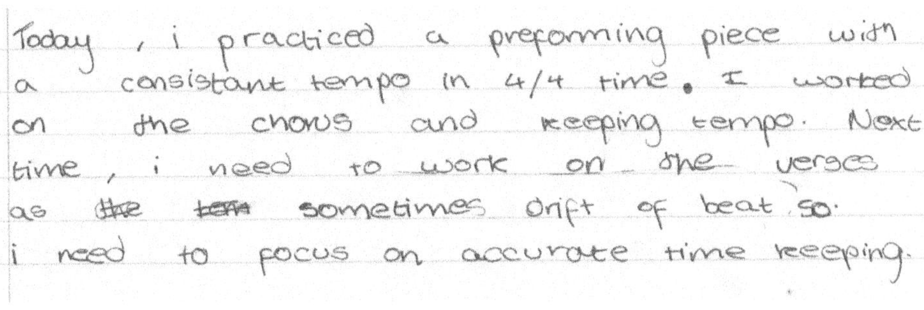

> Today, i practiced a preforming piece with a consistant tempo in 4/4 time. I worked on the chorus and keeping tempo. Next time, i need to work on the verses as the tem sometimes drift of beat so. i need to focus on accurate time keeping.

Figure 15.9 Pupil 6 example exit ticket after a Year 10 solo performing lesson, used with permission

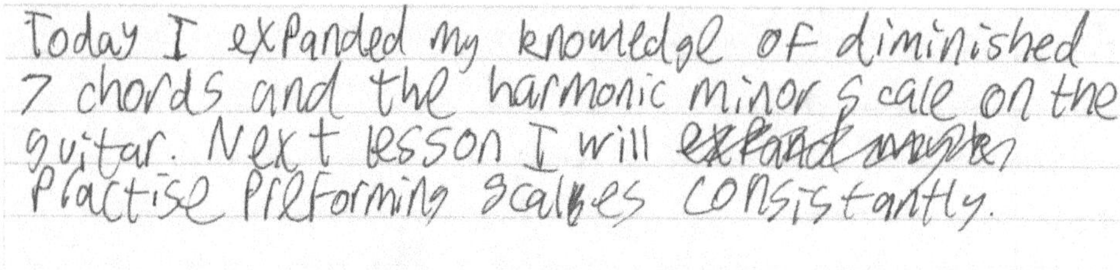

> Today I expanded my knowledge of diminished 7 chords and the harmonic minor scale on the guitar. Next lesson I will ~~expand maybe~~ practise performing scales consistently.

Figure 15.10 Pupil 7 example exit ticket after a Year 10 solo performing lesson, used with permission

consistent tempo going from chorus to verse sections, and how Pupil 7 (Figure 15.10) could be supported with their scale playing.

As cited previously, Ausubel (1968) comments that the most important factor for influencing learning is establishing where the pupils currently are, and it is the teacher's job to discover this and to teach accordingly. As such, by supporting the beginning music teacher to use a technique such as an entrance or exit ticket, not only are they seeing a wider picture by collecting valuable information as to what learning has occurred (whether in the past or during the lesson itself) but, more importantly, they are using the information to make appropriate adjustments to their teaching to better meet pupils' learning needs. The notion of what pupils are going to *learn* and what they are going to *do* needs somewhat unpicking, however. Now do Task 15.3.

Task 15.3 Eliciting and using meaningful evidence to plan next steps in teaching and learning

Ask the beginning music teacher to use the entrance or exit ticket strategy, if they do not do this already. In a follow-up mentor meeting, discuss with them the following reflective questions:

1. What was the beginning music teacher hoping to find out by using this strategy?
2. What did the entrance or exit ticket tell them about teaching and learning that they did not already know?
3. How did the beginning music teacher respond to the information gathered from the tickets?
4. What was the impact of this?
5. How might the use of entrance and/or exit tickets be used even more effectively next time and how could the information gathered be used to better meet pupils' needs?

Seeing lesson planning as a means for what pupils are going to learn not just do

Once pupils' starting points have been established the next step in supporting the beginning music teacher is to consider the notion of "beginning with the end" by sharing and clarifying the learning intention(s) (also commonly referred to as learning objectives or learning outcomes) for the lesson. Writing clear learning intentions is important because, as Wiliam and Leahy (2015, p. 27) make clear:

> ...[b]efore we can find out what our learners are learning, before we can give feedback, before we can engage learners as resources for one another or as owners of their own learning, we have to be clear about where we are going.

Wiggins and McTighe (2005) found the notion of "backwards design" an excellent way to maximise learning; by being clear about what pupils are going to learn at the end of the lesson formative assessment can be used regularly to change the direction of teaching as and when the need arises. Furthermore, since "[t]he indispensable conditions for improvement are that the student comes to hold a concept similar to that held by the teacher" (Sadler, 1989, p. 121) it seems a very good idea for pupils to understand the learning intention(s) behind the lesson's tasks and activities.

Although the purpose of the learning intention(s) is to make explicit what is being learned, this will be very hard for a beginning music teacher and will, therefore, require a lot of support from you; it is easy to say what pupils will be *doing*, but more difficult to say what they are going to *learn* by doing it. Fautley and Savage (2007) provide a very useful model (shown in Figure 15.11) which will help in your discussions with the beginning music teacher to help separate the difference between learning-focused learning intentions and task or activity outcomes (which are "doing" focused). It is important to point out that Fautley and Savage (2007) also include the notion of pupils' prior knowledge, which has been discussed previously in this chapter. This is of immense importance for effective formative assessment to take place; decisions about how to structure and sequence future learning can be appropriately made. In their own words, referring to Figure 15.11:

> [t]he questions in the boxes on the left-hard side of the diagram take you through a series of issues concerned with learning. The boxes on the right of the diagram *inform* [italics in original] your answers to these questions by focusing your attention onto task issues but again, notice that the tasks are there to help with learning.
>
> Fautley and Savage (2007, p. 33)

A learning intention which is too vague, for example, "We are learning how to compose scary music" is not that helpful, but, equally, learning intentions which are too specific like "We are learning how to use high pitch, slow tempo, eerie timbres, silence, quiet and loud dynamics, harsh harmonies within a ternary form structure" encourage "atomistic learning which does not see the bigger picture" (Stobart, 2014, p. 93). With this in mind, when writing clear, learning-centred learning intentions, there are two key aspects which need to be taken into consideration during your discussions with the beginning music teacher.

Following the work of Clarke (2005), the first issue to overcome is including the context within the learning intention itself. For example, in a Year 8 music lesson, a learning intention of "To (be able to) compose a piece of music in the Blues style" would be considered confused. In Clarke's (2005) view pupils who have been working on this, maybe even for several lessons across the half-term, are likely to do well at the end of the unit – but so what? This is a key question for you to discuss with the beginning music teacher because we are not really be

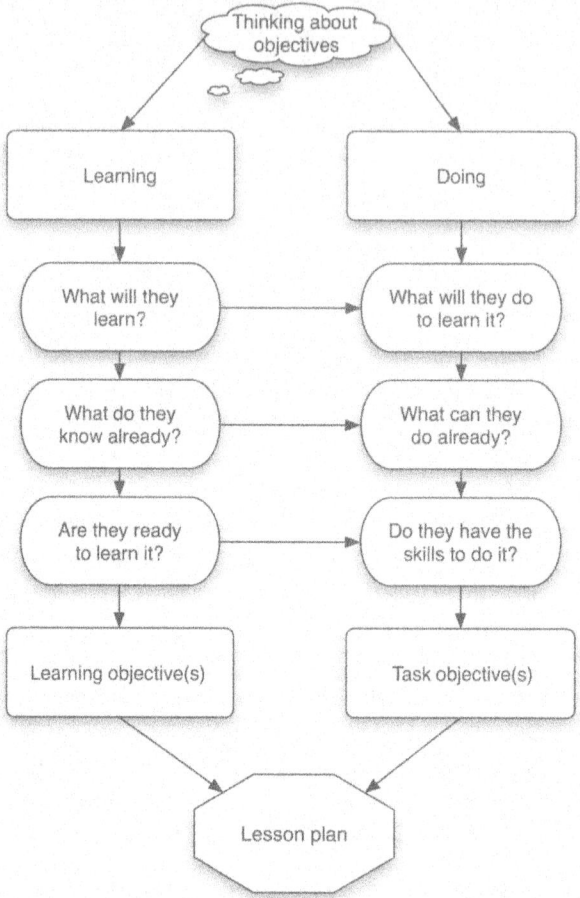

Figure 15.11 Separating *learning* and *doing* within learning intentions (Fautley and Savage, 2007, p. 34, used with permission)

interested in whether pupils can compose in the Blues style *per se*, but, in developing a more wider and holistic understanding of learning overtime, we are more interested in whether the knowledge, understanding and skills pupils have acquired throughout ongoing sequences of lessons can be transferred into other contexts, for example, creating music in a Rock "n" Roll style. Instead, a positive step forward here could be "To (be able to) compose" where "in the Blues style" would be the *context*.

The second point is that there needs to be a clear understanding as to not only what pupils will be *doing* in the lesson (that is, the activities), but what they will be *learning* by doing these activities. For example, the slightly clearer learning intention of "To (be able to) compose" is actually doing-focused not learning-focused. What will pupils be learning by composing? Depending on where this particular learning intention falls within a unit of work, and pupils' prior knowledge, a good example of a learning intention, then, could be "To know how to use melody, chords and a bass-riff effectively". Supporting beginning music teachers in getting learning intentions right is important not only because, in many school policies,

Table 15.1 Examples of confused and clarified learning intentions

	"Confused" learning intention	"Clarified" learning intention	Context used in "confused" learning intention	Possible transferrable context
Listening and appraising	To write a description of Gershwin's *Rhapsody in Blue*	To describe how the elements of music are used	Gershwin's *Rhapsody in Blue*	Describing how elements are used in a piece by Stravinsky
Composing	To create a piece of Blues music	To create a piece of music that includes a bass line, chords and melody	The Blues	Creating a piece of music in Pop style
Performing	To play *Twinkle, Twinkle, Little Star* accurately on the keyboard	To play with accurate fingering	*Twinkle, Twinkle, Little Star* keyboard	Playing Beethoven's *Ode joy*

Source: Hook et al. (2019, p. 39), and used with permission.

they are a requirement for each taught lesson, but, when done well, their clarity lies at the centre of effective formative assessment. In other words, when the beginning music teacher is clear about where learning is heading, they have a much better idea as to how to support pupils in getting there.

To help with your discussions with the beginning music teachers, and based on the work of Hook et al. (2019), Table 15.1 shows examples of how removing the context from the learning intention within the skills of listening, composing and performing can help provide better clarity for what pupils are going to *learn*.

For learning intentions to be clear four considerations are required: they focus on what the pupils will learn not do, they are context free, they reflect the learning that can be achieved in one lesson, and they allow the teacher to identify what pupils should know, understand, or be able to do by the end of the lesson. By working with the beginning music teacher to think and work in this way this allows pupils, as well as the beginning music teacher, to see a wider picture not only about what pupils are learning, but why they are learning it, too. From here, then, it is important to see how musical progress unfolds over time. Now do Task 15.4.

Task 15.4 Writing clear learning intentions

Ask the beginning music teacher to bring with them recent examples of learning intentions which cover a range of foci including listening and appraising, performing and composing, to a mentor meeting. Discuss the following points:

1. Do the learning intentions take into account pupils' prior knowledge?
2. Do the learning intentions follow a logical sequence of musical progression?
3. Are the learning intentions context free?
4. Do they focus on what pupils are going to learn rather than do?
5. In developing a wider picture of ongoing learning at both teacher- and pupil-level, how might these learning intentions be transferred into the next unit of work?

Seeing musical progress as something which happens over a period of time not just in a lesson

Within schools there are three high-frequency assessment-related terminologies used: attainment, achievement, and progress. According to Savage and Fautley (2013), achievement can refer to a pupil's attainment in relation to national standards compared to other schools, attainment can be associated with milestones where marks or grades, for example, are given from assessments; progress, then, can be described as the speed at which pupils move up their attainments from the points at which they started.

Beginning music teachers need to be supported with creating music lessons which incorporate a wide range of musical experiences for learning which include a balanced mixture of, for example, performing, composing, listening and appraising, and social (for example, group work). This is important; as lessons develop overtime, pupils can provide the beginning music teacher with a wealth of information on the work pupils have done and the learning that has occurred which will inform the next steps of pupils' musical journeys. It is important that you work with the beginning music teacher to realise that lesson-by-lesson assessment of pupil progress should be based on developing actual pupil work and not attempting to prove that progress and attainment is, by any means, linear. As Fautley (2010, p. 77) exemplifies:

> A pupil might be thoroughly inspired by a music project on, say, songwriting, and do some really good, original, and interesting work, showing a high level of attainment. The same pupil, for all sorts of reasons could be disengaged by a project on, say, the waltz, and not work at anything like the same level.

Fautley raises an important point because, in terms of musical progression, this means that from one unit of work to another a pupil's progress can actually move backward and forward as well as up and down. The notion of the *Spiral Curriculum* has been explored since the 1960s (for example, Bruner 1960) including within music education (for example, Daubney and Fautley, 2015; Swanwick and Tillman, 1986). A clear point to make is that, from time to time, pupils may appear to "dip" in a new unit of work or when a pupil encounters something which is new to them. "This does not mean that their attainment has worsened, merely that in the specific instance in question the pupil has shifted location on the spiral" (Daubney and Fautley, 2015, p. 6). In Daubney and Fautley's (2015) view, musical learning is built around six-overlapping strands: singing, playing, improvising, composing, critical engagement, and SMSC (Spiritual, Moral, Social and Cultural). Although the first four are self-explanatory, critical engagement includes the notions of, for example, listening, appraising, identifying, describing, evaluating and aural perception. Aspects of SMSC (see, for example, Department for Education, 2014) can also be seen to permeate throughout all aspects of musical learning. The spiral diagram shown in Figure 15.12 illustrates Daubney and Fautley's (2015) six-strands of musical learning, with increasing challenge, as a basis for musical assessment and progression.

In some areas of secondary music education, for example, in England, Key Stage 4 (ages 14-16) and Key Stage 5 (16-18) the skills of performing, composing and listening and appraising are assessed separately as part of examination specifications. This is all well and good, however there are opportunities during Key Stage 3 (ages 11-14), for example, where pupils' knowledge, understanding, and skills can be assessed globally or holistically.

Using Formative Assessment Effectively to See the Wider Picture 199

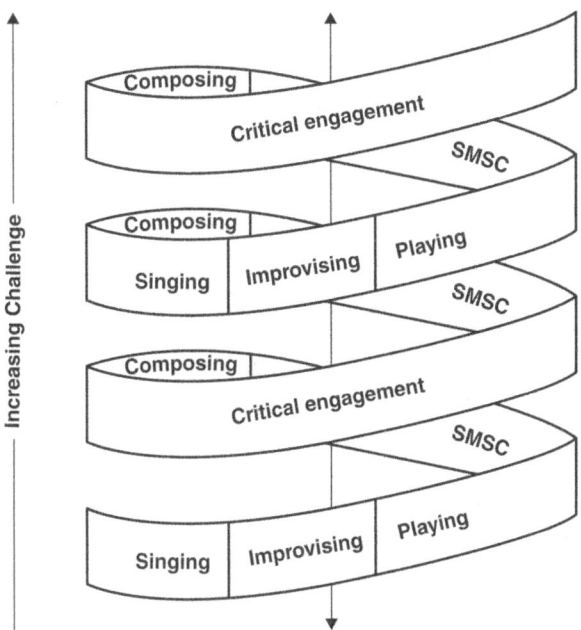

Figure 15.12 A spiral of musical progression (Daubney and Fautley, 2015, p. 6, and used with permission)

In other words, rather than assessing how good a performer a pupil is, we become more concerned which how good a *musician* they are. Supporting the beginning music teacher in taking a holistic approach to classroom-based assessment can see the integration of these different musical skills which stem from creative tasks, such as composing or improvising, as Figure 15.13 exemplifies.

What Figure 15.13 is suggesting is that, in an integrated music education in which learners compose/improvise, perform and listen, the boundaries between these skills disappear. What this means for the classroom is that, when pupils compose, they cannot help but learn as performers and listeners, too (Mills, 1991). Look at Task 15.5 for planning for holistic musical progression.

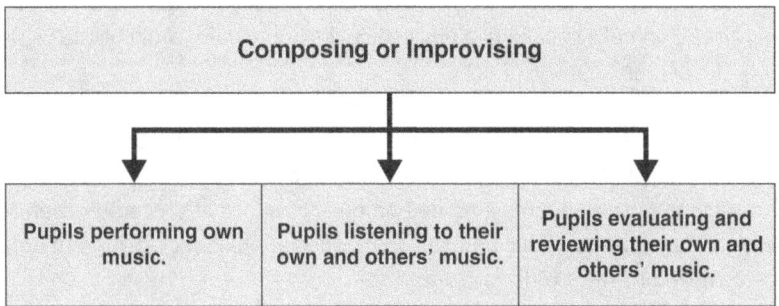

Figure 15.13 How musical skills can be integrated from a composing or improvising stem

> **Task 15.5 Seeing and planning for holistic musical progression**
>
> Ask the beginning music teacher to bring with them their current and following units of work, for a particular class, to a mentor meeting. Discuss the following example questions:
>
> 1. To what extent are pupils receiving a balanced diet of performing, composing, listening and appraising learning activities?
> 2. To what extent are pupils receiving a balanced diet of individual and group work learning activities?
> 3. Is there a leniency towards a particular musical skill? Why might this be?
> 4. Looking across two sequential units of work, what opportunities are there for pupils to transfer their current knowledge, understanding, and skills into new contexts?
> 5. Ask the beginning music teacher to reflect on two previous, sequential units of work. In a class of pupils, did they all progress up the spiral from one unit to another? Did some "dip"? Why might this have been? How might this be overcome next time?

Seeing learning through the eyes of the pupils not just the teacher

Pupil voice can be a powerful formative strategy to help improve learning in the classroom. In fact, research studies (for example, Beaudoin, 2005; Cook-Sather, 2003) found that pupils learn better when they are involved as partners in the education process. This is because, as McIntyre et al. (2007) found, pupils prefer to engage in dialogue which focuses on the learning experiences they receive and, more importantly, how it can be made even better, rather than an opportunity to complain about their teachers. Not only this, but when beginning teachers engage in pupil voice of the learners they teach, they feel much better prepared to teach a diverse range of pupils (Cook-Sather, 2001, 2002). Although pupil voice can be a highly effective tool for teacher development, it can also be a powerful strategy for a pupil's development, also, for example, strengthening their participation skills and increasing leadership abilities (Cushman, 2003). Whilst the information elicited from a pupil voice conversation would be extremely valuable, it can also be time consuming if done too regularly. A particularly useful point to engage in a pupil voice dialogue, then, could be at the time when you observe the beginning music teacher.

The purpose of an observation, at any point in a teacher's career, is to support ongoing professional development. The problem with a single observation, though, is that it can only ever be a mere snapshot of what happens on a day-to-day basis. In other words, within a single lesson being observed, only a limited amount of information can be captured. Pupil voice, then, can be a means of eliciting valuable information about learning to broaden the knowledge-base and to see a wider picture.

With this idea in mind, at Wolgarston High School, Staffordshire, a *Visible Learning* school, Jon Lesniewski (Deputy Headteacher and lead for Teaching and Learning) and myself created

Table 15.2 Pupil voice pre-observation questions used at Wolgarston High School, Staffordshire, used with permission

Key questions for observers	Possible topics for discussion
To what extent are pupils developing as "good" learners?	• Can pupils articulate what they have been learning (rather than doing) in recent lessons? • Can pupils explain how they have used/co-constructed success criteria to meet learning intentions in recent lessons? • Can pupils explain where they are in their learning (based on previous learning intentions) in this class and what their next learning steps are? • Can pupils talk about what tests and assessments they have had recently, what this told them about their current learning, what goals they set themselves/were set by the teacher as a result of the test or assessment, and how this information has impacted on recent lessons?
To what extent is feedback (teacher-pupil, pupil-pupil, pupil-teacher) **elicited and used?**	• What do pupils say about the type of feedback which is typically given by the teacher (oral and in books)? • How does the feedback (whether oral or written) cause pupils to think? • What opportunities are pupils given to respond to feedback? • What opportunities are given for pupils to practise and reinforce the feedback given? • How does the teacher collect and use feedback from their pupils to move teaching and learning forward?
To what extent do pupils believe their teacher identifies with the mindframes for *Visible Learning*?	• Do pupils feel they are challenged during lessons? • Does their teacher model and explain what "success" looks like? • What opportunities are there to learn from other pupils? • Do pupils feel it is okay to make mistakes in lessons?

a series of pre-observation questions to broaden the evidence gained from the lesson observation process where a group of 5-6 pupils, for each teacher being observed, would be asked to talk about their perspectives of the quality of learning they receive. The pupil voice focus-group would typically consist of male and female learners including, for example, a range of high, middle and low abilities, Pupil Premium and Special Educational Needs and/or Disabilities pupils. The list of questions (shown in Table 15.2) would follow a semi-structured format. This is an important consideration because if a pupil within the group says something particularly interesting about classroom learning, follow-up questions could be asked to develop and deepen an understanding of their perceptions and experiences of learning overtime. Try this approach the next time you arrange an observation with the beginning music teacher. Choose/adapt the questions as necessary to suit your own school's context, the pupils in the class, and the beginning music teacher's phase of development.

The followings vignettes (Vignettes 15.1 and 15.2), taken from Wolgarston High School, Staffordshire, illustrate how the use of pupil voice can be a powerful formative tool for both the observer (the mentor) as well as the beginning teacher.

Vignette 15.1 Reflections about pupil voice from an observer's perspective

"A great strength of our new observation process is the pre-lesson discussion with pupils. By asking them questions about the type of feedback they get and value most, along with how this helps to move the learning forward, observers are given a head-start in engaging with the teacher's practice. Similarly, asking pupils where they are in their learning and how they are typically challenged in a lesson helps to give a holistic view of the learning process, as opposed to just a 25-minute snapshot of a lesson (which may or may not be representative of typical practice). The pupils are very honest: they have given us a very fair evaluation of their progress and accurate insights into the 'big picture' of their learning, which more traditional observation processes may miss. It has been incredibly useful to hear about the feedback they get and value most, which has been (perhaps unsurprisingly) the immediate, in-the-moment, minute-by-minute practices which sees the teacher evaluating their impact on the pupils and adjusting their teaching accordingly. To then be able to see highly effective questioning in the lessons themselves only goes to reinforce the point being made by the pupils here, alongside being able to congratulate the teacher on such excellent and valued practice."

Jon Lesniewski (Deputy Headteacher and Lead for Teaching and Learning), Wolgarston High School, Staffordshire, used with permission.

Vignette 15.2 Reflections about pupil voice from a beginning teacher's perspective

"Introducing pupil voice into the observation process has allowed me, as a beginning teacher, to see the wider picture – it has given me a chance to gain feedback not only from my mentor, but perhaps more importantly from the pupils in order to improve teaching and learning in the classroom. Rather than just focusing on my own observations within lessons with regards to learning and using this to adjust my teaching, I am now looking more closely at the pupils' perceptions of learning in the room and using that to alter the learning process to better suit their needs. For example, in recent pupil interviews a number of the pupils expressed that they felt the lessons sometimes moved too quickly and therefore they were not deepening their understanding. As a result, I have adapted my lessons so they include more activities which allow the pupils to deepen and apply their skills. With my mentor's support, I now intend to use pupil voice more within my own lessons so that they know that their perceptions will be taken into account and valued so the process of teaching and learning within the classroom is more of a joint approach – it is *our* classroom, not *my* classroom."

Anonymous beginning teacher, Wolgarston High School, Staffordshire, used with permission.

Having considered the vingettes, now do Tasks 15.6a and 15.6b.

Task 15.6a A group-based pupil voice discussion with the mentor

Organise a discussion with a group of pupils taught by the beginning music teacher. Using (and adapting where necessary) the questions provided in Figure 15.2 above as a starting point, discuss what pupils' perceptions of learning are. What does this information tell you about lesson-by-lesson learning in the classroom? Discuss these views with the beginning music teacher. How can teaching and learning be made even more effective?

Task 15.6b A group-based pupil voice discussion with the beginning music teacher

Ask to beginning music teacher to organise a discussion with a group of students. Using (and adapting where necessary) the questions provided in Figure 15.2 above as a starting point, encourage them to discuss with pupils what their perceptions of learning are. In a follow-up mentoring meeting ask the beginning music teacher to reflect with you on what this information told them about lesson-by-lesson learning in the classroom and how teaching and learning can be made even more effective.

Summary and key points

To support the effective development of the beginning music teacher in seeing the wider picture, your role, as a mentor, should focus on:

- developing their use of in-the-moment (as well as lesson-by-lesson) formative assessment;
- developing effective strategies with them (for example, entrance and exit tickets) to establish differing starting points in pupils' musical learning;
- developing their understanding of the difference between *learning* and *doing* in relation to planning for musical learning;
- developing their activity planning to integrate a variety of musical opportunities; and
- developing an observation system to include pupil voice to support your observations of the beginning music teacher.

Further sources

Daubney, A. and Fautley, M. (2017) *Assessment: Getting it right in a week*. St Albans: Critical Publishing.

A clear and concise book about assessment and how, on a day-to-day basis, it can be made even better.

Evans, J. and Philpot, C. (Eds.) (2009) *A practical guide to teaching music in the secondary school*. Abingdon: Routledge.

Provides valuable support, guidance and creative ideas for teachers with a range of expertise who want to develop their music teaching.

Fautley, M. (2010) *Assessment in music education*. Oxford: Oxford University Press.

This book presents a case for formative assessment, lesson-by-lesson, rather than just summative assessment.

Fautley, M. and Savage, J. (2008) *Assessment for learning and teaching in secondary schools*. Exeter: Learning Matters.

Targeted specifically for beginning teachers, this book centres around the active use of formative assessment through topics such as: diagnosing problems, sharing learning intentions, assessment as a tool for motivation, effective planning, using evidence to adapt teaching, peer- and self-assessment, and learning through dialogue.

Fautley, M. and Savage, M. (2013) *Lesson planning for effective learning*. Maidenhead: Open University Press.

This book is about lesson planning which is an essential component of every teacher's practice.

Wiliam, D. (2018) *Embedded formative assessment*. 2nd edn. Bloomington, IN: Solution Tree Press.

This book shows how integrating classroom formative assessment practices into daily activities which can help substantially increase pupil engagement and the rate of pupil learning.

16 Music teacher health and wellbeing: A practical survival guide for mentor and mentee

Jennifer Rowley

Introduction

How do those responsible for mentoring beginning music teachers promote positive physical and mental health amongst their mentees? This chapter explores the relationship between you, the mentor, and the beginning music teacher and provides a framework for enabling music teacher health and wellbeing. Through an investigation of current practices by mentors in aspects of supporting mentees' overall physical, emotional and mental health wellbeing, this chapter provides practical examples of how to incorporate strategies into everyday life. The framework includes detailed pathways of reducing stressors, seeking support and developing resilience for longevity in a beginning teacher's career including programs such as mindfulness and positive psychology programs with relaxation practices such as Yoga and meditation.

Objectives

At the end of this chapter, you should be able to:

- have a better understanding of the mindfulness framework and positive psychology;
- compare and contrast evidence of current practices by both school and university-based mentors in supporting mentees physical/mental health and promoting healthy practices as beginning teachers;
- apply strategies (the reported practical examples) of how to incorporate a healthy lifestyle into beginning music teacher's everyday life; and
- explore formal programs established to address health and wellbeing (e.g. mindfulness, yoga, meditation).

Before reading further, undertake Task 16.1.

> **Task 16.1 Reflecting on your understanding of mentoring**
>
> Reflect on what you understand by health and wellbeing by considering the following questions:
>
> 1. What do you understand by health and wellbeing?
> 2. In what ways do the various mental and physical health campaigns influence your mentoring practice of beginning music teachers?
> 3. How does your understanding inform your practice as a mentor of beginning music teachers?
> 4. What do you think are the factors impacting attrition of early career teachers?

Background and context

What does promoting positive physical and mental health amongst beginning teachers entail? Globally there is a focus on an individual's health and wellbeing where workplaces are expected to provide employees with support systems. For example, access to no-cost, discrete online phone counselling sessions in large organisations is common place for workers today. For example, the *Are U Ok?* Day is a worldwide initiative aimed at allowing all ages of people to check in with their mental health on a specified day in September. The gender disparity is also equalising as men's health has become more prominent recently with organisations such as Beyond Blue in Australia and *Mo*vember focusing on healthy conversations with and between men.

Traditionally, however, teachers have had fewer formal structures in place to manage their wellbeing and yet today we see services and support campaigns aimed at ensuring acceptance amongst the community for those requiring support. Further to this is the research reporting high teacher attrition rates within the first 5 years of commencing their teaching career (Mason and Poyatos Matas, 2015). One survey found that the two most important reasons for intended early departures were "workload too heavy" and "insufficient recognition and reward" (Mason and Poyatos Matas, 2015, p. 47). The support received in the early years of teaching with a lack of ongoing employment, job security and salary levels with experience have also been identified as factors (Mason and Poyatos Matas, 2015). However, studies also found that practical considerations such as restricted income increments after the first 6 years, job security and work-life balance were lower in teachers' priorities than the personal fulfilment of teaching (Howes and Goodman-Delahunty, 2015, p. 20). So, such issues that relate to professional skills and training, relationships and cultures within a school, personal factors and structural issues such as employment conditions more broadly combine to influence retention and attrition (Mason and Poyatos Matas, 2015).

With the continuation of formal mentoring programs for early career teachers we have seen positive inroads in addressing the issue surrounding teacher's health and wellbeing which has in turn impacted on retention rates (Field et al., 2013). In addition, there has been an increase in programs for beginning music teachers at tertiary (or higher education) institutions that are specific to ensuring their health is not left without support.

Through the lens of the mindfulness framework, we explore the relationship between mentor and mentee for enabling positive musician/music teacher health and wellbeing. This chapter provides practical examples for mentoring beginning music teachers. For example, during an initial teacher education (ITE) program in New South Wales (NSW), Australia, informal conversations with supervising music teachers in secondary schools ($n = 5$) were held where they were asked to describe recent experiences of working alongside the beginning music teacher during the formal professional experience (practicum) placements. In addition, the university (tertiary) mentors ($n = 5$) were asked to comment officially in their designated role as mentors on the physical and mental health of each beginning music teacher over the final placement period of 8 weeks. In the case of tertiary mentors, they are qualified music teachers who are employed casually by the university to support and mentor beginning music teachers throughout the duration of the professional experience. The tertiary mentor visits the beginning teacher in-situ and observes lessons. They are responsible for ensuring that they are progressing through the placement according to the NESA established *NSW Graduate Teacher Professional Standards* and, in tandem with the classroom supervising teacher, they complete a final report.

Before reading further, undertake Task 16.2.

Task 16.2 Understanding the barriers for beginning teacher retention and what can be done to address this

1. Research the current report on teacher retention.
2. List some common barriers for beginning music teachers. Why do you think these barriers occur?
3. Identify some strategies for beginning music teachers on how these barriers might be overcome.

Literature and theoretical framework

Wellbeing is not just another word for physical or mental health. It is about finding balance in body, mind, and spirit so that we feel content, connected, energised, resilient, and safe. The *Framework for Enhancing Student Mental Wellbeing* (shown in Figure 16.1) can help to support healthy people, build healthy places, develop healthy policies and implement healthy practices.

The five aspects of the framework:

1. *Mental health knowledge and skills* is associated with experiences of personal growth, intrinsic motivation, positive relationships, autonomy and competence. A person's state of mental health can fluctuate over time and in response to many factors (e.g. physical health, life events and environmental conditions) that increase protective or risk factors.
2. *Engaging Curricula* addresses the issue of how curriculum be intentionally designed to better support student wellbeing. Through teaching innovation and the intentional design of curricula that are psychologically "resource-rich" there is potential to enhance wellbeing.

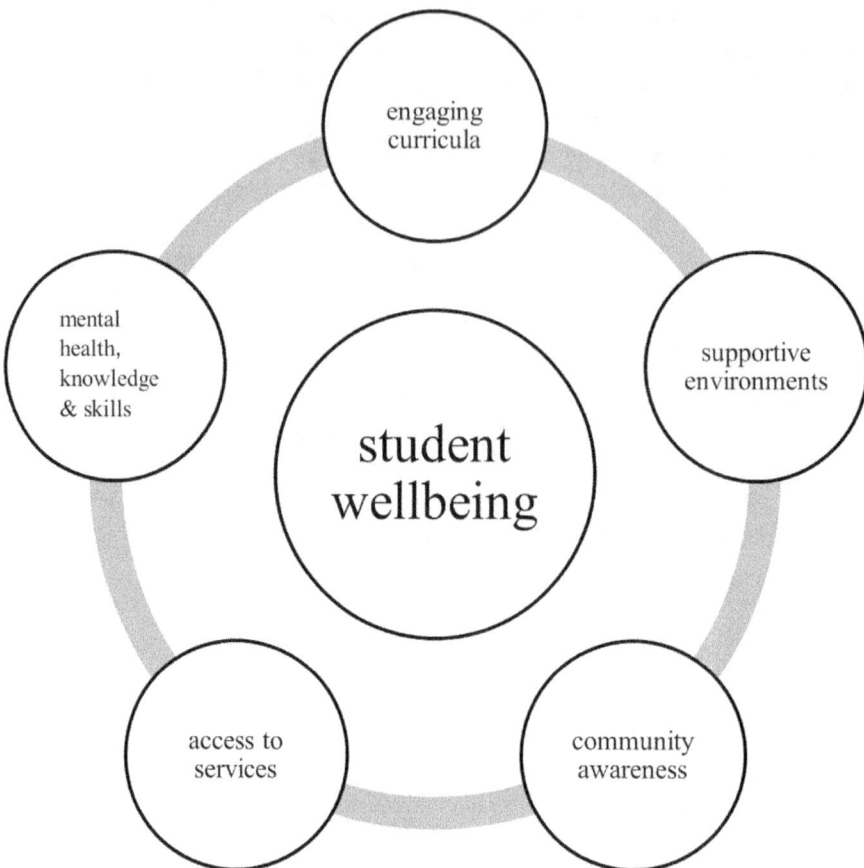

Figure 16.1 Framework for enhancing student mental wellbeing (adapted from Baik et al., 2017)

3. *Supportive environments* put a responsibility on tertiary educators to create learning environments that support wellbeing by creating assessment approaches informed by psychological principles and research to mitigate psychological stressors in the educational environment.
4. *Community awareness* encourages all staff and services in Universities to employ techniques to foster students' autonomous motivation, promote inclusion and belonging, encourage positive relationships, enable autonomy and scaffold competence.
5. *Access to services* is necessary so that students are aware of the support available to them as part of a University community. Services such as counselling, academic support and learning hubs (for example) play a role in both the provision and programs for wellbeing.

Positive mental health is essential for effective learning, and because curriculum design and teaching practices influence mental wellbeing (positively and negatively). Adopting teaching and learning approaches that actively support a beginning teacher's mental health will enhance the wellbeing and educational experiences for all, not just those at risk of experiencing mental health difficulties during their time at university (Norrish et al., 2013). Through an application of the following wellbeing strategies, we can determine how a beginning music teacher is supported through the five aspects of the framework.

Mindfulness

Is a program designed to assist you in focusing on the present? It is the psychological process of purposely bringing your attention to experiences occurring in the present moment without judgment, which can be developed through the practice of meditation and through other training like *Positive Psychology* (discussed later). *Mindfulness* is paying full attention to what is going on in you and outside you, moment by moment, without judgment by observing your thoughts, feelings, and the sensations of taste, touch, smell, sight and sound. You become fully aware of your surroundings and this heightened awareness has shown to improve effects of stress and anxiety. *Mindfulness* can help to feel better and reduce stress as it helps manage these negative thoughts and feelings in a more positive way (Gu et al., 2015). Researchers have studied *Mindfulness* (and related techniques such as relaxation, meditation and yoga) to see if they can help treat various physical and mental health conditions. Meditation can also be used as a relaxation method to relieve stress and anxiety. Practising calm, deep breathing creates physiological changes in the body which may help reduce stress. Relaxation techniques can help to relax the mind and body and also manage some of the symptoms of anxiety and depression. Mindfulness-based stress reduction is a particular type of therapy which incorporates meditation, body awareness and yoga (Gu et al., 2015). Many people who have depression also experience stress and anxiety, so reducing these symptoms could improve their depressive symptoms also. Being mindful involves awareness without judgement or reaction. This may help change people's attitudes towards their feelings or events to be more positive and help them develop better coping skills.

Positive psychology is a program designed specifically to improve wellbeing and is used extensively in Australian schools. It is a scientific approach to studying human thoughts, feelings, and behaviour, with a focus on strengths instead of weaknesses, building the good in life instead of repairing the bad, and taking the lives of average people up to "great" instead of focusing solely on moving those who are struggling up to "normal" (Park and Peterson, 2008). *Positive Psychology* has three central concerns: positive experiences, positive individual traits, and positive institutions. Understanding positive emotions entails the study of contentment with the past, happiness in the present, and hope for the future.

What follows next is a review of the current mentoring literature with subheadings of: mentoring qualities and strategies; health and wellbeing for musicians and music teachers (performance science and student teacher expectations); *Mindfulness*, yoga, meditation and *Positive Psychology*.

Mentoring qualities and strategies

An active mentor usually guides their mentee through insights into their practice by sharing information – often about her/his career. Often a mentor provides guidance, motivation, emotional support, and more often than not acts as a role model to their mentee. The relationship between you, the mentor, and the beginning music teacher can be complex (or simple) depending on expectations. Some mentors may help their mentee with exploring careers, setting goals, developing contacts, and identifying resources.

A good mentor:

- Does not blame – stays neutral.
- Will be a critical friend and give honest answers.
- Is not intimidating – easy to approach and frequently available.
- Has relevant expertise.
- Listens more than they talk.
- Actively questions
- Is enabling, caring, open and facilitative.
- Gives constructive and positive feedback.
- Provides subtle guidance, but ensures to make any decisions.
- Is interested and shows genuine concern.
- Is willing to debate, argue, discuss.

Mentoring beginning teachers is necessary in a climate of unstable teacher retention. For example, an Australian study of 5000 early career teachers and 1000 principals found that retention was linked to teachers' sense of being effective, work satisfaction, a combination of extrinsic and intrinsic rewards and support systems such as induction and mentoring (Mayer et al., 2015).

Health and wellbeing for musicians and music teachers

There is increasing recognition that good mental and physical health consists of the presence of wellbeing. Some beginning music teachers in the initial stages of learning to teach can suffer from burnout and stress at a higher rate than others due to the added burden of rehearsals, late night practising and performance responsibilities (Ballantyne, 2007). Popular health and wellbeing initiatives/strategies for beginning music teachers include:

- Handling stress and dealing with performance anxiety;
- Diagnosis, treatment, rehabilitation and recovery from injury (e.g. prevention of hearing loss);
- Understanding neuroscience and its impact on musical learning;
- The lesson environment and its effect on one's self-esteem and desire to learn;
- The varied uses of technology in the field of wellness;
- Adapting the instrument to the musician; and
- Developing and maintaining a self-care plan.

Mindfulness and yoga

There has been research looking at how *Mindfulness* and meditation affects wellbeing generally (Ivtzan and Lomas, 2016). One systematic review of 21 studies found that mindfulness therapies were effective at reducing depression symptoms in 10 studies, but in four studies the treatment was no more effective than a control condition (Gu et al., 2015). Another meta-analysis of 39 studies found that, in general, mindfulness therapies were moderately effective in reducing depression symptoms (Fischer et al., 2017). In this review, the mindfulness therapies were more effective for people who had a primary diagnosis of clinical depression, compared to people who had another diagnosis (e.g. cancer). Many of the therapies which incorporate *Mindfulness* also include aspects of cognitive therapies as well – for example, cognitive behavioural therapy.

Before reading further, undertake Task 16.3.

Task 16.3 One example of practice

Reflect on the literature you have just read describing effective health and wellbeing practices. What aspects would you identify as being of most use to your work with a beginning music teacher and why? Are there any specific implications to mentoring?

Here is a simple technique of meditation that is similar to those taught in *Mindfulness* and meditation books and courses:

1. Sit in a quiet room in a comfortable position with eyes closed.
2. Choose a word which is relaxing for you (for example, "One" or "Calm") and repeat it silently over and over in your mind. Do not force yourself to concentrate on the word.
3. If your mind wanders, turn your attention back to the word.
4. Do this for around 10-15 minutes each day.

There are a range of support resources and materials that are freely available on the web. For example, a popular App that is often used in conjunction with *Mindfulness* called "Headspace" is a 10-minute meditation program where the first 10 sessions are free and then to continue you pay a service fee.

Yoga is a complementary technique to *Mindfulness* as it centres on strengthening the body and raising awareness and harmony in both the mind and body. Yoga's incorporation of meditation and breathing can help improve a person's mental wellbeing. "Regular yoga practice creates mental clarity and calmness; increases body awareness; relieves chronic stress patterns; relaxes the mind; centres attention; and sharpens concentration" (Liebert, 2010, p. 7). It is also noted in the literature as a natural remedy for anxiety which is a topic to consider when discussing musician and music teacher health as performance anxiety is reported as common to this profession.

This chapter reports a qualitative methodology as a scientific method of observation to gather non-numerical data. Informal conversations with supervising classroom teachers ($n = 5$) and tertiary mentors ($n = 5$) of pre-service music teachers during the final 8 weeks block professional experience (practicum) built a case study reporting strategies for maintaining beginning music teachers' well-being. Through using grounded theory as a general research method, the following strategies were extracted in a process of identifying themes or concepts.

Before reading further, complete Task 16.4.

Task 16.4 Different strategies to support beginning music teachers

- How do you currently support a beginning music teacher's health and wellbeing?
- Which models do you think you might use/want to use in your mentoring? *Yoga*? *Mindfulness*?
- How would you incorporate the *Framework for Enhancing Student Mental Wellbeing* (Baik et al., 2017) into your future mentor planning?

Repeated strategies for supporting a beginning music teacher's health and wellbeing

The following results are reported conversations with supervising classroom teachers (ST) and Tertiary Mentors (TM). Strategies for promoting positive physical and mental health will be summarised from these results.

> ST1: "At the beginning of the teaching round, I think it's important to allow 'prac' students [beginning teachers] to watch for a day or two, then take small groups of students for 5 minutes at a time to start building rapport with students. At the end of the round, it's difficult to judge when to step in and when to let the prac teacher flounder, especially when they run out of activities or energy with 10 minutes left to teach."

ST1 was clearly concerned for the beginning music teacher but felt that "learning by doing" was the best approach so that the pupils developed a rapport. In relation to ensuring the physical health of the mentee in her care, she continues:

ST1: "When prac students are involved in rehearsals and concerts (outside their scheduled teaching time), I believe it's appropriate to let them rest a little in free periods. Some other faculties take the opposite stance and suggest that prac students should to work a full day from the outset, regardless of evening or weekend commitments."

It was interesting to see that ST2 was sharing her 30 plus years of music teaching experience when she talked about her mentee's relationship with the pupils:

ST2: "Don't let anything fester. Strike while the iron is hot. Chase those kids down. If you are going to put them on detention. Go to them and find them."

She was adamant that the best way to maintain your health as a beginning teacher was to take the stress of the classroom management out of your life and that often meant managing the one person in the class that was making life difficult.

ST3 agreed with ST1 by stating that you have to be there for your mentee and remember that it is often a challenging time during the professional experience.

ST3: "Being supportive in your professional manner and highlighting the individual strengths of your PST. Let them know we all have tough days and everyone has them no matter how long you have been teaching. Be tough if you need to be and follow through on threats especially on classroom management."

Following on from this was ST4 who felt mentoring the beginning music teacher through classroom management would significantly reduce stress and allow teaching to flow better.

ST4: "She is well organised and knows her content but needs to time her lessons a little more (ensuring that she doesn't spend too long on one activity and run out of time at the end), and there is a little more work to do regarding dealing with difficult students."

Beyond being there for your beginning music teacher and supporting them with the more challenging pupils, ST5 felt that helping the mentee to plan great lessons would actually reduce stress and promote wellbeing.

ST5: "We worked together before the lesson to 'bulk up' her lesson plan. Generally, she has an overview of the lesson sequence and I am helping her to develop her skills in devising clear outcomes and objectives so that all of her lessons have a goal."

Whilst the supervising teachers mentored to ensure smooth lessons and classroom management, the tertiary mentors (TM) felt they provided the scaffold to the professional approach as a music teacher.

TM1: "Answer any questions from the PST [beginning music teacher] as promptly as possible. I can only meet their concerns when clear communication is established at the very start. This means that at the outset I am prepared to make an extra visit if necessary or if they request it."

Along the same lines was an emphasis on open channels of communication so that an honest assessment of the mentee's progress can be made.

TM2: "I tell my pre-service teachers to buckle up and be very receptive to constructive criticism."

When mentoring her beginning music teacher, TM2 wants to build their self-confidence over the 6 weeks of professional experience as she believes this is the best way to encourage her mentee's wellbeing.

TM2: "Get actively involved in all school extra-curricular and activities so that you show yourself first as a musician. This they can do. The teaching gig is a little harder so building their confidence within a skill they are really good at provides some great motivation to improve their teaching."

TM3 took a similarly active role in ensuring her mentee was motivated to learn the hard stages of teaching.

TM3: "Mentoring and supervision must be undertaken within the framework of National Teaching Standards, which means lots of modelling, peer teaching and assistance provided."

Along with comprehensive written documentation, TM3 believed that her mentee should be provided for at every step of their development in the form of Lesson Observation Reports or other written records of mentoring discussions, goal setting etc.

TM3: "Providing diverse opportunities for the prac student to share active classroom-based programmes (Guitars, Keyboards, drum kits, composition), and a range of co-curricular musical undertakings (Pop Choir, String Ensemble, Band) along with the opportunity for pre-service teachers to experience a range of classes. Also, co-teaching with the student teacher to assist with discipline and so the students can experience a range of classes and teaching opportunities."

This strategy of "at elbow support" by the TM and the ST together in a partnership with the mentee was also the key piece of advice of TM4 who believed the beginning music teacher must be au fait with how to effectively relate to pupils.

TM4: "The music prac teacher needs to know just when and how to engage the students with questioning; how to consider the range of musical knowledge and experience in the classroom, and how to design lessons that are fun."

She regarded the mentoring of her beginning teacher as a formal, mandatory component of their training just like they have to know the curriculum/syllabus implementation.

It was important for TM5 to provide positive feedback to the beginning music teachers and used positive reinforcement because he wanted his mentees to be confident in presenting lesson material, to give clear instructions and to present sound knowledge of technology in lessons.

TM5: "I want to be able to motivate my students [beginning music teachers] through a positive interaction…this is the model for them to use with their class. For example, making behaviour expectations clear. I saw evidence of her acting on my feedback (e.g. time management of lessons) and this I knew helped her to manage her stress."

Before reading further, undertake Task 16.5.

> **Task 16.5 Responsibilities of the mentor and mentee according to the *Framework for Enhancing Student Mental Wellbeing* (Baik et al., 2017)**
>
> In each circle of the *Framework* (see Figure 16.1), there are suggested approaches that you can make operational to provide support to your mentee towards a mutually agreed goal of wellbeing.
>
> 1. Which of the various approaches would you use and why? Please be specific in your response.
> 2. How would you help the mentee to learn a health and wellbeing approach through the model? You could suggest they seek support from friends or family.

Implications for mentoring practice

There were mixed opinions from both the classroom supervising teachers and the tertiary mentors when it came to promoting positive physical and mental health amongst the beginning music teachers. Some believed that they must be able to do what a full-time teacher can do whilst others thought there should be some leniency because they are new to the profession. As one classroom supervising teacher reported, "If we stay late at school one night for rehearsal then I would say to my prac student to come in late the next morning". This may be indicative of how the teacher would act themselves if it fitted in with colleagues. It also shows a respect and responsibility for the mentee in their care. This type of role modelling is a positive aspect for the teacher commencing their teaching career.

Most mentors noted that they would constantly check in on their mentee to ensure there were no signs of overload and, if there was, the mentor would suggest a re-assessment of the beginning teacher's current workload. It was noted that, to be a good mentor, it was important that there was open and honest communication at all times and that this had to be modelled with other teaching colleagues in the school. That constructive criticism and positive feedback was at the forefront and that the mentor identified and worked with mentees' differing needs.

The key take away from the reported strategies by the mentors was not only to be supportive of the beginning music teacher, but also to develop a professional, collaborative, supportive working relationship with them so that they had a model to use when they were in staffroom and working as a teacher. Attention is being paid to the area of support for all beginning teachers and in a study of pre-service music teacher identity, Ballantyne and Zhukov (2017) found that despite the reported "isolation, heavy workload, exhaustion, and lack of work-specific skills most of the [early career] teachers interviewed demonstrated a wide range of professional and personal skills associated with a positive outlook on life and career" (p. 241). This is such a positive result and one of explicit conversations that academics, formal mentoring arrangements and support for the classroom supervising teachers that provides us with evidence of a change.

It was through the clearly defined mentor expectations that the mentee was helped to develop a rapport with pupils and teachers alike and this assisted in their motivation, confidence and engagement in the teaching profession.

Summary and key points

Use *mindfulness*-based strategies to address beginning music teachers' wellbeing as anxiety and stress reduction is reported to improve mental health and wellbeing.

- A mentor who is competent, confident and professional is the best role model for a beginning music teacher.
- Look for evidence of self-evaluation through discussions with the mentee.
- A good mentor makes expectations clear and are always followed through.
- Be positive, encouraging and continually assess progress, particularly when involved in challenging or difficult situations.
- Use the *Framework for Enhancing Student Mental Wellbeing* (Baik et al., 2017) to plan the beginning music teacher's wellbeing strategies.

Further resources

Download the free health and wellbeing apps:

- "Smiling Mind" which is a mindfulness meditation app designed to provide children and adults with mindfulness tools.
- "ReachOut Breathe" is an app designed to help users reduce the physical symptoms of stress and anxiety.
- "Music eScape" taps into your music library and creates a playlist based on your mood.
- "Sleepbot" is a sleep tracking app designed to help users learn more about the quality of their sleep.

REFERENCES

Adams, K. (2019) 'Developing growth mindset in the ensemble rehearsal', *Music Educators Journal*, 105(4), pp. 21-27.

Adams, P. (2001) 'Planning to teach music musically', in Philpott, C. and Spruce, G. (eds.) *Learning to teach music in the secondary school*. Abingdon: Routledge.

Addison, N., Burgess, L., Kinsella, V. et al. (2015) 'Learning in the art and design classroom', in Addison, N. and Burgess, L. (eds.) *Learning to teach art and design in the secondary classroom*. London: Routledge.

Alexander, R. (2008) *Essays on pedagogy*. Abingdon: Routledge.

Allsup, R.E. (2008) 'Creating an educational framework for popular music in public schools: Anticipating the second-wave', in *Visions of research in music education (special edition - Beyond Lucy Green: Operationalizing theories of informal music learning)*, 12, pp. 1-12. Available at: https://digitalcommons.lib.uconn.edu/cgi/viewcontent.cgi?article=1071&context=vrme [accessed: 2 March 2020].

Anderson, A. (2009) *Mighty mentor: Music mentoring at the chalk face*. NAME magazine summer edition. Matlock: National Association of Music Educators.

Anderson, A. (2019) *Happy accidents? Music teacher perceptions of curriculum design at key stage 3 in the English secondary school*. Birmingham: Birmingham City University, unpublished thesis.

Antovic, M. (2009) 'Towards a semantics of music: The 20th century', *Language and History*, 52(1), pp. 119-129.

Applebee, A.N. and Langer, J. (1983) 'Instructional scaffolding: Reading and writing as natural language activities', *Language Arts*, 60(2), pp. 168-175.

Asghar, M. (2013) 'Exploring formative assessment using cultural historical activity theory', *Turkish Online Journal of Qualitative Inquiry*, 4(2), pp. 18-32.

Atkinson, T. and Claxton, G. (2000) *The intuitive practitioner: On the value of not always knowing what one is doing*. Buckingham: Open University Press.

Atlas, G.D., Taggart, T. and Goodell, D.J. (2004) 'The effects of sensitivity to criticism on motivation and performance in music students', *British Journal of Music Education*, 21(1), pp. 81-87.

Austin, J. and Reinhardt, D. (1999) 'Philosophy and advocacy: An examination of preservice music teachers' beliefs', *Journal of Research in Music Education*, 47(1), pp. 18-30.

Ausubel, D. (1968) *Educational psychology: A cognitive view*. New York, NY: Holt, Rinehart & Winston.

Baik, C., Larcombe, W., Brooker, A. et al. (2017) *Enhancing student mental wellbeing: A handbook for academic educators*. Australian Government Department of Education and Training. Available at: https://melbourne-cshe.unimelb.edu.au/__data/assets/pdf_file/0006/2408604/MCSHE-Student-Wellbeing-Handbook-FINAL.pdf [accessed: 27 May 2019].

Bakhurst, D. (2009) 'Reflections on activity theory', *Educational Review*, 61(2), pp. 197-210.

Ballantyne, J. (2007) 'Documenting praxis shock in early-career Australian music teachers: The impact of beginning teacher education', *International Journal of Music Education*, 25(3), pp. 181-191.

Ballantyne, J. and Grootenboer, P. (2012) 'Exploring relationships between teacher identities and disciplinarity', *International Journal of Music Education*, 30(4), pp. 368-381.

Ballantyne, J. and Zhukov, K. (2017) 'A good news story: Early-career music teachers' accounts of their "flourishing" professional identities', *Teacher Education*, 68, pp. 241-251.

Ballantyne, J., Kerchner, J.L. and Aróstegui, J.L. (2012) 'Developing music teacher identities: An international multi-site study', *International Journal of Music Education*, 30(3), pp. 211-226.

Baron, R.A. (1988) 'Negative effects of destructive criticism: Impact on conflict, self-efficacy, and task performance', *Journal of Applied Psychology*, 73(2), pp. 199-207.

Barrett, M. (1992) 'Music education and the natural learning model', *International Journal of Music Education*, 20(1), pp. 27-34.

Bate, E. (2020) 'Justifying music in the national curriculum: The habit concept and the question of social justice and academic rigour', *British Journal of Music Education*, 37(1), pp. 3-15.

Bautista, A. and Wong, J. (2019) 'Music teachers' perceptions of the features of most and least helpful professional development', *Arts Education Policy Review*, 120(2), pp. 80-93.

Beauchamp, C. and Thomas, L. (2009) 'Understanding teacher identity: An overview of issues in the literature and implications for teacher education', *Cambridge Journal of Education*, 39(1), pp. 175-189.

Beauchamp, C. and Thomas, L. (2011) 'New teachers' identity shifts at the boundary of teacher education and initial practice', *International Journal of Educational Research*, 50(1): pp. 6-13.

Beaudoin, N. (2005) *Elevating student voice: How to enhance participation, citizenship, and leadership*. Larchmont, NY: Eye of Education.

Beck, S. (2015) 'The problem of expertise: From experience to skillful practices to expertise: Ecological and pragmatist perspectives', *European Journal of Pragmatism and American Philosophy*, 7(1), p. 15.

Beijaard, D. (2019) 'Teacher learning as identity learning: Models, practices, and topics', *Teachers and Teaching*, 25(1), pp. 1-6.

Benedict, C., Schmidt, P., Spruce, G. et al. (2015) *The Oxford handbook of social justice in music education*. Oxford: Oxford University Press.

Benson, M. (2008) 'Effective mentoring for new music teachers', *Update Applications of Research in Music Education*, 26(2), pp. 42-49.

Berg, M.H. and Rickels, D.A. (2018) 'Mentoring for mentors: The music mentor plus program', *Journal of Music Teacher Education*, 27(2), pp. 39-51.

Bernard, R. (2005) 'Music-making, making selves, making it right: A call for reframing music teacher education', *Action, Criticism, and Theory for Music Education*, 4(2), pp. 2-36.

Bernstein, B. (1996) *Pedagogy. Symbolic, control and identity*. London: Rowman and Littlefield.

Black, P. and Plowright, D. (2010) 'A multi-dimensional model of reflective learning for professional development', *Reflective Practice*, 11(2), pp. 245-259.

Black, P. and Wiliam, D. (2018) 'Classroom assessment and pedagogy', *Assessment in Education: Principles, Policy & Practice*, 25(6), pp. 1-24.

Black, P., Harrison, C., Lee, C. et al. (2003) *Assessment for learning*. Milton Keynes: Open University Press.

Blair, D.V. (2008) 'Mentoring novice teachers: Developing a community of practice', *Research Studies in Music Education*, 30(2), pp. 99-117.

Blakeslee, M. (2004) 'Assembling the arts education jigsaw', *Arts Education Policy Review*, 105(4), pp. 31-36.

Bloom, B., Englehart, M., Furst, E. et al. (1956) *Taxonomy of educational objectives: The classification of educational goals. Handbook 1: Cognitive domain*. New York: Longmans, Green.
Bor, R., Eriksen, C. and Chaudry, S. (2014) *Overcoming stress*. London: Sheldon Press.
Boreen, J. and Niday, D. (2000) 'Breaking through the isolation: Mentoring beginning teachers', *Journal of Adolescent and Adult Literacy*, 44(2), pp. 152-163.
Boulton, H. and Hraniak, A. (2012) 'E-reflection: The development of reflective communities of learning for trainee teachers through the use of shared online web logs', *Reflective Practice*, 13(4), pp. 503-515.
Bowman, W. (2005) 'To what question(s) is music education advocacy the answer?', *International Journal of Music Education*, 23(2), pp. 125-129.
Bowman, W. (2010) 'No one true way: Music education without redemptive truth', in Regelski, T.A. and Gates, J.T. (eds.) *Music education for changing times*. New York: Springer.
Brookfield, S. (2017) *Becoming a critically reflective teacher*. San Francisco: John Wiley and Sons.
Bruner, J. (1960) *The process of education*. Cambridge, MA: Harvard University Press.
Bruner, J.S. (1986) *Actual minds: Possible worlds*. Cambridge, MA: Harvard University Press.
Bruner, J.S. (1996) *The culture of education*. Cambridge MA: Harvard University Press.
Bubb, S. (2007) *Leading and managing continuing professional development*. 2nd edn. London: Paul Chapman Publishing.
Buchan, D.S., Ollis, S. and Young, J.D. (2013) 'High intensity interval running enhances measures of physical fitness but not metabolic measures of cardiovascular disease risk in healthy adolescents', *BMC Public Health*, 13, p. 498.
Buell, C. (2004) 'Models of mentoring in communication', *Communication Education*, 53(1), pp. 56-73.
Bull, A. (2019) *Class, control, and classical music*. Oxford: Oxford University Press.
Bunting, T. (2002) 'The place of composing in the music curriculum', in Spruce, G. (ed.) *Teaching music in secondary schools*. London: Routledge.
Burnard, P. (2012) *Musical creativities in practice*. Oxford: Oxford University Press.
Burnard, P. and Murphy, R. (eds.) (2013) *Teaching music creatively: Learning to teach in the primary school series*. Abingdon: Routledge.
Burnard, P. and Younker, B. (2008) 'Investigating children's musical interactions within the activities systems of group composing and arranging: An application of Engeström's activity theory', *International Journal of Educational Research*, 47(1), pp. 60-74.
Cain, T. (2007) 'Mentoring trainee music teachers: Beyond apprenticeship or reflection', *British Journal of Music Education*, 24(3), pp. 281-294.
Cain, T. and Cursley, J. (2017) *Teaching music differently: Case studies of inspiring pedagogies*. Abingdon: Routledge.
Campbell, J. and van Nieuwerburgh, C. (2018) *The Leader's guide to coaching in schools*. Thousand Oaks, CA: Corwin.
Carter, A. (2015) *Carter review of initial teacher training*. London Department for Education. Available at: https://www.gov.uk/government/publications/carter-review-of-initial-teacher-training [accessed: 24 August 2022].
Cashwell, C. (2020) *Integrating spirituality and religion into counselling: A guide to competent practice*. 3rd edn. Alexandria, VA: American Counselling Association.
Child, A. and Merrill, S. (2005) *Developing as secondary school mentor: A case study approach for trainee mentors and their tutors*. Exeter: Learning Matters.
Cho, C., Ramanan, R. and Feldman, M. (2011) 'Defining the ideal qualities of mentorship: A qualitative analysis of the characteristics of outstanding mentors', *The American Journal of Medicine*, 124(5), pp. 453-458.
Christophersen, C. (2021) 'Educating music teachers for the future: The crafts of change', in Holdhus, K., Murphy, R. and Espeland, M. (eds.) *Music education as craft: Reframing theories and practices*. Cham, Switzerland: Springer.

Clarke, S. (2005) *Formative assessment in the secondary classroom*. London: Hodder and Stoughton.

Clayton, M., Sager, R.D. and Will, U. (2005), 'In Time With The Music: The concept of entrainment and its significance for ethnomusicology', *ESEM CounterPoint, Vol. 1*.

Clift, S. (2012) 'Singing, wellbeing, and health', in MacDonald, R.A.R., Kreutz, G. and Mitchell, L. (eds.) *Music, health, and wellbeing*. Oxford: Oxford University Press, pp. 113-124.

Clutterbuck, D. (2004) *Everyone needs a mentor: Fostering talent in your organisation*. 4th edn. London: Chartered Institute of Personnel and Development.

Coe, R., Aloisi, C., Higgins, S. and Major, L.E. (2014) *What makes great teaching? Review of the underpinning research*.

Cole, M. and Engeström, Y. (1993) 'A cultural-historical approach to distributed cognition', in Solomon, G. (ed.) *Distributed cognitions: Psychological and educational considerations*. Cambridge: Cambridge University Press.

Colwell, R. (2006) 'Assessment's potential in music education', in Colwell, R. (ed.) *MENC handbook of research methodologies*. New York: Oxford University Press.

Conkling, S.W. (2007) 'The possibilities of situated learning for teacher preparation: The professional development partnership', *Music Educators Journal*, 93(3), pp. 44-48.

Conway, C.M. (2008) 'Experienced music teacher perceptions of professional development throughout their careers', *Bulletin of the Council for Research in Music*, 176, pp. 7-18.

Conway, C. (2015a) 'Beginning music teacher mentor practices: Reflections on the past and suggestions for the future', *Journal of Music Teach Education*, 24(2), pp. 88-102.

Conway, C. (2015b) 'The experiences of first-year music teachers: A literature review', *Update: Applications of Research in Music Education*, 33(2), pp. 65-72.

Conway, C. and Christensen, S. (2006) 'Professional development and the beginning music teacher', *Contributions to Music Education*, 33(1), pp. 9-25.

Conway, C., Hansen, E., Schulz, A. et al. (2004) 'Becoming a teacher: Stories of the first few years: Four teachers who are new to the profession share their thoughts about the challenges faced by beginning teachers', *Music Educators Journal*, 91(1), pp. 45-50.

Conway, C.M., Hibbard, S., Albert, D. et al. (2005) 'Professional development for arts teachers', *Arts Education Policy Review*, 107(1), pp. 3-10.

Cooke, C. and Spruce, G. (2016) 'What is a music curriculum?', in Cooke, C., Evans, K., Philpott, C. et al. (eds.) *Learning to teach music in the secondary school*. 3rd edn. Abingdon: Routledge.

Cooke, C., Evans, K., Philpott, C. et al. (eds.) (2016) *Learning to teach music in the secondary school: A companion to school experience*. 3rd edn. Abingdon: Routledge.

Cook-Sather, A. (2001) 'Negotiating worlds of worlds: Writing about students' experiences of school', in Shultz, J. and Cook-Sather, A. (eds.) *In our own words: Students' perspectives on school*. Lanham, MD: Rowan & Littlefield.

Cook-Sather, A. (2002) 'Authorizing students' perspectives: Towards trust, dialogue and change in education', *Educational Researcher*, 31(4), pp. 3-14.

Cook-Sather, A. (2003) 'Re(in)forming the conversations: Student position, power, and voice in teacher education', *Radical Teacher*, 64, pp. 21-28.

Cordingley, P., Higgins, S., Greany, T. et al. (2015) *Developing great teaching: Lessons from the international reviews into effective professional development*. London: Teacher Development Trust.

Creech, A. (2012) 'Interpersonal behaviour in one-to-one instrumental lessons: An observational analysis', *Music Education*, 29(3), pp. 387-407.

CUREE (Centre for the Use of Research and Evidence in Education) (2005) *Mentoring and coaching CPD capacity building project: National framework for mentoring and coaching*. London: Department for Education.

Cushman, K. (2003) *Fires in the bathroom: Advice for teachers from high school students*. New York: The New Press.

Custodero, L.A. (2010) 'Meaning and experience: The musical learner', in Abeles, H.F. and Custodero, L.A. (eds.) *Critical issues in music education: Contemporary theory and practice*. New York: Oxford University Press.

Daloz, L. (2012) *Mentor: Guiding the journey of adult learners*. Hoboken, NJ: Jossey Bass-Wiley.

Dascalu, M., Coman, M., Postelnicua, R. et al. (2014) 'Learning to play a musical instrument in adulthood – Challenges and computer-mediated solutions', *Procedia - Social and Behavioural Sciences*, 142, pp. 311–317.

Daubney, A. and Fautley, M. (2015) *The national curriculum for music: A framework for curriculum, pedagogy and assessment in key stage 3*. Available at: https://www.ism.org/images/files/ISM_A_Framework_for_Curriculum,_Pedagogy_and_Assessment_KS3_Music_Wallchart.pdf [accessed: 24 April 2019].

Daubney, A. and Fautley, M. (2017) *Assessment: Getting it right in a week*. St Albans: Critical Publishing.

Daubney, A. and Mackrill, D. (2017) *Changes in secondary music curriculum over time 2012–2016*. Brighton: University of Sussex.

Davis, V.W. (2017) 'Error reflection', *General Music Today*, 30(2), pp. 11–17.

DeLorenzo, L. (1992) 'Perceived problems of beginning music teachers', *Bulletin of the Council for Research in Music*, 113, pp. 9–25.

Denscombe, M. (2017) *The good research guide*. 6th edn. Maidenhead, UK: Open University Press.

Department for Education (2011) *Teachers' standards: Overview*. London: Crown Copyright.

Department for Education (2013) *Music programmes of study: Key stage 3*. London: Crown Copyright.

Department for Education (2015) *Carter Review of initial teacher training*. Available at: https://assets.publishing.service.gov.uk/government/uploads/system/uploads/attachment_data/file/399957/Carter_Review.pdf [accessed: 19 November 2021].

Department for Education (2016a) *A framework of core content for initial teacher training (ITT)*. London: Crown Copyright.

Department for Education (2016b) *National standards for school-based initial teacher training (ITT) mentors*. London: Crown Copyright.

Department for Education (2016c) *Standards for teachers' professional development*. London: Crown Copyright.

Department for Education (2021) *Model music curriculum: Key stages 1 to 3. Non-statutory guidance for the national curriculum in England*. London: Crown Copyright.

Department for Education and Skills (2006) *Secondary national strategy for school improvement. Foundation subjects: KS3 music*. London: Crown Copyright.

De Shazer, S. (1988) *Clues: Investigating solutions in brief therapy*. New York: Norton.

Devaney, K. (2018). How composing assessment in English secondary examinations affect teaching and learning practices (PhD dissertation). School of Education, Birmingham City University.

Doyle, A.C. (1892/2004) *The adventures of Sherlock Holmes*. London: Collector's Library.

Doyle, W. (1980) *Classroom management*. West Lafayette, IN: Kappa Delta Pi.

Driscoll, L.G., Parkes, K.A., Tilley-Lubbs, G.A. et al. (2009) 'Navigating the lonely sea: Peer Mentoring and collaboration among aspiring women scholars', *Mentoring and Tutoring: Partnership in Learning*, 17, pp. 5–21.

Duffy, K. (2013) 'Providing constructive feedback to students during mentoring', *Nursing Standard*, 27(31), pp. 50–58.

Dweck, C. (2008) 'Can personality be changed? The role of beliefs in personality and change', *Current Directions in Psychological Science*, 17(6), pp. 391–394.

Dweck, C. (2017) *Mindset - updated edition: Changing the way you think to fulfil your potential*. New York: Hachette UK.

Dwyer, R. (2016) *Music teachers values and beliefs*. London: Routledge.
Egan, G. (2002) *The skilled helper: A problem management and opportunity development approach to helping*. 7th edn. Pacific Grove, CA: Brooks Cole.
Eisner, E. (2001) 'Music education six months after the turn of the century', *International Journal of Music Education*, 37(1), pp. 5-12.
Eisner, E.W. (2002) *The arts and the creation of mind*. New Haven, CT: Yale University Press.
Elliott, D. (1986) 'Finding a place for music in the curriculum', *British Journal of Music Education*, 3(2), pp. 135-151.
Elliott, D. (1995) *Music matters: A new philosophy of music education*. Oxford: Oxford University Press.
Elliott, D.J. and Silverman, M. (2015) *Music matters: A philosophy of music education*. 2nd edn. New York: Oxford University Press.
Ellis, A. and Dryden, D. (1997) *The practice of rational emotive behaviour therapy*. 2nd edn. New York: Springer Publishing Company.
Elpus, K. (2007) 'Improving music education advocacy', *Arts Education Policy Review*, 108(3), pp. 13-18.
Emmons, R. and McCullough, M. (2004) *The psychology of gratitude*. New York: Oxford University Press.
Emmons, R.A. and Stern, R. (2013) 'Gratitude as a psychotherapeutic intervention', *Journal of Clinical Psychology*, 69(8), pp. 846-855.
Engeström, Y. (1987) *Learning by expanding: An activity-theoretical approach to developmental research*. Helsinki: Orienta-Konsultit.
Engeström, Y. (2001) 'Expansive learning at work: Toward an activity theoretical conceptualization', *Journal of Education and Work*, 14(1), pp. 133-156.
Engeström, Y. (2009) 'Expansive learning', in Illeris, K. (ed.) *Contemporary theories of learning*. Abingdon: Routledge.
Engeström, Y. and Miettinen, R. (1999) 'Introduction', in Engeström, Y., Miettinen, R. and Punamäki, R.L. (eds.) *Perspectives on activity theory*. Cambridge: Cambridge University Press.
Evans, P. (2015) 'Self-determination theory: An approach to motivation in music education', *Musicae Scientiae*, 36(1), pp. 51-62.
Evans, J. and Philpot, C. (Eds.) (2009) *A practical guide to teaching music in the secondary school*. Abingdon: Routledge.
Fallin, J. and Royse, D. (1994) 'Common problems of the new music teacher', *Journal of Music Teacher Education*, 4(1), pp. 13-18.
Farrell, C. (2018) 'The role of the mentor', in Dikilitas, K., Mede, E. and Atay, D. (eds.) *Mentorship strategies in teacher education*. Hershey, PA: IGI Global.
Fautley, M. (2005) 'A new model of the group composing process of lower secondary school students', *Music Education Research*, 7(1), pp. 39-57.
Fautley, M. (2009) 'Assessment for learning in music', in Evans, J. and Philpott, C. (eds.) *A practical guide to teaching music in the secondary school*. Abingdon: Routledge.
Fautley, M. (2010) *Assessment in music education*. Oxford: Oxford University Press.
Fautley, M. (2012) 'Developing musical leadership', in Price, J. and Savage, J. (eds.) *Teaching secondary music*. London: Sage.
Fautley, M. (2014) 'Assessment of composing in higher education music education: Purposes and practices', in Burnard, P. (ed.) *Developing creativities in higher education music education: International perspectives and practices*. London: Routledge.
Fautley, M. (2015) *Teach through music evaluation report*. London: Trinity Laban Conservatoire of Music and Dance.
Fautley, M. (2018) 'Why music educators really understand skills', *British Journal of Music Education*, 35(1), pp. 1-4.

Fautley, M. and Daubney, A. (2015) *The national curriculum for music: A framework for curriculum, pedagogy and assessment in key stage 3 music*. London: Incorporated Society of Musicians (ISM)/SoundCity: Brighton and Hove.

Fautley, M. and Daubney, A. (2019) *ISM - The National Curriculum for Music.A revised framework for curriculum, pedagogy and assessment in key stage 3 music*. Availabe at: chrome-extension://efaidnbmnnnibpcajpcglclefindmkaj/https://www.ism.org/images/images/ISM_The-National-Curriculum-for-Music-booklet_KS3_2019_digital.pdf [accessed 2 May 25].

Fautley, M. and Kinsella, V. (2016) 'The use of activity theory as an analytical tool for the music learning process,' in Bugos, J. (ed.) *Contemporary research in music learning across the lifespan: music education and human development. Routledge studies in music education*. Abingdon: Routledge.

Fautley, M. and Savage, J. (2007) *Creativity in secondary education*. Exeter: Learning Matters Ltd.

Fautley, M. and Savage, J. (2008) *Assessment for learning and teaching in secondary schools*. Exeter: Learning Matters.

Fautley, M. and Savage, M. (2013) *Lesson planning for effective learning*. Berkshire: Open University Press.

Fautley, M. and Savage, J. (2014) *Lesson planning for effective learning*. Abingdon: Open University Press.

Ferm Almqvist, C., Vinge, J., Väkevä, L. et al. (2017) 'Assessment as learning in music education: The risk of "criteria compliance" replacing "learning" in the Scandinavian countries', *Research Studies in Music Education*, 39(1), pp. 3-18.

Ferm Thorgersen, C. (2014) 'Learning among critical friends in the instrumental setting', *Update - University of South Carolina. Dept. of Music*, 32(2), pp. 60-67.

Field, R., James, R., Buchanan, J. et al. (2013) 'Teacher retention and attrition: Views of early career teachers', *Australian Journal of Teacher Education*, 38(3), pp. 112-129.

Finney, J. (2017) *Music curriculum, pedagogy, assessment and the order of things*. Available at: https://jfin107.wordpress.com [accessed: 30 October 2019].

Finney, J. and Philpott, C. (2010) 'Informal learning and meta-pedagogy in initial teacher education in England', *British Journal of Music Education*, 27(1), pp. 7-19.

Fischer, D., Stanszus, L., Geiger, S. et al. (2017) 'Mindfulness and sustainable consumption: A systematic literature review of research approaches and findings', *Journal of Cleaner Production*, 162(20), pp. 544-558.

Folkestad, G. (2006) 'Formal and informal learning situations or practices vs formal and informal ways of learning', *British Journal of Music Education*, 23(2), pp. 135-145.

Froehlich, H.C. (2007) *Sociology for music teachers: Perspectives for practice*. Upper Saddle River, NJ: Prentice Hall.

Gaunt, H. (2006) Student and teacher perceptions of one to one instrumental and vocal tuition in a conservatoire. Institute of Education, London University.

Gedera, D. (2016) 'The application of activity theory in identifying contradictions in a university blended learning course', in Gedera, D. and Williams, P.J. (eds.) *Activity theory in education*. Rotterdam: Sense Publishers.

Georgii-Hemming, E. (2016) 'Music as knowledge in an educational context', in Georgii-Hemming, E., Burnard, P. and Holgersen, S.-E. (eds.) *Professional knowledge in music teacher education*. Farnham: Routledge.

Ghaye, T. (2010) *Teaching and learning through reflective practice: A practical guide for positive action* (2nd ed.). Abingdon: Routledge.

Gladwell, M. (2009) *Outliers: The story of success*. London: Penguin.

Glaser, B.G. and Strauss, A.L. (1971) *Status passage*. New Brunswick: AldineTransaction.

Green, L. (2006) 'Popular music education in and for itself, and for 'other' music: Current research in the classroom', *International Journal of Music Education*, 24(2), pp. 101-118.

Green, L. (2008) *Music, informal learning and the school: A new classroom pedagogy.* Aldershot: Ashgate.

Gu, J., Strauss, C., Bond, R. et al. (2015) 'How do mindfulness-based cognitive therapy and mindfulness-based stress reduction improve mental health and wellbeing? A systematic review and meta-analysis of mediation studies', *Clinical Psychology Review*, 37, pp. 1-12.

Gudmundsdottir, S. and Shulman, L. (1987) 'Pedagogical content knowledge in social studies', *Scandinavian Journal of Educational Research*, 31(2), pp. 59-70.

Haggard, D.L., Dougherty, T.W., Turban, D.B. et al. (2011) 'Who is a mentor? A review of evolving definitions and implications for research', *Journal of Management*, 37, pp. 280-304.

Hale, J.A. (2008) *A guide to curriculum mapping.* Thousand Oaks, CA: Corwin.

Hallam, S. (2006) *Music psychology in education.* London: Institute of Education.

Hallam, S. (2010) 'The power of music: Its impact on the intellectual, social and personal development of children and young people', *International Journal of Music Education*, 28(3), pp. 269-289.

Hallam, S. and Himonedes, E. (2022) *The power of music. An exploration of the evidence.* Open Book Publishers. Available at: https://www.openbookpublishers.com/books/10.11647/obp.0292 [accessed: 14 May 2025].

Hallam, S. and Rogers, L. (2010) 'Creativity', in Hallam, S. and Creech, A. (eds.) *Music education in the 21st century in the United Kingdom: Achievements, analysis and aspirations.* London: Institute of Education.

Hallam, S., Creech, A. and McQueen, H. (2017) 'Can the adoption of informal approaches to learning music in school music lessons promote musical progression?', *British Journal of Music Education*, 34(2), pp. 127-151.

Harford, J., MacRuairc, G. and McCartan, D. (2010) 'Lights, camera, reflection: Using peer-video to promote reflective dialogue among student teachers', *Teacher Development: An International Journal of Teachers' Professional Development*, 14(1), pp. 57-68.

Hargreaves, D.J., Purves, R.M., Welch, G.F. et al. (2007) 'Developing identities and attitudes in musicians and classroom music teachers', *British Journal of Educational Psychology*, 77(3), pp. 665-682.

Harpaz, Y. (2014) *Teaching and learning in a community of thinking: The third model.* Dordrecht: Springer.

Harrison, J., Dymoke, S. and Pell, T. (2006) 'Mentoring beginning teachers in secondary schools: An analysis of practice', *Teacher and Teacher Education*, 22(8), pp. 1055-1067.

Hattie, J. and Timperley, H. (2007) 'The power of feedback', *Review of Educational Research*, 77(1), pp. 81-112.

Hendricks, K. (2011) 'The philosophy of Shinichi Suzuki: "Music education as love education"', *Philosophy of Music Education Review*, 19(2), pp. 136-154.

Henry, A. (2019) 'A drama of selves: Investigating teacher identity development from dialogical and complexity perspectives', *Studies in Second Language and Learning*, 9(2), pp. 263-285.

Hensley, L. and Munn, K. (2020) 'The power of writing about procrastination: Journaling as a tool for change', *Journal of Further and Higher Education*, 44(10), pp. 1450-1465.

Hesterman, P.K. (2012) 'Growing as a professional music educator', *General Music Today*, 25(3), pp. 36-41.

Hicks, C.D., Glasgow, N.A. and McNary, S.J. (2005) 'Choosing the best strategies for supporting new teachers', in Hicks, C.D., Glasgow, N.A. and McNary, S.J. (eds.) *What successful mentors do: 81 research-based strategies for new teacher induction, training, and support.* Thousand Oaks, CA: Corwin.

Higgins, R. (2000) *Be more critical! Rethinking assessment feedback.* British Educational Research Association Conference, Cadriff University, September 7-10, 2000.

Higgins, M.C. and Thomas, D.A. (2001) 'Constellations and careers: Toward understanding the effects of multiple developmental relationships', *Journal of Organizational Behavior*, 22, pp. 223-247.

Hobbs, V. (2007) 'Faking it or hating it: Can reflective practice be forced?', *Reflective Practice*, 8(3), pp. 405-417.

Hobson, A.J. (2003) *Mentoring and coaching for new leaders*. Nottingham: National College for New Leadership.

Hobson, A. and Malderez, A. (2015) 'Judgementoring and other threats to realising the potential of school-based mentoring in teacher education', *International Journal of Mentoring and Coaching in Education*, 2(2), pp. 89-108.

Hook, P., Booth, N., Price, A. et al. (2019) *SOLO taxonomy in music education: Growing high quality musicians through a reflective learning environment*. New Zealand: Essential Resources Educational Publishers Limited.

Howes, L.M. and Goodman-Delahunty, J. (2015) 'Teachers' career decisions: Perspectives on choosing teaching careers and on staying or leaving', *Issues in Educational Research*, 25(1), pp. 18-35.

Hudson, P. (2012) 'How can schools support beginning teachers? A call for timely induction and mentoring for effective teaching', *Australian Journal of Teacher Education*, 37(7), pp. 71-84.

Hudson, P. (2016) 'Forming the mentor-mentee relationship', *Mentoring & Tutoring: Partnership in Learning*, 24(1), pp. 30-43.

IBO (International Baccalaureate Organisation) (2022) Music subject page. Available at: https://www.ibo.org/programmes/diploma-programme/curriculum/the-arts/music/ [accessed: 2 May 2025].

Incorporated Society of Musicians (2015) *The national curriculum for music: A framework for curriculum, pedagogy and assessment in key stage 3 music*. London: Incorporated Society of Musicians (ISM)/SoundCity: Brighton and Hove.

Incorporated Society of Musicians (2018) *Consultation on the future of music education: Results of the Incorporated Society of Musicians' (ISM) surveys conducted over summer 2018*. Available at: https://www.ism.org/images/images/Future-of-Music-Education-ISM-report-December-2018.pdf [accessed: 29 April 2021].

Isbell, D.S. (2015) 'The socialization of music teachers: A review of the literature', *Update: Applications of Research in Music Education*, 34(1), pp. 5-12.

Ivtzan, I. and Lomas, T. (2016) *Mindfulness in positive psychology: The science of meditation and wellbeing*. New York: Routledge.

Johnson, R. (2010) 'Critically reflective musicianship', in Regelski, T.A. and Gates, J.T. (eds.) *Music education for changing times*. New York: Springer.

Jorgensen, E.R. (2010) 'School music education and change', *Music Educators Journal*, 96(4), pp. 21-27.

Katz, L. (1995) *Talks with teachers: A collection*. Norwood, NJ: Ablex.

Kay, M. (2013) *Sound before symbol: Developing literacy through music*. London: Sage.

Kelly, A.V. (2009) *The curriculum: Theory and practice*. 6th edn. London: Sage.

Kinsella, V. (2015) 'Activity theory', in Addison, N. and Burgess, L. (eds.) *Learning to teach art and design in the secondary school*. London: Routledge.

Kinsella, V. and Fautley, M. (2016) 'The use of activity theory as an analytical tool for the music learning processes', in Bugos, J. (ed.) *Contemporary research in music learning across the lifespan: music education and human development*. Abingdon: Routledge, pp. 26-38.

Kokotsaki, D. and Hallam, S. (2007) 'Higher education music students' perceptions of the benefits of participative music making', *Music Education Research*, 9(1), pp. 93-109.

Kolb, D.A. (1984) *Experiential learning: Experience as the source of learning and development*. Englewood Cliffs, NJ: Prentice-Hall.

Kolman, J.S., Roegman, R. and Goodwin, A.L. (2017) 'Learner-centered mentoring: Building from student teachers. Individual needs and experiences as novice practitioners while MTs play many crucial', *Teacher Education Quarterly*, 44(3), pp. 93-117.

Kroll, J. (2016) 'What is meant by the term group mentoring?', *Mentoring and Tutoring: Partnership in Learning*, 24, pp. 44-58.

Krueger, P.J. (1996) 'Becoming a music teacher: Challenges of the first year', *Dialogue in Instrumental Music*, 20(2), pp. 88-104.

Kula Ünver, S. (2018) 'The knowledge quartet in the light of the literature on subject matter and pedagogical content knowledge', *Acta Didactica Napocensia*, 11(2), pp. 27-42.

Kwami, R. (1998) 'Non-western musics in education: Problems and possibilities', *British Journal of Music Education*, 15(2), pp. 161-170.

Lamont, A. (2002) 'Musical identities in the school environment', in MacDonald, R., Hargreaves, D.J. and Miell, D. (eds.) *Musical identities*. Oxford: Oxford University Press.

Lamont, A., Hargreaves, D.J., Marshall, N. et al. (2003) 'Young people's music in and out of school', *British Journal of Music Education*, 20(3), pp. 1-13.

Larivee, B. (2000) 'Transforming teaching practice: Becoming the critically reflective teacher', *Reflective Practice*, 1(3), pp. 293-307.

Lehmann, A.C., Sloboda, J.A. and Woody, R.H. (2007) *Psychology for musicians: Understanding and acquiring the skills*. Oxford: Oxford University Press.

Lejonberg, E., Elstad, E. and Christophersen, K. (2015) 'Mentor education: Challenging mentors' beliefs about mentoring', *International Journal of Mentoring and Coaching in Education*, 4(2), pp. 142-158.

Leont'ev, A.N. (1978) *Activity, consciousness, and personality*. Englewood Cliffs, NJ: Prentice-Hall.

Lerch, A., Arthur, C., Pati, A. and Gururani, S. (2019) "Music Performance Analysis: A Survey", 20th International Society for Music Information Retrieval Conference, Delft, The Netherlands, 2019.

Liebert, M.A. (2010) 'The health benefits of yoga and exercise: A review of comparison studies', *The Journal of Alternative and Complementary Medicine*, 16(1), pp. 3-12.

London, M. (1995) 'Giving feedback. Source-centred antecedents and consequences of constructive and destructive feedback', *Human Resource Management Review*, 5(3), pp. 159-188.

López-Íñiguez, G. (2017) 'Constructivist self-regulated music learning', *Finnish Journal of Music Education*, 20(1), pp. 134-138.

López-Íñiguez, G. and Pozo, J.I. (2016) 'Analysis of constructive practice in instrumental music education: Case study with an expert cello teacher', *Teaching and Teacher Education*, 60, pp. 97-107.

Malmberg, I. (2017) 'Transitions between art and pedagogy: Mentoring music teacher novices in Austria', *Global Education Review*, 4(4), pp. 39-53.

Malmberg, I. (2018) 'Auf einer mehrspurigen Autobahnbrücke. Die Statuspassage am Beginn des Musiklehrberuf', in Krettenauer, T., Schäfer-Lembeck, H.-U. and Zöllner-Dressler, S. (eds.) *Musiklehrer*innenbildung. Veränderungen und Kontext: Beiträge der Kooperativen Tagung München 2018*. München: Allitera.

Mark, M.L. (2005) 'Why does our profession need advocacy?', *International Journal of Music Education*, 23(2), pp. 95-98.

Marsh, K. (2013) 'Exploring children's musical play', in Burnard, P. and Murphy, R. (eds.) *Teaching music creatively: Learning to teach in the primary school series*. Abingdon: Routledge.

Marshall, N.A. and Hargreaves, D.J. (2008) 'Teachers' views of the primary-secondary transition in music education in England', *Music Education Research*, 10(1), pp. 63-74.

Mason, S. and Poyatos Matas, C. (2015) 'Teacher attrition and retention research in Australia: Towards a new theoretical framework', *Australian Journal of Teacher Education*, 40(11), pp. 45-66.

Mayer, D., Allard, A., Bates, R. et al. (2015) *Studying the effectiveness of teacher education - final report*. Geelong: Deakin University.

Maynard, T. and Furlong, J. (1995) 'Learning to teach and models of mentoring', in Kerry, T. and Shelton-Mayes, A. (eds.) *Issues in mentoring*. London: Routledge, pp. 10-14.

McIntyre, D., Pedder, D. and Rudduck, J. (2007) 'Pupil voice: Comfortable and uncomfortable learnings for teachers', *Research Papers in Education*, 20(2), pp. 149-168.

McPhail, G. (2017) 'Powerful knowledge: Insights from music's case', *The Curriculum Journal*, 1(1), pp. 1-15.

Measor, L. and Woods, P. (1984) *Changing schools*. Milton Keynes: Open University Press.

Mena, J., Hennissen, P. and Loughran, J. (2017) 'Developing pre-service teachers' professional knowledge of teaching: The influence of mentoring', *Teaching and Teacher Education*, 66, pp. 47-59.

Merrion, M. (1996) 'Classroom management for beginning music educators', in Spruce, G. (ed.) *Teaching music*. London: Routledge.

Mills, J. (1991) 'Assessing musical performance musically', *Educational Studies*, 17(2), pp. 173-181.

Mills, J. (2005) *Music in the school*. Oxford: Oxford University Press.

Mills, J. and Paynter, J. (eds.) (2008) *Thinking and making: Selections from the writings of John Paynter on music education*. Oxford: Oxford University Press.

Ministry of Education and Research (2010) *Differentiated primary and lower secondary teacher education programmes for year 1-7 and years 5-10*. Oslo: Ministry of Education and Research.

Montgomery, D. (2012) *Helping teachers develop through classroom observation*. Abingdon: Routledge.

Munroe, A.M. (2019) 'Keeping my head above water: The influence of context on the concerns of a novice urban music teacher', *Visions of Research in Music Education*, 33, pp. 1-23.

Murphy, C. (2002) 'How far do test of musical ability shed light on the nature of musical intelligence?', in Spruce, G. (ed.) *Aspects of teaching secondary music: Perspectives on practice*. London: Routledge.

Murphy, R. (2007) 'Harmonizing assessment and music in the classroom', in Bresler (ed.) *International handbook of research in arts education*. Dordrecht: Springer, p. 361.

Music Commission (2019) *Returning our ambition for music learning. Every child taking music further*. Available at: chrome-extension://efaidnbmnnnibpcajpcglclefindmkaj/https://www.musicmark.org.uk/wp-content/uploads/Music-Commission-Report.pdf?x48237. [accessed: 2 May 2025].

National Curriculum Council (1992) *Music non-statutory guidance*. York: National Curriculum Council.

National Foundation for Educational Research (2008) *Mentoring and coaching for professionals: A study of the research evidence*. London: Teaching and Development Agency.

National Oak Academy (2020) *Music secondary key stage 3: Curriculum plan 2020-21*. Version 1.0. London: NOA. Available at: https://classroom.thenational.academy/subjects-by-key-stage/key-stage-3/subjects/music [accessed: 1 November 2023].

Nelson-Jones, R. (2015) *Nelson-Jones' theory and practice of counselling and psychotherapy*. 6th edn. London: Sage.

New Teacher Centre (2011) *NTC continuum of mentoring practice*. Santa Cruz: New Teacher Center.

Norrish, J.M., Williams, P., O'Connor, M. et al. (2013) 'An applied framework for positive education', *International Journal of Wellbeing*, 3(2), pp. 147-161.

Oates, T. (2011) 'Could do better: Using international comparisons to refine the national curriculum in England', *Curriculum Journal*, 22(2), pp. 121-150.

OFSTED (2009) *Making more of music: An evaluation of music in schools 2005/8*. London: OFSTED. Available at: https://dera.ioe.ac.uk/308/1/Making%20more%20of%20music.pdf [accessed: 24 August 2022].

OFSTED (2012) *Music in schools: wider still and wider. Quality and inequality in music education 2008-2011*. London: OFSTED. Available at: https://assets.publishing.service.gov.uk/government/uploads/system/uploads/attachment_data/file/413347/Music_in_schools_wider_still__and_wider.pdf [accessed: 24 August 2021].

OFSTED (2018a) *Curriculum research: Assessing intent, implementation and impact*. London: Crown Copyright. Available at: https://www.gov.uk/government/publications/curriculum-research-assessing-intent-implementation-and-impact [accessed: 30 October 2019].

OFSTED (2018b) *Six models of lesson observation: An international perspective*. Manchester: Office for Standards in Education, Children's Services and Skills.

OFSTED (2019a) *Inspecting the curriculum*. London: Crown Copyright. Available at: https://assets.publishing.service.gov.uk/government/uploads/system/uploads/attachment_data/file/814685/Inspecting_the_curriculum.pdf [accessed: 23 April 2021].

OFSTED (2019b) *Busting the 'intent' myth*. London: Crown Copyright. Available at: https://educationinspection.blog.gov.uk/2019/07/01/busting-the-intent-myth/ [accessed: 30 October 2019].

OFSTED (2019c) *School inspection handbook*. London: Crown Copyright.

Ohio Department for Education (2015) *Ohio standards for professional development*. Columbus, OH: Department for Education.

O'Leary, M. and Gewessler, A. (2014) 'Changing the culture: Beyond graded lesson observations', *Adults Learning*, 25, pp. 38-41.

Olsson, B. (2001) Scandinavia. In: D. J. Hargreaves and A. C. North (Eds.), Musical development and learning: The international perspective (pp. 175-186). London, UK: Continuum.

Pajares, M.F. (1992) 'Teachers' beliefs and educational research: Cleaning up a messy construct', *Review of Educational Research*, 62(3), pp. 307-332.

Palmer, P. (2011) 'Revisiting the 'P' in the PRACTICE coaching model', *The Coaching Psychologist*, 7(2), pp. 156-158.

Palmer, P. and Cooper, C. (2013) *How to deal with stress*. 3rd edn. London: Kogan Page.

Palmer, S. (1990) 'Stress mapping: A visual technique to aid counselling or training', *Employee Counselling Today*, 2(2), pp. 9-12.

Palmer, S. and Whybrow, A. (eds.) (2018) *Handbook of coaching psychology: A guide for practitioners*. 2nd edn. London: Routledge.

Park, N. and Peterson, C. (2008) 'Positive psychology and character strengths: Application to strengths-based school counselling', *Professional School Counselling*, 12(2), pp. 85-92.

Paynter, J. (1992) *Sound and structure*. Cambridge: Cambridge University Press.

Paynter, J. (1994) 'The composer as educator: Things that matter', in Mills, J. and Paynter, J. (eds.) *Thinking and making*. Oxford: Oxford University Press.

Pea, R.D. (1993) 'Practices of distributed intelligence and design for education', in Salomon, G. (ed.) *Distributed cognitions: Psychological and educational considerations*. Cambridge: Cambridge University Press.

Pellegrino, K. (2009) 'Connections between performer and teacher identities in music teachers: Setting an agenda for research', *Journal of Music Teacher Education*, 19(1), pp. 39-55.

Pellegrino, K. (2011) 'Exploring the benefits of music-making as professional development for music teachers', *Arts Education Policy Review*, 112(2), pp. 79-88.

Pellegrino, K., Conway, C.M. and Si Millican, J. (2017) 'Tenure and promotion experiences of music teacher educators: A mixed-methods study', *Journal of Music Teacher Education*, 27(2), pp. 82-99.

Peterson, C. and Seligman, M. (2004) *Character strengths and virtues*. Washington, DC: American Psychological Association/Oxford University Press.

Philpott, C. (2010) 'The sociological critique of curriculum music in England: Is radical change possible?', in Wright, R. (ed.) *Sociology and music education*. 1st edn. Farnham: Ashgate.

Philpott, C. (2016) 'The what, how and where of musical learning and development', in Cooke, C., Evans, K., Philpott, C. et al. (eds.) *Learning to teach music in the secondary school*. 3rd edn. Abingdon: Routledge.

Philpott, C. and Evans, K. (2016) 'Creativity and music education', in Cooke, C., Evans, K., Philpott, C. et al. (eds.) *Learning to teach music in the secondary school*. 3rd edn. Abingdon: Routledge.

Philpott, C. and Kubilius, (2015) 'Social justice in the English secondary music classroom', in Benedict, C., Schmidt, P., Spruce, G. et al. (eds.) *The Oxford handbook of social justice in music education*. Oxford: Oxford University Press.

Philpott, C. and Spruce, G. (eds.) (2012) *Debates in music teaching*. Abingdon: Routledge.

Philpott, C. and Spruce, G. (2021) 'Structure and agency in music education', in Wright, R., Johansen, G., Kanellopoulos, P. et al. (eds.) *The Routledge handbook to sociology of music education*. Abingdon: Routledge.

Pitts, S. (2012) *Chances and choices: Exploring the impact of music education*. New York: Oxford University Press.

Pitts, S.E. (2017) 'What is music education for? Understanding and fostering routes into life-long musical engagement', *Music Education Research*, 19(2), pp. 160-168.

Plummeridge, C. (2001) 'The place of music in the school curriculum', Learning to Teach Music in the Secondary School (1st edition), Abingdon: RoutledgeFalmer.

Pohio, K. (2016) 'Activity theory tools', in Gedera, D. and Williams, P.J. (eds.) *Activity theory in education*. Rotterdam: Sense Publishers.

Pollard, A. (2014) *Reflective teaching in schools*. 4th edn. London: Bloomsbury.

Postholm, M.B. (2015) 'Methodologies in cultural-historical activity theory: The example of school-based development', *Education Research*, 57(1), pp. 43-58.

Priest, P. (2002) 'Putting listening first: A case of priorities', in Spruce, G. (ed.) *Aspects of teaching secondary music: Perspectives on practice*. London: Routledge.

Priestley, M., Biesta, G. and Robinson, S. (2015) *Teacher agency: An ecological approach*. London: Bloomsbury.

QCA (2004) *Music 2002/3 annual report on curriculum and assessment*. London: QCA.

Ragins, B. (2016) 'From the ordinary to the extraordinary: High quality mentoring relationships at work', *Organizational Dynamics*, 45, pp. 228-244.

Regelski, T.A. (1986) 'A sound approach to sound composition', *Music Educators Journal*, 72(9), pp. 41-45.

Regelski, TA. (2009) 'The ethics of teaching as profession and praxis', *Visions of Research in Music Education*, 13, pp. 1-34.

Reif, F. (2008) *Applying cognitive science to education: Thinking and learning in scientific and other complex domains*. Cambridge, MA: MIT Press.

Reimer, B. (2005) 'The danger of music education advocacy', *International Journal of Music Education*, 23(2), pp. 139-142.

Richter, D., Kunter, M., Lüdtke, O. et al. (2013) 'How different mentoring approaches affect beginning teachers' development in the first years of practice', *Teaching and Teaching Education*, 36, pp. 166-177.

Robson, C. and McCarten, K. (2016) *Real world research*. 4th edn. Oxford: John Wiley and Sons.

Rowland, T., Huckstep, P. and Thwaites, A. (2005) 'Elementary teachers' mathematics subject knowledge: The knowledge quartet and the case of Naomi', *Journal of Mathematics Teacher Education*, 8(3), pp. 255-281.

Sadler, D.R. (1989) 'Formative assessment and the design of instructional systems', *Instructional Science*, 18, pp. 119-144.

Savage, J. (ed.) (2013) *The guided reader to teaching and learning music*. Abingdon: Routledge.

Savage, J. and Barnard, D. (2019) *The state of play - a review of music education in England 2019*. Musicians Union. Available at: https://musiciansunion.org.uk/MusiciansUnion/

media/resource/Guides%20and%20reports/Education/MU_The-State-of-Play_WEB.pdf?ext=.pdf [accessed: 15 August 2023].

Savage, J. and Fautley, M. (2013) *A to z of teaching*. Berkshire, UK: Open University Press.

Scharmer, C. (2018) *Theory U: Leading from the future as it emerges*. 2nd edn. Oakland, CA: Berrett-Koehler.

Schartel, S.A. (2012) 'Giving feedback – An integral part of education', *Best Practice & Research Clinical Anaesthesiology*, 26(1), pp. 77–87.

Schmidt, M. (2012) 'Transition from student to teacher: Preservice teachers' beliefs and practices', *Journal of Music Teacher Education*, 23(1), pp. 27–49.

Schmidt, P. and Robbins, J. (2011) 'Looking backwards to reach forward: A strategic architecture for professional development in music education', *Arts Education Policy Review*, 112(2), pp. 95–103.

Schön, D. (1983) *The reflective practitioner*. Aldershot: Academic Publishing.

Searby, L.J. (2016) *Best Practices in mentoring for teacher and leader development*. Charlotte, NC: Information Age Publishing (Perspectives in Mentoring).

Seligman, M., Railton, P., Baumeister, R. *et al.* (2016) *Homo prospectus*. London: Oxford University Press.

Sexton, F. (2012) 'Practitioner challenges working with informal learning pedagogies', *British Journal of Music Education*, 29(1), pp. 7–11.

Shulman, L. (1986) 'Those who understand: Knowledge growth in teaching', *Educational Researcher*, 15(1), pp. 4–14.

Shulman, L. (1987) 'Knowledge and teaching: Foundations of the new reform', *Harvard Educational Review*, 57(1), pp. 1–23.

Sindberg, L. (2011) 'Alone all together – The conundrum of music teacher isolation and connectedness', *Bulletin of the Council for Research in Music Education*, 189, pp. 7–22.

Singapore Management University (2019) MODULE II The Teacher As A Curriculum Planner. Available at: https://www.scribd.com/document/671842238/MODULE-II-the-Teacher-as-a-Curriculum-Planner#:~:text=1.,creating%20technology%2Dintegrated%20lesson%20plans [accessed: 2 May 2025].

Small, C. (1987) *Music of the common tongue*. London: Calder Riverrun.

Small, C. (1998) *Musicking: The meanings of performing and listening*. Hanover, NH: Wesleyan University Press.

Smith, R. and Gallagher, K. (2019) 'The experience of OFSTED: Fear, judgement and symbolic violence', in Bennet, P. and Smith, R. (eds.) *Identity and resistance in further education*. London: Routledge.

Spruce, G. (2002) Ways of thinking about music: political dimensions and educational consequences. In: G. Spruce (Ed.) Teaching Music in Secondary Schools: A reader, 1st ed., London: RoutledgeFalmer, pp, 3-24.

Spruce, G. (2012) 'Musical knowledge, critical consciousness and critical thinking', in Philpott, C. and Spruce, G. (eds.) *Debates in music teaching*. London: Routledge.

Spruce, G. (2016) 'Culture, society and musical learning', in Cooke, C., Evans, K., Philpott, C. *et al.* (eds.) *Learning to teach music in the secondary school*. 3rd edn. Abingdon: Routledge.

Spruce, G. (2017). 'The power of discourse: Reclaiming social justice from and for music education', *Education 3-13*, 45(6), pp. 720–733.

Spruce, G. with Matthews, F. (2012) 'Musical ideologies, practices and pedagogies', in Philpott, C. and Spruce, G. (eds.) *Debates in music teaching*. Abingdon: Routledge.

Spruce, G., Stanley, A. and Li, M. (2021) 'Music teacher professional agency as challenge to music education policy', *Arts Education Policy Review*, 122(1), pp. 65–74.

Stierer, B. and Antoniou, M. (2004) 'Are there distinctive methodologies for pedagogic research in higher education?', *Teaching in Higher Education*, 9, pp. 275–285.

Stobart, G. (2014) *The expert learner: Challenging the myth of ability*. Maidenhead: Open University Press.
Strong, M. and Baron, W. (2003) 'An analysis of mentoring conversations with beginning teachers: Suggestions and responses', *Teaching and Teacher Education*, 20(1), pp. 47-57.
Swanwick, K. (1979) *A basis for music education*. Windsor: NFER.
Swanwick, K. (1988) *Music, mind, and education*. London: Routledge.
Swanwick, K. (1992) 'Music education Before the national curriculum', in Spruce, G. (ed.) *Teaching music*. Abingdon: Routledge.
Swanwick, K. (1994) *Musical knowledge: Intuition, analysis and music education*. London: Routledge.
Swanwick, K. (1996) 'Music education before the national curriculum', in Spruce, G. (ed.) *Teaching music*. London: Routledge.
Swanwick, K. (1999) *Teaching music musically*. London: Routledge.
Swanwick, K. (2012) *Teaching music musically*. Abingdon: Routledge.
Swanwick, K. and Tillman, J. (1986) 'The sequence of musical development: A study of children's composition', *British Journal of Music Education*, 3(3), pp. 305-339.
Sweller, J. (1988) 'Cognitive load during problem solving: Effects on learning', *Cognitive Science*, 12(2), pp. 257-285.
Symonds, J. (2015) *Understanding school transition: What happens to children and how to help them*. London: Routledge.
The State Education Department/The University of the State of New York (2011) *The New York state mentoring standards*. Albany, NY: The State Education Department/The University of the State of New York.
Thompson, L.K. (2007) 'Considering beliefs in learning to teach music', *Music Educators Journal*, 93(3), pp. 30-35.
Van Driel, J.H. and Berry, A. (2012) 'Teacher professional development focusing on pedagogical content knowledge', *Educational Researcher*, 41(1), pp. 26-28.
van Es, E. (2012) 'Examining the development of a teacher learning community: The case of a video club', *Teacher and Teacher Education*, 28(2), pp. 182-192.
van Nieuwerburgh, C. (ed.) (2016) *Coaching in professional contexts*. London: Sage.
Vygotsky, L. (1978) Mind in society. Cambridge, MA: Harvard University Press.
Webster, P. (1990) 'Creativity as creative thinking', *Music Educators' Journal*, 76(9), pp. 22-28.
Welch, G., Purves, R., Hargreaves, D. *et al*. (2011) 'Early career challenges in secondary school music teaching', *British Educational Research Journal*, 37(2), pp. 285-315.
Welsch, R. and Devlin, P. (2012) 'Developing preservice teachers' reflection: Examining the use of video', *Action Teacher Education*, 28(4), pp. 53-61.
West, C. and Clauhs, M. (2015) 'Strengthening music programs while avoiding advocacy pitfalls', *Arts Education Policy Review*, 116(2), pp. 57-62.
Westerlund, H. (2008) 'Justifying music education: A view from here-and-now value experience', *Philosophy of Music Education Review*, 16(1), pp. 79-95.
Westerlund, H. (2012) 'What can a reflective teacher learn from philosophies of music education', in Philpott, C. and Spruce, G. (eds.) *Debates in music teaching*. Abingdon: Routledge.
Whitmore, J. (2017) *Coaching for performance: The principles and practice of coaching and leadership*. 5th edn. London: Nicolas Brealey Publishing.
Wiggins, G. and McTighe, J. (2005) *Understanding by design*. New York: Prentice Hall.
Wiliam, D. (2015) Changing what teachers do is more important than changing what they know. Available at: https://www.dylanwiliamcenter.com/changing-what-teachers-do-is-more-important-than-changing-what-they-know/ [last accessed 24 april 2019].

Wiliam, D. (2016) *Leadership for teacher learning*. West Palm Beach, FL. Learning Sciences International.

Wiliam, D. (2018) *Embedded formative assessment*. 2nd edn. Bloomington, IN: Solution Tree Press.

Wiliam, D. and Leahy, S. (2015) *Embedding formative assessment*. West Palm Beach, FL: Learning Sciences International.

Williams, D.A. (2019) *A different paradigm in music education: Re-examining the profession*. New York: Routledge.

Wilson, V. (2014) 'Examining teacher education through cultural historical activity theory', *Teacher Education Advancement Network (TEAN) Journal*, 6(1), pp. 20-29.

Winch, C. (2013) 'Curriculum design and epistemic ascent', *Journal of Philosophy of Education*, 47(1), pp. 128-146.

Winch, C. (2017) 'Knowing 'Wh' and knowing how: Constructing professional curricula and integrating epistemic fields', *Journal of Philosophy of Education*, 51(2), pp. 351-369.

Wolf, M. and Younie, S. (2018) 'Overcoming barriers: Towards a framework continuing professional development to foster teaching sound-based music', *Journal of Music, Technology & Education*, 11(1), pp. 83-101.

Wolf, M. and Younie, S. (2019) 'The development of an inclusive model to construct teacher's professional knowledge: Pedagogic content knowledge for sound-based music as a new subject area', *Organised Sound*, 24(3), pp. 274-288.

Wood, D. (1991) 'Aspects of teaching and learning', in Light, P., Sheldon, S. and Woodhead, M. (eds.) *Learning to think*. London: Routledge.

Wood, D.J., Bruner, J.S. and Ross, G. (1976) 'The role of tutoring in problem solving', *Journal of Child Psychiatry and Psychology*, 17(2), pp. 89-100.

Wyse, D., Hayward, L. and Pandya, J. (eds.) (2016) *The Sage handbook of curriculum, pedagogy and assessment*. London: Sage.

Yeo, N. F. (2017) *The Infallible Protagonist - a study of complexity theory and rehearsal dynamics in monodrama*. University of Sydney. DMA Thesis.

Yeo, N., Mohler, S., Paxton, I., Kwan, H.H.T., Massey, L. and Hallworth, T. (2022) '"The connection itself was the project": Capstone experiences for emerging professional musicians through WIL', *Student Success*, 13(3), pp. 37-45.

Yeo, N. F. and Rowley, J. (2018) 'Reflections on a three-way mentoring program using e-Portfolios: I Pagliacci (Leoncavallo) under the Buddy Inclusion Project', in *MISTEC 2018. Music in Schools and Teacher Education Commission*. Prague, Czech Republic. International Society for Music Education (ISME).

Yeo, N.F. and Rowley, J. (2020) ''Putting on a show' non-placement WIL in the performing arts: Documenting professional rehearsal and performance using ePortfolio reflections', *Journal of University Teaching & Learning Practice*, 17(4), pp. 1-19.

Zeserson, K., Welch, G., Burn, S. et al. (2014) *Inspiring music for all: Next steps in innovation, improvement and integration*. Paul Hamlyn Foundation review of music in schools. Available at: https://www.phf.org.uk/wp-content/uploads/2014/07/Inspiring-Music-for-All.pdf [accessed: 24 August 2022].

URLs

https://teachtalkmusic.wordpress.com/2016/09/03/what-is-ks3-music-education-for/ [accessed: 1 May 2021].

www.musicmark.org.uk/resources/10-things-schools-should-know-about-learning-music/ [accessed: 1 May 2021].

AUTHOR INDEX

Adams, K. 51
Adams, P. 96, 126
Addison, N., Burgess, L., Kinsella, V. and Kenning, D. 175
Alexander, R. 161
Allsup, R. E. 36, 68
Anderson, A. 105, 121, 126
Antovic, M. 158
Applebee, A. N. and Langer, J. 158, 159
Asghar, M. 173
Atkinson, T. and Claxton, G. 113
Atlas, G. D., Taggart, T., and Goodell, D. J. 139
Austin, J. and Reinhardt, D. 34
Ausubel, D. 188, 194

Baik, C., Larcombe, W., Brooker, A., Wyn, J., Allen, L. and Brett, M. 208, 212, 215, 216
Bakhurst, D. 173
Ballantyne, J. 57, 58, 210
Ballantyne, J. and Grootenboer, P. 37
Ballantyne, J., Kerchner, J. L., and Aróstegui, J. L. 28
Ballantyne, J. and Zhukov, K. 25, 215
Baron, R. A. 141
Barrett, M. 96
Bate, E. 35, 98
Bautista, A. and Wong, J. 38
Beauchamp, C. and Thomas L. 24, 27
Beaudoin, N. 200
Beck, S. 155
Beijaard, D. 19
Benedict, C., Schmidt, P., Spruce, G. and Woodford, P. G. 163
Benson, M. 57, 59

Berg, M. H. and Rickels, D. A. 59
Bernard, R. 25
Bernstein, B. 28
Black, P., Harrison, C., Lee, C., Marshall, B. and Wiliam, D. 137
Black, P. and Plowright, D. 169
Black, P. and Wiliam, D. 187
Blair, D. V. 59
Blakeslee, M. 35
Bloom, B., Englehart, M. Furst, E., Hill, W., and Krathwohl, D. 157
Booth, N. 186, 187
Boreen, J. and Niday, D. 73-75
Boulton, H. and Hraniak, A. 169
Bowman, W. 2, 33-34, 39
Brookfield, S. 153
Bruner, J. 124, 126, 198
Bubb, S. 121
Buell, C. 74-77
Bull, A. 21
Bunting, T. 130
Burnard, P. 159, 165
Burnard, P. and Murphy, R. 129, 159
Burnard, P. and Younker, B. 175

Caddick, P. 169
Cain, T. 76
Cain, T. and Cursley, J. 98
Campbell, J. and van Nieuwerburgh, C. 73-80
Carter, A. 37, 42, 44, 46-48, 54
Child, A. and Merrill, S. 14
Cho, C., Ramanan, R. and Feldman, M. 14
Christophersen, C. 119
Clarke, S. 195

Author Index

Clift, S. 1
Clutterbuck, D. 11-14
Cole, M. and Engeström, Y. 174-175
Colwell, R. 137
Conkling, S. W. 33
Conway, C. 51, 72-73
Conway, C. and Christensen, S. 121
Conway, C., Hansen, E., Schulz, A., Stimson, J. and Wozniak-Reese, J. 37
Conway, C. M. 38
Conway, C. M., Hibbard, S., Albert, D., and Hourigan, R. 39
Cook-Sather, A. 200
Cooke, C. and Spruce, G. 122
Cooke, C., Evans, K., Philpott, C. and Spruce G. 124, 129, 132, 164
Cordingley, P., Higgins, S., Greany, T., Buckler, N., Coles-Jordan, D., Crisp, B., Saunders, L. and Coe, R. 15
Costantino, T. and Bresler, L. 137
Creech, A. 139
Cushman, K. 200
Custodero, L. A. 116

Dalladay, C. 28
Daloz, L. 11, 14, 166-167
Dascalu, M., Coman, M., Postelnicua, R. and Nichifor, C. 145
Daubney, A. and Fautley, M. 119, 142, 154, 168, 198, 199, 203
Daubney, A. and Mackrill, D. 126
Daubney, A., Spruce, G. and Annetts, D. 32
Davis, V. W. 51
de Bruin, L. R. 72
DeLorenzo, L. 72
Denscombe, M. 150-151, 153
Devaney, K. 175
Doyle, A. C. 113
Doyle, W. 110
Driscoll, L. G., Parkes, K. A., Tilley-Lubbs, G. A., Brill, J. M. and Pitts Bannister, V. R. 6
Duffy, K. 140
Dweck, C. 51, 64
Dwyer, R. 21, 23

Egan, G. 77
Eisner, E. 33, 35

Eisner, E. W. 35
Elliott, D. 122, 156, 157
Elliott, D. J. and Silverman, M. 33, 35-37, 39-40
Elpus, K. 32, 35
Engeström, Y. 97, 173-175
Engeström, Y. and Miettinen, R. 173
Evans, J. and Philpot, C. 204
Evans, P. 96, 136

Fallin, J. and Royse, D. 72
Farrell, C. 41, 44, 46- 49, 51, 54
Fautley, M. 28, 96, 100-101, 107, 123, 126, 158, 160-162, 176, 186, 191, 204
Fautley, M. and Daubney, A. 119, 139, 142, 155, 164, 168
Fautley, M. and Kinsella, V. 175
Fautley, M. and Savage, J. 115, 116, 195, 196, 204
Ferm Almqvist C., Vinge J., Väkevä L. and Zandén, O. 137
Ferm Thorgersen, C. 143
Field, R., James, R., Buchanan, J., Prescott, A., Schuck, S., Aubusson, P. and Burke, P. 206
Finney, J. 122
Finney, J. and Philpott, C. 24
Fischer, D., Stanszus, L., Geiger, S., Grossman, P. and Schrader, U. 211
Folkestad, G. 35, 36
Froehlich, H. C. 122

Gaunt, H. 139
Gedera, D. 173-174
Georgii-Hemming, E. 110
Gladwell, M. 145
Glaser, B. G. and Strauss, A. L. 49
Green, L. 21, 35-37, 146
Gu, J., Strauss, C., Bond, R. and Cavanagh, K. 209, 211
Gudmundsdottir, S. and Shulman, L. 145, 146

Haggard, D. L., Dougherty, T. W., Turban, D.B and Wilbanks, J. E. 6
Hale, J. A. 126
Hallam, S. 32-33, 52, 96, 100
Hallam, S., Creech, A. and McQueen, H. 35
Hallam, S. and Himonedes, E. 1
Hallam, S. and Rogers, L. 158
Harford, J., MacRuairc, G. and McCartan, D. 171

Author Index

Hargreaves, D. J., Purves, R. M., Welch, G. F. and Marshall, N. A. 38
Harpaz, Y. 162-164
Harrison, J., Dymoke, S. and Pell, T. 70, 73
Hattie, J. and Timperley H. 137, 139, 141-142
Hendricks, K. 146
Henry, A. 29
Hesterman, P. K. 33, 38
Hicks, C. D., Glasgow, N. A. and McNary, S. J. 73
Higgins, M. C. and Thomas, D. A. 7
Higgins, R. 140
Hobbs, V. 169, 179
Hobson, A. and Malderez, A. 121
Hobson, A. J. 70
Hook, P., Booth, N., Price, A. and Fobister, L. 197
Howes, L. M. and Goodman-Delahunty, J. 206
Hubbard 62
Hudson, P. 57, 59
Hudson, P. 71, 79

Isbell, D. S. 43, 45
Ivtzan, I. and Lomas, T. 210

Johnson, R. 38
Jorgensen, E. R. 38

Katz, L. 11-12, 14, 167-169, 180
Kay, M. 146
Kelly, A. V. 122, 154, 158
Kinsella, V. 173, 176-177
Kinsella, V. and Fautley, M. 181
Kolb, David A. 60, 62-63, 67, 159
Kolman, J. S., Roegman, R., and Goodwin, A. L. 51
Kroll, J. 6
Krueger, P. J. 72
Kula Ünver, S. 149
Kwami, R. 159-160

Lamont, A. 122, 157
Lamont, A., Hargreaves, D. J., Marshall, N. and Tarrant, M. 135
Larivee, B. 29
Lehmann, A. C., Sloboda J. A. and Woody, R. H. 96
Lejonberg, E., Elstad, E. and Christophersen, K. 121
Leont'ev, A. N. 173
Lerch, A., Arthur, C., Pati, A., Gururani, S. 134
Liebert, M. A. 211

London, M. 141
López-Íñiguez, G. 139
López-Íñiguez, G. and Pozo, J. I. 139
Loughran, J. 113

Malmberg, I. 43, 45, 49
Mark, M. L. 32
Marsh, K. 159
Marshall, N. A. and Hargreaves, D. J. 135
Mason, S. and Poyatos Matas, C. 206
Mayer, D., Allard, A., Bates, R., Dixon, M., Doecke, B., Kline, J., Kostogriz, A., Moss, J., Rowan, L., Walker-Gibbs, B., White, S. and Hodder, R. 210
Maynard, T. and Furlong, J. 8, 11, 14-15
McIntyre, D., Pedder, D. and Rudduck, J. 200
McPhail, G. 127
Measor, L. and Woods, P. 135-136
Mena, J., Hennissen, P. and, Loughran, J. 169
Merrion, M. 113
Mills, J. 158, 163, 199
Mills, J. and Paynter, J. 157-158
Montgomery, B. L. 6-7
Montgomery, D. 143
Munroe, A. M. 72
Murphy, C. 98
Murphy, R. 137

Norrish, J. M., Williams, P., O'Connor, M. and Robinson, J. 209

O'Leary, M. and Gewessler, A. 150-151
Oates, T. 122
Olsson, B. 137

Pajares, M. F. 34
Park, N. and Peterson, C. 209
Paynter, J. 98
Pea, R. D. 161
Pellegrino, K. 20, 25, 38
Pellegrino, K., Conway, C. M. and Si Millican, J. 72
Philpott, C. 22, 99, 121-123, 127
Philpott, C. and Evans, K. 101, 137
Philpott, C. and Kubilius, J. 129
Philpott, C., Price, C. and Lewis, M. 99
Philpott, C. and Spruce, G. 19, 28, 165
Pitts, S. 33-35, 40
Plummeridge, C. 121

Author Index

Pohio, K. 175
Pollard, A. 7
Postholm, M. B. 175
Priest, P. 96
Priestley, M., Biesta, G. and Robinson, S. 28

Ragins, B. 14
Regelski, T. A. 25, 154, 157
Reif, F. 111
Reimer, B. 33
Richter, D., Kunter, M., Lüdtke, O., Klusmann, U., Anders, A. and Baumert, J. 73
Robson, C. and McCarten, K. 150-151
Rowland, T., Huckstep, P. and Thwaites, A. 144, 147-148

Sadler, D. R. 140, 195
Savage, J. 96, 131, 165
Savage, J. and Barnard, D. 32
Savage, J. and Fautley, M. 198
Scharmer, C. 74
Schartel, S. A. 137
Schmidt, M. 34
Schmidt, P. and Robbins, J. 38
Schön, D. 12, 109-111, 118
Searby, L. J. 2
Sexton, F. 36
Shaw, M. and Redfern, C. 116
Shulman, L. 46, 128-129, 133, 147
Sindberg, L. 52
Small, C. 21, 36, 156
Smith, R. and Gallagher, K. 150
Spruce, G. 20, 22, 97-99, 102, 123, 132
Spruce, G., Stanley, A. and Li, M. 28
Spruce, G. with Matthews, F. 21, 115
Stierer, B. and Antoniou, M. 154
Stobart, G. 195
Strong, M. and Baron, W. 71, 75-77

Swanwick, K. 20, 25-26, 36-37, 96-98, 100-101, 117, 156-157
Swanwick, K. and Tillman, J. 156-157, 198
Sweller, J. 111
Symonds, J. 135

Thompson, L. K. 33-34, 38

Van Driel, J. H. and Berry, A. 59
van Es, E. 171
van Nieuwerburgh, C. 77-79
Vygotsky, L. 55, 172-173

Wagoner. C.L. 25
Webster, P. 97
Welch, G., Purves, R., Hargreaves, D. and Marshall, N. 37-38
Welsch, R. and, Devlin, P. 171
West, C. and Clauhs, M. 32-33
Westerlund, H. 33-34, 109, 115, 134
Wiggins, G. and McTighe, J. 195
Wiliam, D. 179, 187, 2014
Wiliam, D. and Leahy, S. 195
Williams, D. A. 33
Wilson, V. 173-174
Winch, C. 155
Wolf, M. and Younie, S. 50
Wood, D. 98
Wood, D. J., Bruner, J. S. and Ross, G. 155
Wyse, D., Hayward, L. and Pandya, J. 158

Yeo, N. F. 64
Yeo, N. F. and Rowley, J. 57-58, 60, 67
Yeo, N., Mohler, S., Paxton, I., Kwan, H.H.T., Massey, L. and Hallworth, T. 63

Zeserson, K., Welch, G., Burn, S., Saunders, J. and Himonides, E. 32, 35

SUBJECT INDEX

activity theory 166, 172-174, 176-178, 181
advocacy 31-34, 40
agency 19, 27-30, 89, 109, 129, 131-132
assessment 7, 20, 28, 47-48, 52, 98-99, 102, 128, 134, 140-141, 143, 186, 198-199, 201, 208, 21; baseline 135-136; criteria 133-134, 137-140, 142, 160, 162-163; formative 115, 117, 146-147, 149, 162, 175, 185-188, 195, 197, 203; resources on 107, 119, 132, 142, 203-204; summative 146, 149, 187

burn-out 25, 57, 58, 60, 81, 82, 210

circular mentoring 57-67
classroom management 59, 108, 112-114, 119, 212-213
community of practice 59, 67
curriculum xvii, 14, 34-36, 59, 95, 103, 117, 121, 127, 129-132, 154-155, 198, 207, 214; design 120-125, 127-128, 132, 208; intent 103, 106; ISM curriculum 138-139; knowledge 133, 146, 149; model music curriculum 35, 95, 98, 105, 121, 157; music curriculum general 32, 100, 117, 121-123, 126-132, 168, 188; national curriculum 95, 105, 123-124; resources on 119, 132, 142

data 135-136, 138, 140, 150, 160, 171, 211
discussion 10, 12-13, 34-36, 38-39, 42, 68, 95, 97-100, 103, 115-116, 119-123, 126, 129-132, 140, 147, 152, 166, 168-173, 176, 178-181, 195, 197, 201-203, 214, 216

enculturation 20, 21, 22, 23, 127

feedback xviii, 2, 29, 37, 40, 47, 67-68, 70, 75, 91, 104, 121, 123, 133-134, 136, 138, 150-152, 171, 177, 179-180, 195, 201-202; constructive 140-141, 210, 215; effective 134, 139, 140-142; lesson 130, 132; positive 66, 75, 144, 210, 214, 215; principles of 48-49, 140; reflective 120, 151

ideology 20-23, 132
impact of mentoring 5, 15, 41-44, 46-54, 73, 80; on career 7, 66-67, 72, 206; on identity 19, 21, 23, 27, 30; on practice 14, 39, 84, 92, 97, 99, 201; on teaching 12, 31-33, 37, 168, 202
impact of music teaching 26, 33, 160

knowledge i, ii, xvii, xviii, 2, 6, 7, 9, 14-15, 26, 28, 35, 42, 44, 51-52, 58, 60, 67, 73, 77, 95-96, 102-106, 118, 122, 127, 137, 139, 140-141, 145, 147, 151-152, 155, 156, 160, 162-164, 168-169, 175, 189, 198, 200, 207; curriculum knowledge 129, 132-133, 146, 149; knowledge of learners and their characteristics 133, 135-136, 142; knowledge transformation 147-148; musical knowledge 19-20, 23, 28, 34, 39, 73, 97, 98-101, 103-104, 107, 115, 122-123, 129, 130, 141, 149, 153-154, 156, 158, 176, 214; pedagogic content knowledge 46-47, 50, 128, 133; pedagogic knowledge 46, 99, 133; prior knowledge 39, 104, 195-197; subject knowledge 31, 37, 39-40, 100, 128, 133

learning and doing 108, 116, 119, 196, 203
lesson plans 81, 90, 104, 123-124

mentoring models 5, 8, 11, 57, 60
mindfulness 83, 205, 207, 209-212

Subject Index

musical values 20, 22-23
musicianship 31, 36-40, 45, 57, 69, 72, 100, 106

observation 42-43, 46, 49, 60, 63, 70, 96, 98, 104-105, 113, 119, 129, 143-144, 146, 148-153, 156, 172, 186, 187, 200-203, 214; observation process 149, 151, 153, 202; observing 2, 12, 108, 113, 118, 143, 144, 209

pedagogy 28-29, 31, 35-38, 40, 46-47, 110, 117, 119, 124, 126, 129, 143, 145, 153-154, 158, 163-165
performance: classroom performance 134, 137, 138-139, 142; musical performance 24, 44, 45, 52, 49, 64, 65, 68, 72, 76, 96, 103, 133-136, 140-141, 145, 149, 162-163, 186-187; performance anxiety 50, 51, 83, 163, 159, 210-211; performance curation 57-58, 60-61, 67; teacher performance 48, 81-82, 84, 90, 116, 143
professional development 8, 10, 15, 31, 37-40, 79, 103, 106, 121, 179, 200
programmes of study 124, 130
progression 35, 37, 39, 40, 97, 148, 168, 176-177, 186, 197-200
pupil voice 200-203

questioning 9, 27, 73, 89, 132, 134, 142, 166, 172-173, 180, 189, 191, 202

reflection xvii, 6, 7, 10, 12, 14, 23-24, 29, 34, 37-39, 41-42, 46-47, 49, 50-51, 54, 59-60, 63-64, 67, 71, 76-77, 79, 80, 82, 88, 89-91, 97, 98, 108-111, 114-118, 120, 124, 131-133, 137-138, 142, 151-153, 166, 168-172, 176, 178-179, 181, 188, 193, 202; critical reflection 152, 135, 166, 169, 172, 176; reflective diary 84, 89; self-reflection 24, 41, 59, 64, 151, 179

research methods 150, 153
roles 5, 8, 21, 25, 44, 47-50, 52-54, 57-58, 60, 62, 65-67, 161, 174, 177

schemes of work 35, 117, 123, 124, 129, 131-132, 148, 176
skills xvii, xviii, 6-8, 19, 20, 23, 25-26, 32, 34-37, 39, 42-43, 45-47, 51, 57-60, 62-65, 68-70, 73-75, 77, 79-80, 84-85, 93, 95-97, 99, 100, 101-107, 112, 126, 130, 137, 139, 140-143, 145-147, 153, 156, 158, 166, 169, 170-172, 176, 196-200, 202, 206-207, 209, 213, 215

teacher identity 19-20, 25, 27, 29-30, 43, 75, 215
training 2, 7, 9, 14, 34, 41, 42, 43, 45, 50, 54, 57, 58, 59, 81, 90, 91, 95, 99, 103, 114, 115, 119, 120, 123, 127, 128, 129, 130, 144, 145, 186, 206, 209, 214; mentor training 41, 42, 90-91; teacher training 2, 7, 9, 14, 43, 45, 50, 54, 57-58, 95, 99, 103, 114-115, 119-120, 123, 127-129, 144, 186, 214
transition 6, 37, 43, 46, 49, 120, 135, 174

understanding i, ii, xvii, xviii, 2, 5, 7, 9, 14-15, 19-20, 29-39, 45, 48, 52-53, 69-76, 79-80, 89, 93, 95, 96, 97, 102-105, 107, 110, 120, 122-124, 126, 129, 132, 137-141, 143, 145, 148-149, 151, 156-158, 162-163, 166-167, 169, 176, 180, 186, 189-191, 196, 198, 200-203, 205-207, 209-210; musical understanding 26, 28, 35-36, 99, 100-101, 103, 105, 106-107, 130

wellbeing 1, 2, 32, 38, 59, 70, 73, 76, 79, 81, 91-92, 139, 205-212, 213, 215, 216

For Product Safety Concerns and Information please contact our EU representative GPSR@taylorandfrancis.com
Taylor & Francis Verlag GmbH, Kaufingerstraße 24, 80331 München, Germany

www.ingramcontent.com/pod-product-compliance
Lightning Source LLC
Chambersburg PA
CBHW080612230426
43664CB00019B/2871